£4.25 TW/6

THE HAPPY MAN

NORWEGIAN UNIVERSITIES PRESS

Distribution offices

NORWAY:

KARL JOHANSGATE 47, OSLO

UNITED KINGDOM:

16, PALL MALL, LONDON S. W. 1

THE HAPPY MAN

STUDIES IN THE METAMORPHOSES
OF A CLASSICAL IDEAL

by

MAREN-SOFIE RØSTVIG

VOLUME I

1600-1700

2nd edition

NORWEGIAN UNIVERSITIES PRESS

1962

OSLO STUDIES IN ENGLISH, NO. 2

Publications of the British Institute in the University of Oslo

General editors:
Professor Lorentz Eckhoff, 1953-55

Since 1955:
Professor Paul Christophersen - Professor Kristian Smidt

First published 1954
Revised Edition 1962
© The University of Oslo 1962

THE HAPPY MAN, VOL. II: 1700-1760
appeared in 1958 as No. 8 in this series.

Printed on a grant from
The Norwegian Research Council for Science
and the Humanities

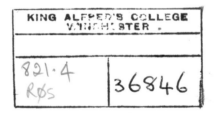
Printed in Norway by
AKTIETRYKKERIET I TRONDHJEM
TRONDHEIM

To the Memory of

EDWARD NILES HOOKER

CONTENTS

PREFACE

The question of what constitutes human happiness and under what conditions it may be obtained, has obviously stirred the minds of men in all ages. This is a study of a single such prescription for the achievement of happiness; originally created by Horace and Virgil on the basis of partly Stoic and partly Epicurean ideas, it came to attract many European poets of the seventeenth and eighteenth centuries. Its finest English exponents are Milton, Marvell, and Thomson. In the eighteenth century the popularity of Milton's companion poems and of James Thomson's *The Seasons* was such that numerous imitations were written, on the Continent as well as in England. The example set by James Thomson was particularly influential, and the manner in which he exploited the ancient formula will therefore be of some importance for our understanding of eighteenth-century poetry. Andrew Marvell's 'The Garden' enjoyed no such fame, but had to wait for the present century before its unique qualities were properly appreciated. To many readers today it is possibly the best-loved single lyric from its period. Two advantages are gained by placing Marvell's poem in the context of the tradition outlined in this study: the interpretation of the more difficult passages is facilitated, at the same time that one realises more clearly what constitutes Marvell's unique personal contribution to the tradition within which he was writing.

It is true that some of the poems discussed in these pages will fall lamentably short of the excellence encountered in a Milton or a Marvell. However, a selection of such poetry had to be included in order to show the surprising pervasiveness of this poetic tradition, and the way in which new motifs were constantly added to the classical core. Unless we are also prepared to study the works of those poets who are no longer read and enjoyed, we shall cut ourselves off from important clues to a proper understanding of the poetry which truly matters. The more obscure poets may sometimes reveal how a tradition is born, or how it is interpreted by succeeding generations of poets, *before* this interpretation appears in the works of the major poets.

Although a certain amount of identity or sameness is required before one can assign a body of poetry to a specific literary tradition, our main concern will be with change rather than with permanence. Once the nature of our tradition has been established, it will be our task to observe how succeeding generations re-interpret the old formula in the light of their own ruling ideas.

The study of change, or growth, is always absorbing. In the history of literature perhaps the most intriguing change is the transition from Neoclassical to Romantic attitudes. The average textbook presentation of this change is too well known to be referred to here. It will be sufficient to recall how a passion for solitude and for rural retirement has been closely associated with the Romantic movement, and that this movement is often described as a sudden revolt against the town-bred manners and preferences of the past. This study, however, shows that there is no such clear-cut line of division between Romantics and Neoclassicists — that, on the contrary, a love of solitude and rural retirement lies at the heart of the Neoclassical creed. It will also show that as far as the attitude to rural life is concerned, the transition from Neoclassical to Romantic is a question of continuous development and not of a sudden and dramatic change. Indeed, the development is so gradual that it is difficult to identify any one particular point at which the Neoclassical tradition of the Happy Man turned into its Romantic counterpart. Other scholars have reached similar conclusions about the nature of the change which occurred in the second half of the eighteenth century. There is more continuity than one has been led to believe. William Blake, surprisingly enough, is a case in point. Thus Josephine Miles has shown that there is a clear connection between Blake's poetry — so far considered as a unique isolated manifestation of Romantic energy — and the well-known sublime strain in eighteenth-century poetry.[1] Even Blake's pronounced individualism has been recognised as a culmination of an important eighteenth-century trend.[2]

It is clearly high time that our concept of Neoclassical literature should become richer and more varied. Instead of labelling any poem about rural retirement as 'pre-Romantic', one ought to change one's definition of Neoclassicism in a manner which admits the inclusion of such poetry. This can be done by distinguishing between a typically Neoclassical attitude towards rural life, and one which is typically Romantic. Although there is a stretch of common ground between the two, there is a clear difference between the extreme left and the extreme right which will serve to point the contrast.

Finally one word about the connection between the poetry of human happiness and the poetry of nature. Whenever a poet attributes an important part of his happiness to his experience of the rural scene, the *beatus ille* tradition merges with the tradition of the descriptive poem. It is scarcely possible to draw a sharp line of distinction between the two, nor is it desirable. Horace himself was by no means indifferent to the rural setting; many of his lyrics contain beautiful vignettes of field and forest. His philosophy of happiness, on the other hand, focussed squarely on moral issues, so that the setting itself formed no important part of his argument. The religious or philosophic bias of many seventeenth- and eighteenth-century poets, however, caused them to invest the rural scene with secret powers or qualities capable of inducing a certain state of mind in the beholder. In many cases the very perception of the significance of the landscape of retirement came to be viewed as the mechanism whereby happiness was achieved. In this manner the *beatus ille* tradition led directly to the creation of descriptive poetry. In the early eighteenth century

9

the same tradition also provided men like Timothy Nourse and Stephen Switzer with their most powerful arguments in favour of landscape gardening. A study of the *beatus ille* tradition in English poetry is therefore also a study of the poetic approach to the rural scene.

The criterion employed in my selection of poems is fairly simple: indebtedness to classical sources must be discovered in the argument, preferably also in the phrasing. While most seventeenth-century poets adhere closely enough to a classical pattern to make identification easy, the tradition was so well established by the time of Dyer and James Thomson that it is treated with a freedom which tends to obscure the connection. This is clearly why so many eighteenth-century *beatus ille* echoes have remained unidentified; they are perceptible only to the eye of one who has traced the line of growth from the roots into the very branches.

This second, revised edition differs markedly from the first. It is in parts much abbreviated, in parts enlarged by substantial additions. It is nevertheless still largely based on the research once carried out at the Henry E. Huntington Library and Art Gallery of San Marino, California, on grants from the Marsden Foundation and from the United States Government. This has been supplemented by work done at the Bodleian Library and the British Museum Library. I am glad to have this opportunity of expressing my sincere appreciation of the facilities which I have enjoyed at these institutions. My greatest intellectual debt is to the late Professor Edward Niles Hooker for patient advice and friendly encouragement at all times.

I am grateful to the editor of *English Studies* for permission to include material from two articles on Marvell.

The publication of this second edition was made possible by a grant from The Norwegian Research Council for Science and the Humanities.

M. S. R.

January, 1962

CHAPTER I

THE HAPPY MAN
SOURCES AND ARGUMENTS

A classical scholar would be quite right if he were to deny that there is such a thing as an easily defined *beatus ille* tradition in the literature of Antiquity. This 'tradition' was created neither by Horace nor Virgil, but rather by their Renaissance admirers and imitators. The manner in which this was done must therefore be briefly explained.

One can distinguish between three stages in the development of our tradition: (1) The composition of neo-Latin poetry in imitation of classical passages in praise of country life; (2) the publication, in vernacular translation, of such passages, and (3) the composition of original *beatus ille* poems in the vernacular. This sequence is roughly chronological, the first indications of an interest in *beatus ille* sentiments being found in the neo-Latin poetry of the Humanists.

It is well known that literary fashions in England lagged behind those of the Continent. While the English *beatus ille* poem is a definite seventeenth-century creation, Continental poets began to take an interest in this part of the classical heritage already in the preceding century. Thus Carol Maddison, in her study of the ode, quotes a number of neo-Latin Renaissance poets who praised retirement in the manner of Horace.[1] Crinito, who flourished in the second half of the fifteenth century, praised retirement and the golden mean in three of his odes, and similar sentiments mark the poetry of Ludovico Ariosto (1474-1533), Marc Antonio Flaminio (1498-1550), Camillus Capilupus (*Capiluporum Carmina*, 1590), and Bernardino Rota (1509-1575). In the seventeenth century the Horatian odes of Casimire Sarbiewski (published 1625 and 1628) proved extraordinarily influential.

The lyrics of the 'divine Casimire' single out *beatus ille* motifs with much greater frequency than had previously been the case and also fuse them more fervently with Christian ideas. Although I cannot pass any literary judgment on the merit of Sarbiewski's neo-Latin odes, in the context of this study, at least, his work is more significant than that of his predecessors. It was also more significant to his contemporaries, who praised the Polish poet in the warmest possible terms. His formal excellence, so they said, was equalled only by his high moral seriousness, and it was part of this seriousness to focus decisively on those motifs which form the subject-matter of this inquiry.

Among Continental vernacular poets Petrarch was the first to take a sustained interest in *beatus ille* motifs. His essay on the solitary life contains a number of quotations from Horace concerning his Sabine farm, and several of his poems and letters were written in praise of solitude. The Pléiade focussed on such motifs to a not inconsiderable extent, and by 1583 enough poetry had been written along these lines in France to provoke an anthology of poetry on country life. The finest single French collection appeared in 1618 with Racan's *Stances à Tircis*.

So much for the Continental background. Since our main task in this chapter is to give a survey of the classical sources for the tradition, we turn at once to the English translators of such poems, letting them perform the introduction.

Our two crucial dates are 1621 and 1668, the first being the date of publication of John Ashmore's *Certain Selected Odes of Horace*, the second that of Abraham Cowley's essays and discourses.

Out of the nineteen odes translated by Ashmore, five deal with *beatus ille* sentiments. Ashmore's large appendix, however, is more interesting than the main body of his book. This appendix consists solely of *beatus ille* poetry divided into a pagan and a Christian section, the former being headed 'The Praise of a Country Life', the latter 'Of a Blessed Life'. Here, then, is evidence

14

that by 1621 at least one English translator had thumbed through the works of Horace, Virgil, Martial, and the humanists to discover passages written in praise of country life. It is possible that Ashmore may have borrowed his selection from a similar Continental publication, but this is of minor importance. The main point is that Ashmore's volume is the first English collection of classical *beatus ille* passages in translation. The pagan section contains translations from Martial, Virgil, and Marc Antonio Flaminio; the second, Christian section from Flaminio again, and Georg Fabricius.

Ashmore's choice from Martial is his epigram 'De Rusticatione' (IV, 90), where the Latin poet describes the course of a happy day — a device which was to become a favourite with the English poets. Horace, too, had employed this device in his second Epode. Ashmore's choice from Virgil is the crucial passage from his second *Georgic*, to which the translator gave the title *Vitae Rusticae Laus*. The ode by Flaminio is a conscious imitation of the Horatian rural ode; it paints an appealing lyric picture of the delights of country life. A pastoral note is perceptible, but the main emphasis is nevertheless on actual country life and not on an idealised abstraction. This *L'Allegro* aspect of the *beatus ille* tradition is apparent also in the translations from Martial and Virgil.

Ashmore's poetry is admittedly poor, and his volume is inaccessible to most. It will therefore be wiser to turn at once to Abraham Cowley for our first introduction to the tradition which we are to pursue through the literature of nearly two centuries. In doing so we shall be forced to abandon the chronological approach, and we shall also have to take into account the fact that Cowley's translations are biassed; he adds and expands substantially, inserting passages which reflect the attitude of his own generation. However, these drawbacks are more than compensated for by the circumstance that his selection of classical sources is the most comprehensive in the annals of English literature, that his translations are as inspired as those of Ashmore are humdrum, and that the prose essays in which these translations are embedded, present a searching analysis of the philosophy expressed by the classical poets.

Cowley's essays are usually considered from the point of view of prose style, in the development of which they form an important stage. They are justly famous for the manner in which the author pursues a graceful conversational pattern, thus establishing a trend which English prose was to follow in the years to come. Except for their references to Cowley's own life, their contents seem to have stirred little interest. Even a cursory reading at once reveals the fact that they are organised around a single idea — that of human happiness. They are, in fact, a prose commentary on, or exposition of, the *beatus ille* tradition. The prose and the verse present one sustained philosophic argument. This argument centres on the familiar Stoic paradox concerning the Great Man and the Happy Man. While the former, in having all, has nothing, the latter, in having nothing, has all.

The initial essay on liberty[2] goes straight to the psychological nexus in its insistence on happiness being a question of intellectual and emotional liberty. A person, as well as a nation, should be *sibi imperiosus*, should be governed, that is, by laws of his own making. The majority of men, however, are slaves to the three great tyrants — ambition, covetousness, and voluptuousness. To be properly free, and therefore happy, a man must liberate himself from the dominion of these three vices, and must learn to remain content with what he has. This Stoic argument, which supports the Christian position so strongly, is at the very heart of the tradition of the Happy Man, whether the author be Virgil, Horace, or Martial. It is given poignant expression in Martial's epigrams, from which Cowley selected three as a fitting conclusion to his essay. Cowley's translation paints the picture of the *beatus vir* with vigorous strokes. His main characteristics are mental independence and emotional equilibrium; since he enjoys freedom

16

from slavery not only to other men, but also to his own passions, he is the prototype of the free man. His pleasures, though simple, are very real:

> Let gay and toilsome Greatness others please,
> He loves of homely Littleness the Ease.
> Can any Man in guilded Rooms attend,
> And his dear hours in humble visits spend;
> When in the fresh and beauteous Fields he may
> With various healthful pleasures fill the day?
> If there be man (ye Gods) I ought to hate,
> Dependance and Attendance be his Fate.
> Still let him busie be, and in a crowd,
> And very much a Slave, and very Proud.

Two further epigrams underline the same point. 'Would you be free?' If so, then be content to live in a small house and to look upon 'thy beechen bowl' without sighing for one of gold. 'If in thy Mind such power and greatness be, / The *Persian* King's a Slave compar'd with Thee.' To these translations Cowley added an original Pindaric ode 'Upon Liberty', which paints vivid and impressive pictures of the slavery endured by all who succumb to the lure of the flesh, of money, or ambition. These contrast strongly with the appealing description of the happy life, enjoyed in Horatian fashion in the company of a few good friends.

Cowley throughout supports the argument by means of classical quotations, largely of a Stoic character. Thus he quotes Seneca's well-known paradox that a great fortune is a great servitude, and repeats Horace's query: *Quisnam igitur Liber? Sapiens, sibi qui Imperiosus* (Sat. II, 7). Suddenly breaking into poetry, Cowley inserts his own version of this definition. The Wise Man is he

> Who governs his own course with steady hand,
> Who does Himself with Sovereign Pow'r Command;

Whom neither Death nor Poverty does fright,
Who stands not aukwardly in his own light
Against the Truth: who can when Pleasures knock
Loud at his door, keep from the Bolt and Lock:
Who can, though Honour at his Gate should stay
In all her Masking Cloaths, send her away,
And cry, Be gone, I have no mind to Play.

Although the sentiments are those of Horace, the manner is entirely Cowley's own. Thus Horace is content to say:

83   Sapiens; sibi qui imperiosus;
Quem neque pauperies, neque mors, nec vincula terrent:
Responsare cupidinibus, contemnere honores
86   Fortis, & in seipso totus.[3]

Cowley's rendering is far more passionate than the original and enriched by forceful, concrete details. Among the early exponents of the *beatus ille* philosophy, none embraced the classical ideal with more fervour than Cowley. He reveals an almost abandoned passion for it, a recklessness to quit the world and be done with it, which in its own way seems as headlong as those passions which he condemned so severely. Horace would surely have queried the spirit in which the Englishman wrote his essays and translations; it is not sufficiently dispassionate to suit the ideas expressed. With the desperate urge of the frustrated lover, Cowley asks to be delivered from covetousness, ambition, and sensual desires in order to obtain true freedom.

Cowley was in a good position to draw convincing pictures of the plight of the Great Man, having served at the court of the exiled Stuarts. 'Of Liberty' satirically outlines the wretched existence of the Great Man, besieged as he is by suitors of every kind (many of them impertinent), guarded with crowds and shackled with formalities. 'A hundred businesses of other men . . . fly

SAPIENTIAE LIBERTAS

Emblem inspired by Horace's Satire II, 7 ('Quisnam igitur liber? sapiens, sibi
qui imperiosus...'). The regal figure of the Stoic wise man tramples under
foot various symbols of honour and power. He is threatened by imprisonment,
death, love, greed, and fickle fortune, yet remains aloof. The palm trees are
traditional symbols of the righteous man, whom nothing can depress ('Iustus
ut palma florebit').

continually about his Head and Ears, and strike him in the Face like Doors.' The day is completely lost in empty formalities:

> The half Hat, the whole Hat, the half Smile, the whole Smile, the Nod, the Embrace, the positive Parting with a little Bow, the Comparative at the middle of the room, the Superlative at the door; and if the Person be *Pan huper sepastus*, there's a *Huper-superlative* ceremony then of conducting him to the bottom of the stairs, or to the very Gate: as if there were such Rules set to these *Leviathans* as are to the Sea, *Hitherto shalt thou go, and no further. Perditur haec inter miseros Lux,* Thus wretchedly the precious day is lost.

This lively description of seventeenth-century graded formality explains part of the reason why Cowley's generation tended to favour the classical philosophy of the Happy Man. Troubled periods will often favour a cultural or chronological primitivism, ascribing happiness to earlier periods or to a life of rustic simplicity which mirrors the purity of earlier ages. The times of the Emperor Augustus and the seventeenth century in England were curiously alike in certain respects. The truckling courtier, the man out to seek preferment, the abandoned sensualist and the haughty aristocrat stirred the anger of Cowley, as it did that of Horace and Martial. And Cowley, like Virgil and Horace, focusses on the crowded anteroom as the outward and visible sign of greatness:

> Let's begin with him by break of day: For by that time he's besieged by two or three hundred Suitors; and the Hall and Antichambers (all the Outworks) possest by the Enemy; as soon as his Chamber opens, they are ready to break into that, or to corrupt the Guards, for entrance. This is so essential a part of Greatness, that whosoever is without it, looks like a fallen Favourite, like a person disgraced, and condemned to what he please all the morning.

In his second *Georgic* Virgil had pointed out that one of the blessings of the Happy Husbandman was his freedom from importunate suitors. In Cowley's translation (appended to the essay 'Of Agriculture'): . . . no morning Tide of Clients comes, / And fills the painted Channels of his rooms, / Adoring the rich Figures as they pass.' Instead his 'calm and harmless life' abounds with 'substantial blessedness'. Cowley's own Pindaric apostrophe to Liberty elaborates this idea further:

> 'Tis Morning; well; I fain would yet sleep on;
>   You cannot now; you must be gone
>   To Court, or to the noisie Hall:
> Besides, the Rooms are crowded all;
>   The stream of Business does begin,
> And a Spring-Tide of Clients is come in.
> Ah cruel Guards, which this poor Prisoner keep!
>   Will they not suffer him to sleep?
> Make an Escape, out at the Postern fleet,
> And get some blessed Hours of Liberty,
> With a few Friends, and a few Dishes Dine,
>   And much of Mirth, and moderate Wine.
> To thy bent mind some relaxation give,
> And steal one day out of thy life to live.
> Oh happy man (he cries) to whom kind Heaven
>   Has such a Freedom always given!
> Why, Mighty Mad[m]an, What should hinder thee
>   From being every day as free?
> . . . .
> He's no small Prince, who every day
>   Thus to himself can say,
> Now will I sleep, now eat, now sit, now walk,
> Now meditate alone, now with Acquaintance talk.

Although the connection with Horace and Virgil is obvious, one feels that Cowley's poem was primarily prompted by personal experience. One is tempted to say that his essays embody deeply

personal experience, and that the classical quotations and translations were added to invest his own passionate rejection of contemporary society with greater authority. This seems confirmed
by the autobiographical essay 'Of my Self', where the poet confesses that he has always felt aversion for 'the glories' or 'business'
of the world.

'Of Obscurity' and 'Of Greatness' carry on the argument presented in the initial essay, and so their chief interest consists in
the further addition of classical sources. Thus the former quotes
the line which Pope was to have inscribed above the entrance
to his grotto: *Secretum iter, & Fallentis semita vitae.*[4] Cowley
quotes Broome's translation ('... a Life, led as it were by stealth')
and adds:

> The meaning of all this is no more than that most vulgar saying,
> *Bene qui latuit, bene vixit,* He has lived well, who has lain well
> hidden. Which if it be a truth, the world (I'll swear) is suffi-
> ciently deceived: For my part, I think it is, and that the pleas-
> antest condition of life is, *in incognito.* ... This innocent
> Deceiver of the World; as *Horace* calls him, this *Muta persona,*
> I take to have been more happy in his Part, than the greatest
> Actors that fill the Stage with show and noise, nay, even than
> *Augustus* himself, who askt with his last breath, whether he had
> not played his *Farce* very well.

A single translation concludes the essay, a passage from Seneca's
Thyestes, Act II. I quote merely a few lines:

> Upon the slippery tops of humane State,
>   The guilded Pinnacles of Fate,
> Let others proudly stand, and for a while
>   The giddy danger to beguile,
> With Joy and with disdain look down on all,
>   Till their Heads turn, and down they fall.
> . . . .
> Here wrapt in th'Arms of Quiet let me lye;
> Quiet, Companion of Obscurity.

21

Here let my life, with as much silence slide,
As Time that measures it does glide.

This chorus was translated so frequently in the course of the century that its popularity must have been notorious.

'Of Greatness' again compares the Great Man and the Happy Man. 'When you have pared away all the Vanity, what solid and natural contentment does there remain which may not be had with Five hundred pounds a year?' Hence a stately palace is rejected in favour of 'a convenient Brickhouse, with decent Wainscot, and pretty Forest-work Hangings'. This ideal may perhaps strike a modern reader as fairly ambitious, but Horace had definitely specified a decent house and an adequate competence, both of which ought to be inherited to avoid wasting time on earning the money. Next one must consider that the audience to which Cowley addressed himself would have viewed an income of £ 500 as a very modest one. The essay ends with a translation of Horace's well-known Ode III, 1 — *Odi profanum vulgus & arceo.*

In the essays 'Of Agriculture' and 'The Garden' denunciation of false values yields to praise of what is genuine. 'Of Agriculture' is perhaps the most important of all the essays. In it, Cowley proceeds to a fuller discussion of what constitutes human happiness. As we have already guessed, the Happy Man can be one of two things: either a gentleman-philosopher who retires to his rural estate, or a humbler husbandman-farmer without much insight into abstract philosophy:

> The first wish of *Virgil* (as you will find anon by his Verses) was to be a good Philosopher; The second a good Husbandman; and God ... dealt with him just as he did with *Solomon*; because he prayed for Wisdom in the first place, he added all things else . . . He made him one of the best Philosophers, and the best Husbandmen, and to adorn and communicate both those faculties, the best Poet: He made him besides all this a rich man, and a man who desired to be no

richer. *O fortunatus nimium, & bona qui sua novit:* To be a Husbandman, is but a retreat from the City; to be a Philosopher, from the World, or rather, a Retreat from the World, as it is mans; into the World, as it is Gods.

However, since only very few have the intellectual capacity for philosophy, Cowley concludes that 'the best mixture of humane affairs that we can make, are the employments of a Countrey life.' In support of this view, Cowley proceeds to quote Columella, who called a country life the 'nearest neighbour, or rather next in Kindred to Philosophy', as well as Varro and Cicero to the same effect. After underlining the usefulness of this sort of life, its innocence, its pleasant character, its antiquity, Cowley proceeds to outline his famous plan for agricultural colleges. In the course of his plea for such institutions Cowley observes that husband-men 'are without dispute, of all men the most quiet and least apt to be inflamed to the disturbance of the Common-wealth.' Although all other trades actively supported the cause of Parliament, 'I do not remember the Name of any one Husbandman who had so considerable a share in the twenty years ruin of his Countrey, as to deserve the Curses of his Countrey-men.'

The point is perhaps an obvious one, but it should be stressed. Cowley's argument reflected a fairly general sentiment among Anglicans and Royalists, and it is probably in this one circumstance more than in any other that the major reason must be found for the sudden popularity of the *beatus ille* philosophy in the seventeenth century. This popularity becomes marked after 1630, while a veritable peak is reached in the 'fifties and 'sixties. That it was more than just a poetic motif is shown by Cowley's essays, and this will be shown to be true also of poets like Henry Vaughan, Mildmay Fane and others. This had to be so. Before a poetic motif can become truly important to a generation, the philosophy which it expresses must correspond to a deeply felt need of the individual and of his age.

Cowley concludes his essay by pointing out how Virgil and

23

Horace both refused to enter into employment which would have made great public figures out of them, instead preferring a retired rural existence. Horace is viewed as the next best poet in the world to Virgil, whom, however, he far exceeds in the quantity of lines and poems devoted to the subject of the happiness of a simple country life (*parva rura*). Hence Cowley adds: 'If I should produce all the passages of this excellent Author upon the several Subjects which I treat of in this Book, I must be obliged to translate half his Works.' By way of compromise, Cowley selects one ode, one satire, and one epistle, wisely forbearing to quote 'the suffrages of all other Poets, which may be found scattered up and down through all their writings, and especially in Martials.' Horace was a clear favourite with Cowley, who refers to him as 'that person whom you and I love very much, and would believe as soon as another man.'

The appended translations should be closely studied, since they offer the most important classical sources for the motif of the Happy Man. A passage from Virgil's second *Georgic* comes first. It falls logically into four parts: (1) Lines 458-74 in praise of the husbandman, (2) lines 475-89, where Virgil expresses his desire to penetrate the secrets of the universe (*rerum cognoscere causas*), (3) lines 490-512, where the Happy Man is the Stoic Wise Man, and (4) lines 513-40, where Virgil again turns to the husbandman as the prototype of human happiness. The husbandman and the philosopher-poet are apostrophised in phrases that were to re-echo down the centuries:

458   O fortunatos nimium, sua si bona norint,
459   agricolas!
490   felix, qui potuit rerum cognoscere causas . . .
493   fortunatus et ille, deos qui novit agrestis . . .

Cowley's translation displays its accustomed vigour. Each statement capable of it, is dramatised and made more emphatic. Thus Virgil's seventeen lines are expanded into twenty-eight.

1   Oh happy, (if his happiness he knows)
        The Countrey Swain! on whom kind Heav'n bestows
        At home all Riches that wise Nature needs;
        Whom the just Earth with easie plenty feeds.
5   'Tis true, no morning Tide of Clients comes,
        And fills the painted Channels of his rooms,
        Adoring the rich Figures as they pass,
        In Tap'stry wrought, or cut in living Brass;
        Nor is his Wooll superfluously dy'd
10   With the dear Poyson of *Assyrian* pride:
        Nor do Arabian Perfumes vainly spoil
        The Native Use and Sweetness of his Oil.
        Instead of these, his calm and harmless life
        Free from th' alarms of fear, and storms of strife,
15   Does with substantial blessedness abound,
        And the soft wings of Peace cover him round:
        Through Artless Grots the murm'uring waters glide,
19   . . . and his ground
20   With lowing Herds, and bleating Sheep does sound;
        And all the Rivers and the Forests nigh,
        Both Food and Game, and Exercise supply.
        Here a well hard'ned active youth we see,
        Taught the great Art of chearful Povertie.
25   Here, in this place alone, there still do shine
        Some streaks of Love both Humane and Divine;
        From hence *Astraea* took her flight, and here
28   Still her last Footsteps upon Earth appear.

Cowley underlines the contrast between a natural and an artificial environment when he refers to the rooms of the Great Man as 'painted Channels', contrasting these with the 'Artless Grots' of the country-side. Virgil's text merely refers to the proud portals which disgorge a tide of visitors, and to caves or caverns without underlining their artlessness. This conflict between art and Nature was to be felt with increasing strength, and ultimately led to the adoption of landscape gardening in the 1730's. A second discrepancy between Virgil and Cowley is discovered in the use of the term 'Countrey Swain' for *agricola*. The former conjures up pastoral associations quite out of place in a context where the emphasis is squarely on farmers and farming. The phrase 'easie plenty' in line 4 tends in the same direction and accords poorly with the 'well hard'ned active youth' and the 'chearful Poverty' of lines 23-24. Virgil's phrase is *facilem victum*, i. e. food easily obtained at home in contrast to dainty rarities. Cowley's paradoxical juxtaposition of an 'easie plenty' with 'chearful Povertie' was to remain inherent in the English version of the *beatus ille* tradition. A number of poets went so far in stressing the soft and pleasant aspects of country life that the austerity of the Happy Man was quite transformed into a refined Epicureanism. Lines 15-16 offer yet another example of the intrusion of softer terms than are warranted by the original. If one compares translations or imitations of this particular Virgilian passage dating from the first half of the century — for example Ashmore's — one finds a realistic note more in keeping with the original text.

In the lines which follow Virgil expresses his own desire for knowledge of the universe; if incapable of such an elevation, he prays for the privilege of living among running streams and dells:

45   In the next place, let Woods and Rivers be
        My quiet, though unglorious destinie.
        In Life's cool vale let my low Scene be laid;
48   Cover me, Gods, with *Tempe*'s thickest shade.

The philosopher-poet and the husbandman are thus bracketed together as first and second choice because they share the same Stoic fortitude; they are *sibi imperiosi* and not the playthings of fickle fate or superstitious fears. The difference between them is simply this, that the philosopher-poet, by virtue of his insight into the causes of things, is even more invulnerable and inde-

MEDIIS TRANQUILLUS IN UNDIS

This emblem gives a dramatic presentation of Horace's Ode III, 3 ('Iustum & tenacem propositi virum...'). The poised scales symbolise the balanced mind of the Stoic wise man, who remains unperturbed in the midst of the havoc wrought by earthquake, fire, and war.

pendent than the husbandman. He represents a higher, because
conscious level of happiness, while the husbandman is scarcely
aware of it (*sua si bona norint*). Virgil's description of these two
types of human happiness is worth studying in detail:

49   Happy the man, I grant, thrice happy he,
Who can through gross effects their causes see:
Whose courage from the Deeps of knowledge springs,
Nor vainly fears inevitable things;
But does his walk of virtue calmly go,
Through all th'Alarms of Death and Hell below.

55   Happy! but next such Conqu'erors, happy they,
Whose humble life lies not in Fortunes way.
They unconcern'd from their safe distant seat

58   Behold the Rods and Scepters of the great.
   . . . .

63   Them never yet did strife or av'arice draw,
Into the noisy Markets of the Law,
   . . . .

67   Duty for Natures Bounty they repay,
And her sole Laws religiously obey.
  Some with bold labour plough the faithless main,

70   Some rougher storms in Princes Courts sustain.
Some swell up their slight Sails with pop'ular fame,
Charm'd with the foolish whistlings of a Name.
Some their vain Wealth to Earth again commit;
With endless cares, some brooding o'er it sit.

75   Countrey and Friends are by some wretches sold,
To lye on *Tyrian* Beds, and drink in Gold;
No price too high for profit can be shown;
Not Brothers blood, nor hazards of their own.
Around the World in search of it they roam,

80   It makes ev'n their Antipodes their home.
Meanwhile the prudent Husbandman is found,

In mutual duties driving with his ground,
. . . .
89 All sorts of Fruit crown the rich *Autumns* pride:
 And on a swelling Hill's warm stony side,
 The pow'erfull Princely Purple of the Vine,
 Twice dy'd with the redoubled Sun, does shine.
 In th' evening to a fair ensuing day,
 With joy he sees his Flocks and Kids to play;
95 And loaded Kyne about his Cottage stand,
 Inviting with known sound the Milkers hand;
 And when from wholsome labour he doth come,
 With wishes to be there, and wisht for home,
 He meets at door the softest humane blisses,
100 His chaste wifes welcome, and dear Childrens kisses.
 When any Rural Holy-days invite
 His Genius forth to innocent delight,
 On Earths fair bed beneath some sacred shade,
 Amidst his equal friends carelessly laid,
105 He sings thee *Bacchus* Patron of the Vine,
 The Beechen Bowl foams with a flood of Wine,
 Not to the loss of reason or of strength:
 To active games and manly sport at length
 Their mirth ascends, and with fill'd veins they see,
110 Who can the best at better Tryals be.
 Such was the life the prudent *Sabins* chose,
112 From such the old *Hetrurian* virtue rose.

Virgil's *laus et vituperatio* is adorned by forceful, concrete examples. We are made to share the intellectual excitement of the philosopher who ponders the causes of things (such as the connection between the waxing and waning of the moon and the tides of the sea), and we appreciate the moral superiority of the man who from his 'safe, distant seat' beholds the 'Rods and Scepters of the great'. Virgil's persuasiveness is great; the innocent

AGRICULTURAE BEATITUDO

Emblem picture in illustration of Horace's praise of the Happy Husbandman
in his second Epode. In the background, a besieged town and a storm-tossed
ship contrast strongly with the peaceful rural scene.

delight of rural holidays and the placid labour of the farmer form a compelling contrast to those who sell even their country and their friends in order to 'lye on *Tyrian* Beds, and drink in Gold'. One notices that the emphasis is not solely on the intellectual or moral superiority of the Happy Man; his pleasures are also seen to give more genuine, more lasting joys. Stoic and Epicurean elements therefore combine.

The next translation is of Horace's second Epode, whose initial words — *beatus ille qui* — have provided a suitable name for the tradition of which it is such an important part.

A classical scholar will know that the lines in praise of rural obscurity and simplicity are spoken by a usurer, and that Horace ends his poem by showing how the usurer's love of money after all prevails over his theoretical insight into the nature of human happiness. His resolution to retire into the country is forgotten the next day, when he proceeds to re-invest his fortune. Cowley omits the satirical conclusion, so that only the praise itself is left. Perhaps he felt that no satire should be allowed to obscure the message of the poem. Unlike Virgil, Horace is concerned with the husbandman only; there is here no hint of the greater glories of the life of the retired philosopher-poet:

1   Happy the Man whom bount'eous Gods allow
           With his own hands Paternal Grounds to plough!
           Like the first golden Mortals happy he
           From Bus'ness and the cares of Money free!
5   No humane storms break off at Land his sleep,
           No loud Alarms of Nature on the deep,
           From all the cheats of Law he lives secure,
           Nor does th'affronts of Palaces endure.
           . . . .
15   He sees the lowing Herds walk o'r the Plain,
           Whilst neighb'ring Hills low back to them again:
           And when the Season Rich as well as Gay,

All her Autumnal Bounty does display,
How is he pleas'd th' encreasing Use to see
20   Of his well trusted Labours bend the Tree?
Of which large shares, on the glad sacred days
He gives to Friends, and to the Gods repays.
With how much joy does he beneath some shade
By aged Trees reve'rend embraces made,
25   His careless head on the fresh Green recline,
His head uncharg'd with Fear or with Design?
By him a River constantly complains,
The Birds above rejoyce with vari'ous strains,
And in the solemn Scene their *Orgies* keep
30   Like Dreams mixt with the Gravity of sleep,
Sleep which does always there for entrance wait,
And nought within against it shuts the Gate.
    Nor does the roughest season of the Sky,
Or sullen *Jove* all sports to him deny.
35   He runs the Mazes of the nimble Hare,
His well-mouth'd Dogs glad concert rends the Air;
Or with game bolder, and rewarded more
He drives into a Toil, the foaming Bore.
Here flies the Hawk t'assault, and there the Net
40   To intercept the trave'ling Foul is set.
And all his malice, all his craft is shown
In innocent Wars, on Beasts and Birds alone.
   . . . .
45   And if a chast, and clean, though homely wife
Be added to the blessings of this life,
   . . . .
53   Who waits at door against her Husband come
From rural duties, late, and wearied home,
55   Where she receives him with a kind embrace,
A chearful Fire, and a more chearful Face;
And fills the Bowl up to her homely Lord,

And with domestique plenty loads the Board:
Not all the lustful Shel-fish of the Sea,
60   Drest by the wanton hand of Luxury,

. . . .

63   Are at the Princely Tables better cheer,
64   Than Lamb and Kid, Lettice and Olives here.

There is much less vituperation here than in Virgil's passage. Horace's second Epode focusses almost entirely on the pleasant aspects of country life, describing in minute detail the varying occupations of the day and of the succeeding seasons. Horace's Happy Man begins his day by attending to the cattle, his fruit trees, and his bees; at noon he rests underneath an aged tree, lulled to sleep by birds and murmuring streams. At this point Cowley inserts a passage of his own. While Horace merely states that it is pleasant to lie beneath some ancient ilex-tree or on the matted turf, Cowley stresses the softness of the scene by adding a number of details. Thus he invests his husbandman with a 'careless head' 'uncharged with Fear or with Design'; he lets the birds keep *'Orgies'* in the tree tops, and he depicts sleep as a perpetual suitor who is never rejected. In the evening the husbandman returns home, tired out, and is cheered by his wife and children. She it is who pens the cattle at night, milks the cows, and finally draws the wine for her husband's table. She provides *dapes inemptas,* that is, unbought victuals, the produce of the farm itself. Simple though it is, this produce nevertheless is better than the luxurious dainties placed on the tables of the great.

The similarity between Virgil's and Horace's praise of the happy husbandman is obvious; both stress much the same features, as was only to be expected. Virgil's picture of happiness, however, is much more comprehensive, and is also more sharply contrasted with various examples of human folly.

The second Epode is followed by a translation of part of Horace's Satire II, 6. Cowley's concern is with the charming fable

31

of the country mouse, and this is too well known to require extended quotation and comment. Suffice it therefore to mention that the tree in which the country mouse lives, is referred to as his 'antient and Hereditary House'; that he himself is frugal and grave, but that he finally is corrupted by the Epicurean arguments of his city visitor, and by his subtle flattery:

> Why should a Soul, so virtu'ous, and so great,
> Lose it self thus in an obscure retreat?
> Let savage Beasts lodge in a Country Den,
> You should see Towns, and Manners know, and Men:
> And taste the gene'rous Luxu'ry of the Court,
> Where all the Mice of quality resort.
> . . . .
> Since Life is so uncertain, and so short,
> Let's spend it all in feasting and in sport.

The true Happy Man (who does not realise his happiness) swallows the bait, and proceeds to abandon himself to all the false pleasures proposed by his companion. However, his blindness is of short duration. When the servants and the dogs arrive 'With hid'eous noise', he prays the gods to restore him to his former happy state: 'With peace, let Tares and Acorns be my food!'

Horace's Epistle I, 10 is a letter written by a rural dweller to his friend in town. The sentiments of this epistle inspired more imitations than perhaps any other poem by Horace. This may be partly due to the attraction of the informal epistolary style, but the contents were also bound to appeal to the Neoclassical mind. The writer belittles the empty pleasures of the town and extols the true joys of a country life. The 'wild Luxury' of city dwellers can never compete with 'those true joys' which 'Nature did to mankind recommend'. In the country one has pure water and real trees; in the city one must be content with the water which struggles to burst its leaden pipes, while the trees

planted amid the columns of the inner court are but poor imitations of proper fields and forests. The golden mean is recommended; a man's fortune should fit him like a shoe. It should
neither pinch him, nor sit so loosely that it trips him up. 'My
dearest friend stop thy desires at last, / And chearfully enjoy the
wealth thou hast.'

Cowley's rendering is fairly faithful, but he consciously emphasises and elaborates the contrast between what is natural and
what is artificial. The following passage is expanded by various
insertions:

> Would I a house for happiness erect,
> Nature alone should be the Architect.
> She'd build it more convenient, than great,
> And doubtless in the Countrey chuse her seat.
>
> . . . .
>
> Does Art through Pipes a purer Water bring,
> Than that which Nature strains into a spring?
> Can all your Tap'stries or your Pictures show
> More beauties than in Herbs and Flow'ers grow?
> Fountains and Trees our weari'd Pride do please,
> Ev'n in the midst of gilded Palaces.
> And in your Towns that prospect gives delight,
> Which opens round the Countrey to our sight.

Cowley definitely contrasts 'Art' with 'Nature', while Horace's
prime concern is to recommend obedience to the laws of Nature:

> Vivere naturae si convenienter oportet,
> Ponendaeque domo quaerenda est area primum;
> Novistine locum potiorem rure beato?

True, Horace, too, contrasts that which is natural with that which
is artificial, but he does not base his preference for the former on
a new aesthetic. Cowley has twisted the Stoic advice to live according to Nature into something of an aesthetic manifesto as

well. That which is a virtuous life is at the same time a more beautiful and truly pleasant existence. 'Flee grandeur', is Horace's advice, 'Though humble be your home, yet in life's race you may outstrip kings and the friends of kings' (*fuge magna: licet sub paupere tecto / reges et regum vita praecurrere amicos*). Cowley transforms the humble home into a highly desirable dwelling:

> An humble Roof, plain Bed, and homely board,
> More clear, untainted pleasures do afford,
> Than all the tumult of vain greatness brings
> To Kings, or to the Favourites of Kings.

The tendency to fuse ethics and aesthetics as yet is only tentative, but some two generations later it was to prevail in the philosophy of the Earl of Shaftesbury and in the vogue for landscape gardening.

A translation of Cowley's own *laus agriculturae*, taken from his Latin poem on plants, concludes the essay on agriculture. The passage is an obvious counterpart to Virgil's similar digression in the second *Georgic*:

> Blest be the man (and blest he is) whom e're
> (Plac'd out of the roads of Hope or Fear)
> A little Field, and little Garden feeds;
> The Field gives all that frugal Nature needs,
> The wealthy Garden lib'erally bestows
> All she can ask, when she luxurious grows.

Then follows the classical example of the honest husbandman turned emperor, fetched from the plough, and always consumed with longing for his former simple life: 'Unwillingly, and slow, and discontent, / From his lov'd Cottage, to a Throne he went.' To this is added the story of the obscure and happy husbandman Aglaeus, whose innocent existence is strongly contrasted with the viciousness of the rich king Gyges. When the latter goes to see the man whom the oracle had pronounced the happiest in his kingdom, he encounters a man busily working 'With his own hands in his own little ground.'

While the essay on agriculture combines two of the three stages outlined at the beginning of this chapter — translations from the Latin, or from neo-Latin poetry — the third stage (free composition in the vernacular) is illustrated by the essay on 'The Garden'. This essay is Cowley's bid for fame as the English Horace or Maro. The prose exposition is brief — a single page in my folio edition of 1700 — while his own Pindaric ode on gardens consists of eleven long stanzas covering five pages.

The essay is one sustained personal confession from author to reader, a confession of worldly failure and subsequent determination to seek happiness in obscurity. This determination is presented as the author's true ambition, as the desire which he has always had, but which he has been stupid enough to abandon in favour of corrupt desires. 'I never had any other desire so strong, and so like to Covetousness as that one which I have always had that I might be Master at last of a small house and large Garden . . .' Although he has completed the hardest part of his reformation, which consists in 'abandoning all ambitions and hopes in this World', yet he still remains 'in the Inn of a hired House and Garden, among Weeds and Rubbish.' He has 'gone out from *Sodom*', but as yet has not arrived. Turning to his friend, John Evelyn, Cowley praises him for having realised the best that a man can hope for, and adds: 'All that I my self am able yet to do, is only to recommend to Mankind the search of that Felicity, which you instruct them how to Find and to Enjoy.'

Cowley reserved his best rhetoric for his poem, where he addresses Evelyn as the prototype of the Happy Man. Since Cowley's original poetry will be considered in Chapter IV, suffice it to state here that Cowley adds the Christian argument that rural retirement leads to religious insight. 'Of Solitude' goes beyond the classical ideal in insisting on complete retirement, devoted to intellectual activities ('Cogitation is the thing which distinguishes the Solitude of a God from a wilde Beast.').

The remaining essays ('Of Avarice', 'The dangers of an Honest man in much Company', 'The shortness of Life and uncertainty of Riches', 'The danger of Procrastination', and 'Of my Self') stick more closely to the classical argument and contribute further translations from Martial, Claudian, and Horace.

'Of Avarice' touches on an idea frequently expressed by Horace, to wit that avarice is perhaps the most serious destroyer of human happiness. The translations from Horace's first Satire (lines 1-79) and Ode III, 16, stress the importance of being content with one's lot. The former also emphasises the beauty and purity of Nature's produce:

> Fond man! what good or beauty can be found
> In heaps of Treasure buried under ground?
> Which rather than diminisht e're to see
> Thou wouldst thy self too buried with them be:
> And what's the diff'erence, is't not quite as bad
> Never to Use, as never to have Had?
> In thy vast Barns millions of Quarters store,
> Thy Belly for all that will hold no more
> Than mine does . . .
> Do you within the bounds of Nature live,
> And to augment your own you need not strive,
> One hundred Acres will no less for you
> Your Life's whole business than ten thousand do.
> But pleasant 'tis to take from a great store;
> What, Man? though you're resolv'd to take no more
> Than I from a small one? if your Will
> Be but a Pitcher or a Pot to fill,
> To some great River for it must you go,
> When a clear Spring just at your feet does flow?

36

Give me the Spring which does to humane use
Safe, easie, and untroubled stores produce,
He who scorns these, and needs will drink at *Nile,*
Must run the danger of the Crocodile,

. . . .

The only true, and genuine use is this,
To buy the things which *Nature* cannot miss
Without discomfort, Oyl, and vital Bread,
And Wine, by which the Life of Life is fed.
And all those few things else by which we live;
All that remains is Giv'en for thee to Give;
If Cares and Troubles, Envy, Grief and Fear,
The bitter Fruits be which Fair Riches bear;
If a new Poverty grow out of store;
The old plain way, ye Gods, let me be Poor.

These arguments are repeated in Cowley's paraphrase of Horace's
Ode III, 16. The Pindaric form is not exactly congenial to the
contents, but one cannot deny that it invests the poem with a
certain fervour and vehemence. Its main idea can be expressed
by the well-known paradox: *magnas inter opes inops* (Amidst
the rich abundance poor):

Sellars and Granaries in vain we fill,
    With all the bounteous Summers store,
    If the Mind thirst and hunger still,
The poor rich Man's emphatically poor.
. . . .

A Field of Corn, a Fountain and a Wood,
    Is all the Wealth by Nature understood.
. . . .

    Much will always wanting be,
To him who much desires. Thrice happy He
To whom the wise indulgency of Heaven,
With sparing hand, but just enough has given.

As Horace phrased it:

> Multa petentibus
> Desunt multa. Bene est, cui Deus obtulit
> Parca, quod satis est, manu.

This is the only true desire: *quod satis est,* and nothing more. And *satis* is found in 'A Field of Corn, a Fountain and a Wood'.

Cowley's disgust with the contemporary scene comes powerfully to the fore in the essay on 'The dangers of an Honest man in much Company'. Like the essay on solitude, it rejects society and expresses an intellectual kind of cultural primitivism. Cowley refers slightingly to the boast of philosophy and eloquence 'that they first congregated men disperst, united them into Societies, and built up the Houses and the Walls of Cities.' Instead he wishes that 'they could unravel all they had woven; that we might have our Woods and our Innocence again instead of our Castles and our Policies.' Even the countryside has become corrupt: 'I thought when I went first to dwell in the Countrey, that without doubt I should have met there with the simplicity of the old Poetical Golden Age . . . but to confess the truth, I perceived quickly, by infallible demonstrations, that I was still in old England.'

Claudian's epigram on the old man from Verona concludes the essay:

> Happy the Man who his whole time doth bound
> Within th' inclosure of his little ground.
> Happy the Man, whom the same humble place,
> (Th' hereditary Cottage of his Race)
> From his first rising infancy has known,
> And by degrees sees gentle bending down,
> With natural propension to the Earth
> Which both preserv'd his Life, and gave him Birth.
> . . . .
> He never heard the shrill alarms of War,

38

SORS SVA QVEMQVE BEAT

Baucis and Philemon, because contented with their humble lot, are the happiest
of mortals and for this reason are visited by Jove and Mercury.

Or the worse noises of the Lawyers Bar.
No change of Consuls marks to him the year,
The change of seasons is his Calendar.
The Cold and Heat, Winter and Summer shows,
Autumn by Fruits, and Spring by Flow'rs he knows.
He measures Time by Land-marks, and has found
For the whole day the Dial of his ground.
A neighbouring Wood born with himself he sees,
And loves his old contemporary Trees.

. . . .

About the spacious World let others Roam,
The Voyage Life is longest made at home.

'The danger of Procrastination' argues along the lines suggested
by Martial's Epigrams V, 59 and II, 90:

V, 59   To morrow you will Live, you always cry;
In what far Countrey does this Morrow lye,
That 'tis so mighty long e'r it arrive?

. . . .

II, 90   Wonder not, Sir . . .
That I make haste to live, and cannot hold
Patiently out, till I grow Rich and Old.
Life for Delays and doubts no time does give,
None ever yet made haste enough to Live.

. . . .

My humble thoughts no glittering roofs require,
Or Rooms that shine with ought but constant Fire.
I well content the Avarice of my sight
With the fair gildings of reflected Light:
Pleasures abroad, the sport of Nature yields
Her living Fountains, and her smiling Fields.
And then at home, What pleasure is't to see
A little cleanly chearful Familie?
Which if a chaste Wife crown, no less in her

> Than Fortune, I the Golden Mean prefer.
> Too noble, nor too wise, she should not be,
> No, not too Rich, too Fair, too Fond of me.
> Thus let my life slide silently away,
> With Sleep all Night, and Quiet all the Day.

Two further epigrams by Martial are found added to the essay 'Of my Self', one of which (Epigram X, 47) is without doubt the most famous of all Martial's epigrams in favour of a country life. The reason why it was translated, paraphrased and imitated with such frequency may have been that it presents an easily adaptable formula:

> Since dearest Friend, 'tis your desire to see
> A true Receipt of Happiness from Me;
> These are the chief Ingredients . . .

The subsequent picture of a happy life is attractive in its snugness and its insistence on true pleasures in moderation. The first stipulation is that one should possess an estate sufficient for the upkeep of a family:

> Take an Estate neither too great nor small,
> Which *Quantum Sufficit* the Doctors call.
> Let this Estate from Parents care descend;
> The getting it too much of Life does spend.
> . . . .
> Let constant Fires the Winters fury tame;
> And let thy Kitchens be a Vestal Flame.
> Thee to the Town let never Suit at Law,
> And rarely, very rarely Business draw.
> Thy active Mind in equal Temper keep,
> In undisturbed Peace, yet not in sleep.
> Let Exercise a vigorous Health maintain,
> Without which all the composition's vain.

In the same weight Prudence and Innocence take,
And of each does the just mixture make.
But a few friendships wear, and let them be
By Nature and by Fortune fit for thee.
Instead of Art and Luxury in food,
Let Mirth and Freedom make thy Table good.

. . . .

Be satisfi'd and pleas'd with what thou art;
Act chearfully and well th' allotted part,
Enjoy the present Hour, be thankful for the Past,
And neither fear, nor wish th' approaches of the last.

In these epigrams by Martial one readily recognises the origin and inspiration of Pomfret's *The Choice* (1700), a type of poem which became exceedingly popular around the turn of the century.

Abraham Cowley's essays have contributed no less than eighteen classical sources for the tradition of the Happy Man, the two most important passages being Horace's second Epode and Virgil's praise of the *agricola* in *Georgics* II. The nature of the entire tradition could be deduced from these two passages alone. Their introductory words were echoed by English poets in every possible phrasal variation and were so well known that they sufficed as thematic indication. Next in importance are Horace's rural odes (of which Cowley selected III, 1 and III, 16) and epistles (I, 10 and I, 18). Of these, Epistle I, 10 was to prove as inspiring as the second Epode. Finally come the numerous epigrams by Martial — seven in all (X, 47 and II, 90 being the most important) — one epigram by Claudian, and the chorus from the second act of Seneca's *Thyestes*.

On reading through these translations one is surprised at the sense of unity conveyed by such a heterogeneous collection. There is nevertheless variety within this unity. While all agree in condemning the false pleasures of the world, associating these with

41

life in town and at court, and with mental blindness and instability, the formula for happiness is by no means identical. One can
distinguish between five basic variants or motifs which may occur
separately, or in conjunction with one or more of the other motifs.

(1) The first motif states that happiness is a question of
internal peace. The Happy Man is he who, having nothing, yet
has all, because he is completely self-possessed and serene. He
is *sibi imperiosus*.

(2) The second motif places the Happy Man on a Sabine farm,
arguing that *internal* and *external* peace can best be achieved in
the obscure life of the husbandman (*parva rura*).

(3) The third motif is an expansion of the first. It states that
a supreme type of mental serenity is achieved by the man who
obtains a knowledge of the universe by studying the 'causes of
things'.

(4) The fourth motif changes the emphasis away from the
parva rura by stipulating that a country life offers truer and more
genuine pleasures than can be found at court or in cities. Rural
scenes, too, are more genuinely beautiful.

(5) The fifth motif goes farther still by proclaiming that a
veritable Golden Age or Earthly Paradise can be found among
scenes of happy rural innocence.

Motifs 1 and 2 are Stoic in character, and the poetry in which
they are found is austere in mood. The third is intellectual in its
austerity, while the fourth and fifth admit Epicurean ideas, but
are not necessarily associated with this philosophy only. Although
these attribute sensuous enjoyment to rural life, they are nevertheless capable of a spiritual, religious interpretation. The common
factor for motifs Number 1 and 2 is *contentment*, for motif
Number 3 *intellectual knowledge*, and for Numbers 4 and 5 *purer*
and *truer pleasures*.

On re-reading the translations from Horace, one realises that
most of them feature motifs 1 and 2 in conjunction, and that 4
is frequently added. This is true of the second Epode and of

Epistle I, 10. Motif 3, on the other hand, is found only in Virgil, Horace having little or no interest in abstract philosophical speculation on the causes of things. Virgil's *o fortunatos nimium* passage is therefore the most varied or comprehensive; it stresses 1, 2, 3, and 4 heavily, and touches on 5 in passing. The idea that rural life constitutes a sort of Golden Age belongs in the context of Virgil's *Eclogues* rather than in his *Georgics,* but the soft or pleasant aspects of country life are described so appealingly by both Virgil and Horace, that one readily understands how it came to form a part of the *beatus ille* formula. If one places a Virgilian eclogue next to Horace's second Epode one realises that the gap, after all, is not so great.

If one were to discuss these motifs in terms of the type of Happy Man suggested by each, one could say that to the first motif corresponds the figure of the Stoic Wise Man (*sapiens, sibi qui imperiosus*); to the second that of the Happy Husbandman; to the third the figure of the Lucretian philosopher-poet; to the fourth the gentleman-farmer or gentleman-philosopher who delights in the society of a few well-chosen friends, while the fifth conjures up the picture of a prelapsarian Adam, or a voluptuous innocent. Many of these figures overlap; the Stoic Wise Man merges with the Happy Husbandman, or again with the gentleman-philosopher whose greatest delight is in simple fare and choice company. Motifs 1 and 5 are apparently irreconcilable; the austerity of the former would seem to exclude the voluptuousness implied by the concept of the Golden Age. However, as soon as this concept is interpreted in the direction of a spiritual symbolism, that is, as soon as the Golden Age turns into a spiritual garden inside which a union with God may be achieved, its sensuousness can be reconciled with a complete austerity regarding mere earthly objects or passions.

Our tradition is therefore a complex one, and it is no doubt this complexity which accounts for its sustained popularity for nearly two centuries. By emphasising one motif at the expense of another, or by adding new motifs to the classical core, the individual poet could fashion the tradition according to his own needs and interests. The age loved nothing better than paraphrase with a difference, the classical texts being so well known that the slightest deviation would be immediately apprehended and relished.

The way in which our tradition hovers between a Stoic and an Epicurean or again a mystic interpretation was particularly conducive to changes in emphasis. The early seventeenth century favoured a Stoic or neo-Stoic bias, so that the softer *carpe diem* tendency inherent in the *beatus ille* message had to wait for the new intellectual climate of the Restoration before it was accepted and developed. Indeed, a poet like Dryden went so far that he denied the presence of Stoic ideas altogether, maintaining that Horace's philosophy of happiness was completely Epicurean. However, before this happened, many poets had invested the rural scene with a religious significance; in the 'forties and 'fifties some of them combined an utterly sensuous description of this scene with a mystic interpretation along lines suggested by *Canticles,* the connecting link possibly being Virgil's fifth eclogue as interpreted by those who believed that it contained true prophetic insight into the Christian mysteries.

The balance between description and argument is struck differently by different poets. The tradition itself leans in both directions, Virgil perhaps favouring argument more strongly than Horace, whose best argument is often an appealing description of life on his Sabine farm. Many readers will surely agree that the most appealing passages are those which describe the course of a happy day, stressing the pleasant family life of the husband-man, his healthy rural occupations, his peaceful environment, and the convivial joys of rural holidays. One may call this the *L'Allegro* aspect of the tradition, the *locus classicus* being Horace's second Epode. Although the landscape of retirement was not as important to Horace as to his English imitators, no *beatus ille* poem is complete without its charming genre pictures from rural life. We have also seen how Cowley fastened on Horace's comparisons between the purity of fields and woods and the dirt and noise of the city, expanding such passages and underlining them heavily.

The strong intellectual note struck by Virgil is unique; there is nothing in Horace to match Virgil's interest in the causes of things. As the seventeenth century wore on and merged with the eighteenth, the growing interest in science was to lead to increasing emphasis on this intellectual aspect of Virgil's praise of the happy life. By the time of James Thomson the quest for a clear perception of the structure of the Universe had become the dominating motif in the presentation of *beatus ille* sentiments, even when the poet imitated is Horace, and not Virgil. Thus one early eighteenth-century imitator of Horace takes care to equip his Sabine farm with a telescope for the study of celestial phenomena. Nothing could reveal more clearly how the English poets had come to think in terms of one coherent tradition, so that it scarcely mattered if Horace was given a Virgilian desire for complete knowledge of the universe.

Cowley's translations have shown that a variety of poetic forms could be employed to present *beatus ille* motifs, so that one could write in almost any mood or style. Horace mastered both the lyric and the epistle; Virgil, on the other hand, introduced his *laus agricolae* into his georgic poem, thus permitting a leisured exposition within the framework of a lengthy descriptive poem with didactic intent. The English poets were to exploit all these forms.

In each of these three genres the manner is subtly different. Although loaded with philosophic ore, the Horatian odes and epodes offer an utterly lyrical presentation of the joys of rural retirement. The closest equivalents, in English, are Milton's com-

45

panion poems, Andrew Marvell's 'The Garden', and John Dyer's 'Grongar Hill'. These are original creations along lines suggested by the Horatian rural lyric. Pope's 'Ode to Solitude' is less well known, but deserves mention for its successful rendering of the form of the Sapphic ode. The main difficulty of the rural ode is to reconcile the claims of philosophy with those of the lyric poem. This is no easy matter. It is therefore scarcely surprising that so many poets followed the example of Abraham Cowley, who avoided the problem by rendering the strictly regular Horatian ode in irregular pseudo-Pindarics. The objection to this solution is that the loose and enthusiastic manner of this form violates the measured spirit of the original. However, it is much simpler to argue in loose Pindarics, and I suppose that this is why arguments tend to prevail in this type of poem. Poets who tried to preserve the regular form of the Horatian ode often resorted to tetrameter couplets. In the eighteenth century many rural poems were labelled 'odes' which, properly speaking, are nothing but epistles. The epistolary presentation of *beatus ille* sentiments was bound to be more popular, because more easy. It is often a dreary task to peruse such epistles, great numbers of which appeared in the early years of the eighteenth century. However, there are also examples of a truly poetic handling of the genre; thus William Habington's rural epistles from the reign of Charles I are particularly fine.

The Virgilian habit of placing *beatus ille* passages in long descriptive-didactic poems was popularised by James Thomson, who exploited this technique in *The Seasons*.

Beatus ille themes are rarely encountered in satires or epigrams. Pope glances at them in passing, and he often assumes that their philosophy is shared by all sane men everywhere. However, like so many of his contemporaries, Pope preferred to incorporate such themes in his loco-descriptive poem, *Windsor Forest*.

Finally a word about a genre which often was, and still is, confused with that of the rural ode. This is the pastoral. The two must be kept separate. The rural ode is realistic, while the pastoral idealises; the one describes a real Sabine farm, the other an Arcadian never-never-land. One must, on the other hand, be aware of the fact that the two genres often were confused, so that *beatus ille* arguments could be employed in critical expositions of the pastoral. This is done by Rapin in his treatise *De Carmine Pastorali* (translated by Thomas Creech in 1684). Pope knew too much to do this; his pastorals are proper pastorals, and he reserved the *beatus ille* themes for use in odes and in loco-descriptive poetry. The fifth motif, which identifies the rural scene with the Golden Age, was particularly apt to cause generic confusion, and Marvell's 'The Garden' for this reason has often been considered a pastoral, rather than the rural ode which it indubitably is. If we keep the contrasting generic characteristics firmly in mind, it will be sufficiently easy to differentiate between proper rural odes, pastorals, and hybrids. Hybrids are particularly frequent in the early years of the seventeenth century, before the *beatus ille* tradition became sufficiently familiar to lead to a rejection of sonnets and pastorals in favour of odes and epistles. When the poets of the reign of Charles I abandoned Petrarch and Theocritus and instead turned to Horace for inspiration, this was in no small measure due to the consuming interest which this generation felt for his rural philosophy, and for the consummate skill with which he embodied this philosophy in lyric and epistolary form.

After this introductory survey of Abraham Cowley's *Essays and Discourses* (1668), the nature and the extent of the *beatus ille* tradition should be clear, and it should now be possible to pursue this tradition chronologically through the seventeenth and eighteenth centuries.

Despite the heterogeneity of the sources selected by Cowley, his treatment of them has succeeded in imposing a high degree of unity. Behind Cowley's selection of sources, and his interpretation of them, was the desire (strong enough to amount to a

47

passion) to defend a certain attitude to life and to society. Cowley needed the moral support of Martial, Claudian, Seneca, Horace, and Virgil in presenting his negative evaluation of contemporary life. Judging from his tone of voice it is possible that he was more concerned with a rejection of civilisation as he knew it, than with the acceptance of a new ideal. His desire to leave the world and be well rid of it may have been stronger than his belief in the superior virtue and happiness of a country life. Indeed, his discovery of the moral decadence also of country folk, and his subsequent decision to remain where he was, regardless of this keen disappointment, points in this direction.

To understand the fervour with which a poet like Cowley embraced the creed of rural retirement, one or two features of the contemporary scene must be called to mind. Cowley's disgust with the over-elaborate social code of his day and particularly with all the paraphernalia of greatness, has already been discussed. To this must be added the cruel impact of the Civil War upon men of moderation, and the influence of the split between Anglican and Puritan. That a Stoic desire to 'lie at rest amid the waves' should prevail at a time when political and religious conflict led to open war, is logical enough, but one must also recall how *peace* came to be a term used for propaganda purposes by those who rallied around the Crown after 1630. The writing of poetry in praise of a peaceful rural retirement must therefore have been practically tantamount to a confession of loyalty to the Crown. This is true to such an extent that one is tempted to view the classical figure of the Happy Man as a conscious counterpart to the Puritan concept of the Christian pilgrim or warrior. The Puritan concept of a happy life was that of the good pilgrim who is always on the road from this world to the next, engaged in a never-ending battle with Satan and the unregenerate Adam in his own flesh. The Puritan served God actively through his calling, and so the peaceful enjoyment of woods and fields and gardens was not for him. To him, rather, peace was something

to be deeply suspected as a temptation of the devil: 'Only the
wicked are at peace; the elect are always at grips with the fiend
in their bowels.' Although the Puritan rejection of the world may
seem to have much in common with Cowley's attacks on ambition,
covetousness, and lust, the aim and the motivation are totally
different. Instead of focussing his eyes on the epic battle between
Christ and the devil in the vast theatre of the soul of man, the
Royalist poet fixed his attention on the classical figure of the
Horatian husbandman, happy in his retirement from the world
of soldiers, merchants, lawyers, and fickle princes. *Sibi vivere*
became his watchword, and the *vestigia ruris* of the husbandman
were accepted as the only valid symbols of peace and contentment.
Against the Puritan creed of a highly emotional conversion and
subsequent daily exposure in the eternal battle between good and
evil, he pitted the Stoical exhortation never to give in to passion
or fanaticism, but always to preserve a soundly balanced mind
untouched by the vicissitudes of life, and to seek *mediocritas*
rather than honour or fame. To many Royalist poets, Horace's
second Epode and Virgil's second *Georgic* must have seemed a
classical counterpart to the wisdom of the Bible. This is particularly true of those poets who, like Vaughan and Marvell, combined
the *beatus ille* tradition with Christian ideas. To a man like Izaak
Walton the beauty of holiness was evident not only in the ritual
of the Church of England, but also in the contemplative solitude
of the country-side. How well Walton expressed the mood of his
times is obvious from the great popularity of his *Compleat Angler*
(1653).

The Horatian appeal to the moral authority of the individual
— *sapiens sibi qui imperiosus* — was bound to attract a period as
individualistic as the seventeenth century. Both Anglicans and
Puritans appealed to the inner authority: *intra te quaere Deum*
(John Smith). For this reason private meditation or contemplation became extraordinarily important. As we shall soon see, the
early stages of the *beatus ille* tradition in England are marked by

49

the frequent introduction of the motif of solitary contemplation. Cowley devoted an entire essay to the topic of solitude. Also the lives of men were marked by this tendency towards introvert speculation. Milton spent years of his life in intellectual retirement, and the circle which formed around Lord Falkland at Great Tew was similarly inspired. One of the members of this circle, John Hales, refused the offer of a ministry to pursue a life of quiet meditation and devotion. Like Horace, Hales scorned 'the common voice of multitudes and majorities', and held that nothing would serve 'but to know things yourselves'. A man should know the truth of his own heart, and so accordingly 'determine of his own way, whatsoever the judgment of his superiors be.' Henry More, the Cambridge Platonist, is completely in accord with Horace when he states that the greatest advantage of riches lies in the fact that they make a person fully master of his own time. However, when he adds that 'the best improvement of this time is the Contemplation of God and Nature', he speaks with the voice of his own age.

Cowley's complete rejection of society forms a strong contrast to the attitude of the preceding generation. It is sufficient to recall how the Elizabethan world view postulated a secret correspondence between the order of society and the world order in general. When the order of society is seen as a reflection of the universe to the extent that disorder in one sphere calls forth disorder in the other, the life of the individual can be justified only in so far as it conforms to this order. Between the world view of Shakespeare and of Cowley the gap is so wide that it is difficult to realise that Cowley's generation followed hard upon the heels of that of the dramatist. When the largely medieval world view of the Renaissance was replaced by a completely new science of the universe, the relationship of the individual to society was loosened. If there was no divine correspondence between society and the order of the universe, why should the individual be tied to an observance of obsolete civil codes? Under the impact of the revolution usually associated with the name of Copernicus, men began to realise their relative insignificance in the scheme of things and the precariousness of their position in a world where everything was subject to change and decay. The subsequent natural desire to establish a private refuge led directly to an acceptance of the philosophy of life expounded by Abraham Cowley.

Finally a word about the insanitary conditions in the towns. Plague and other epidemical diseases were frequent, and the stench from the open sewers added to the discomfort caused by an air full of soot and smoke. A man like Sir William Temple was so 'sensible extreamly to good air and smells' that he once spent five years on his estate without once visiting London. Under such conditions a country life was bound to seem attractive, and a man like Izaak Walton turned his back on town the moment he had earned enough to devote the rest of his days to the quiet joys of the country-side. Dudley North, in his *Forest of Varieties* (1645), combined his aversion for the polluted air of London with his Royalist hatred of the upstart shopkeepers. Wise men 'will not make themselves a silly prey to the proud Shopkeeper, who playes the Spider in the Cobweb, and is now become as familiar as hee was wont to be humble and crouching.' Nor will they 'buy ill ayre, strait lodging, ill drinke, and little good company so deare'. North comments unfavourably on the 'enforced neatnesse' of city dwellers, the 'importunate visits' to which they are exposed, the lack of good exercise, and 'a sootie Ayre, such as the thickest rined vegetables rather pine then live in.'[5] The most famous account of the polluted air of London is, of course, John Evelyn's *Fumifugium* (1661), whose hopeful sub-title reads: 'the Inconvenience of the Aer and Smoak of London dissipated.' The inconvenience, alas, tended to increase rather than diminish, so that Timothy Nourse at the turn of the century repeated and redoubled Evelyn's complaint.[6]

We see, then, how a number of compelling trends combined in the first half of the century to create a favourable attitude towards the ideas so passionately expounded by Abraham Cowley. The pronounced individualism of this period was perhaps the strongest force; it manifests itself in a general tendency to favour solitary introspection, whether of an intellectual or a religious kind, and in a solution of the ties between the individual and society. This tendency was further encouraged by the destruction of the old world view with its emphatic code of social and political conformity, and by the disruptive effect of civil dissension and civil war. The aversion usually felt, especially among loyalists and men of moderation, for London as a centre of dissent, added its influence, together with the fact that any recommendation of a peaceful, rational way of life constituted a declaration in favour of Church and Crown.

CHAPTER II

FIRST BEGINNINGS, 1600-1625

There are few, if any, examples of *beatus ille* poetry composed before the death of Queen Elizabeth. Any anthology of sixteenth-century poetry will show that the classical motif of *contentment* was well-known and popular, but this virtue is never primarily attributed to a country life, and this development must occur before one can speak about *beatus ille* poetry proper. Thus *England's Parnassus* (1600) reveals a surprising lack of interest in country life. This anthology is a poetic encyclopedia where quotations are ranged according to subject-matter in alphabetical sequence. Ten quotations deal with the virtue of contentment, but all of them associate this virtue with Stoic wisdom or with the mean estate in general; they do not echo the belief that it can be found only within the confines of an English Sabine farm.

The first few poems which can be said to touch on our tradition, are scattered phenomena. Moreover, their *beatus ille* sentiments are incidental and seldom form the core of the poetic message. The main interest lies elsewhere. Then, thirdly, the sentiments are poorly presented because the poetic form is highly unsuited; sonnets, songs, and pastorals pervert the realistic *beatus ille* mood into one of poetic compliment or again into an idealised abstraction. On other occasions the mood will be that of a passionate religious rejection of the world, so that the more joyous aspects of the *beatus ille* message are completely lost.

Among the pastoral poems of *England's Helicon* (1600) William Byrd's lines on 'The Herdsman's Happy Life' introduce ideas related to the Horatian tradition. Byrd's herdsman is a real figure, not an idealised allegorical personification, and his happy life is contrasted with that of the great trouble-makers of this world

— princes, lawyers, and merchants. All this is according to the classical prescription, yet the fact that the poem is a song obscures the intended realism and surrounds the herdsman with the halo of the pastoral shepherd:

> Oh, happy who thus liveth!
> Not caring much for gold;
> With clothing which sufficeth,
> To keep him from the cold.
> Though poor and plain his diet,
> Yet merry it is and quiet.[1]

Quiet peacefulness is the key concept also of Francis Thynne's epigrams on 'The Court and Countrey' and 'Quiet and Rest' (*Emblemes and Epigrams*, 1600; Epigrams 71 and 76), and of the 'Picture of an happy Man' penned by John Davies of Hereford,[2] whose death occurred in 1618. The same is true of Sir Henry Wotton's 'Character of a Happy Life',[3] written around 1614. The main stress, in all these poems, is on the contented and unmoved mind. They have little to say about a rural setting or about rural activities.

'The Happy Life' by William Browne (1591-1645?) can best be described as a pious pastoral with elements taken from the rural ode:

> O blessed man! who, homely bred,
> In lowly cell can pass his days,
> Feeding on his well-gotten bread;
> And hath his God's not others' ways . . .
>
> His threshold he doth not forsake,
> Or for the city's cates, or trim;
> His plough, his flock, his scythe, and rake,
> Do physic, clothe, and nourish him.

By some sweet stream, clear as his thought,
He seats him with his book and line;
And though his hand have nothing caught,
His mind hath whereupon to dine.[4]

The same pious bias is found in Browne's apostrophe to the husbandman in the third song of the second book of *Britannia's Pastorals* (1616). Lines 287-450 attribute to the Stoic husbandman the ability to indulge in introspective searchings of his own soul:

O happy men! you ever did possess
No wisdom but was mix'd with simpleness;
So wanting malice and from folly free,
Since reason went with your simplicity,
You search'd yourselves if all within were fair,
And did not learne of others what you were.

(lines 435-440)

John Dennys's *Secrets of Angling* (1613) in the same manner associates the rural dweller with pious contemplation of 'the World and his Creator'.

The sonnets of William Drummond of Hawthornden (1585-1659) occasionally recommend a religious withdrawal into rural solitude in terms indebted to classical poetry. There are at least two such echoes in the following sonnet:

Thrice happie hee who by some shadie Groue,
Farre from the clamorous World, doth liue his owne,
Though solitarie, who is not alone,
But doth conuerse with that Eternall Loue:
. . . .
How sweet are Streames to Poison drunke in Gold?
 The World is full of Horrours, Troubles, Slights,
 Woods harmlesse Shades haue only true Delights.[5]

57

The line about poison drunk in gold reflects the *ut gemma bibat* of Virgil's *Georgics*, II, 506, while the third line recalls Seneca's well-known statement — *Nunquam minus solus quam cum solus.*

Drummond's 'Hymne of True Happinesse' (*Flowres of Sion*, 1623) may be an answer to Horace's second Epode. Like Horace, Drummond lets the argument be spoken by a person, in his case a nymph. This nymph is the daughter of '*Iordans* sacred Streames', and the embodiment of beauty, innocence, and piety. Her lecture on human happiness to begin with agrees with the pagan poet in its rejection of all worldly ambition:

> Not happie is that Life
>   Which yee as happie hold,
>   No, but a Sea of feares, a field of Strife,
>   Charg'd on a Throne to sit
>   With Diadems of Gold,
>   Preseru'd by Force, and still obseru'd by Wit:
> Huge Treasures to enioy,
>   Of all her Gemmes spoyle *Inde*,
>   All *Seres* silke in Garments to imploy,
>   Deliciously to feed,
>   The Phenix plumes to finde
>   To rest vpon, or decke your purple Bed.

The subsequent rejection of the intellectual pursuit of knowledge of the universe as a source of happiness denotes a conscious departure from Lucretius and Virgil and may be aimed at their portrayal of the happy life:

> Nor can it Blisse you bring,
>   Hidde Natures Depthes to know,
>   Why Matter changeth, whence each Forme doth spring;
>   Nor that your Fame should range,
>   And after-Worlds it blow

From *Tänäis* to *Nile*, from *Nile* to *Gange*.
All these haue not the Powre
  To free the Minde from feares,
  Nor hideous horror can allay one howre,
  When Death in steele doth glance,
  In Sicknesse lurke or yeares,
  And wakes the Soule from out her mortall Trance.

Then follows the true definition of happiness:

No, but blest Life is this,
  With chaste and pure desire,
  To turne vnto the Load-starre of all Blisse,
  On GOD the Minde to rest,
  Burnt vp with sacred Fire,
  Possessing him, to bee by him possest.
  . . . .
To hatch no base Desires
  Or Gold or Land to gaine,
  Well pleas'd with what by Vertue one acquires,
  To haue the Wit and Will
  Consorting in one Straine,
  Than what is good to haue no higher skill.

True love should burn the soul 'with fairest Beames', turning it
towards 'that uncreated Sunne' which reveals such beauty that
all lookers-on would 'pine and die for loue'.

Swift is your mortall Race,
  And glassie is the Field,
  Vaste are Desires not limited by Grace;
  Life a weake Tapper is,
  Then while it light doth yeeld
  Leaue flying ioyes, embrace this lasting Blisse.

The mute creation has listened to this discourse and affirms its truth: 'Birds sang from euery Wood, / And Ecchoes rang, this was true Happinesse.'

To summarise: the pastoral or religious contexts of the poetry so far considered have tended to obscure or obliterate the proper rural note, while the forms employed — songs, sonnets, or pastorals — have been utterly unsuited.

It is therefore with considerable interest that we next turn to the works of Ben Jonson, who is perhaps the first English poet — certainly the first major English poet — to write a proper *beatus ille* poem.

Ben Jonson (1572?-1637) was drawn to Horace not only as a poet, but as a moralist. In his *Discoveries* he confessed that to him Horace was 'the best master, both of vertue, and wisdome; an excellent, and true judge upon cause, and reason.' His version of Horace's second Epode is excellent, despite the fact that it is a completely faithful rendering of the original. By the time of Cowley, paraphrase was the popular way of translating, but Ben Jonson demanded, and achieved, exactness. This exactness is evidenced by the very form, which is that of the elegiac couplet:

1   *Happie* is he, that from all Businesse cleere,
         As the old race of Mankind were,
     With his owne Oxen tills his Sires left lands,
         And is not in the Usurers bands:
5   Nor Souldier-like started with rough alarmes,
         Nor dreads the Seas Inraged harmes:
     But flees the Barre and Courts, with the proud bords,
8   And waiting Chambers of great Lords.[6]

Ben Jonson's translation of Martial's Epigram X, 47 has similar virtues; the diction is pleasantly colloquial, and full of pregnant phrasings which present the thought with force and with precision:

The Things that make the happier life, are these,
Most pleasant Martial; Substance got with ease,
Not labour'd for, but left thee by thy Sire;
A Soyle, not barren; a continewall fire;
Never at Law; seldome in office gown'd;
A quiet mind; free powers; and body sound;
A wise simplicity; freindes alike-stated;
Thy table without art, and easy-rated:
Thy night not dronken, but from cares layd wast;
No sowre, or sollen bed-mate, yet a Chast;
Sleepe, that will make the darkest howres swift-pac't;
Will to bee, what thou art; and nothing more:
Nor feare thy latest day, nor wish therefore.[7]

The poetic compliment to Sir Robert Wroth[8] is Ben Jonson's original contribution to the poetry concerned with the Happy Husbandman. For this poem Ben Jonson chose the same metre which he had employed in his translation of Horace's second Epode; furthermore, it contains clear verbal echoes from Horace's poem, and its overriding purpose is to present Sir Robert as an English counterpart to the Horatian Happy Man. For these reasons the poem must unquestionably be classified as an epode. Horace's epodes contain more argument than his odes, and form a transitional stage between the epistolary and the lyric form. A certain amount of generic doubt is therefore inevitable, but a closer comparison between the lines to Sir Robert and Horace's second Epode will settle the issue. Ben Jonson's interest in the genre is proved by the eleventh poem in *The Forrest*, which is identified as an epode, the metre in this case being pentameters interlaced with trimeters.

If one places Ben Jonson's translation side by side with his poem to Sir Robert Wroth, one discovers that not only are the metre and the sentiments the same, but that the very structure is identical. The same ideas are presented in roughly the same sequence. Both Horace and Ben Jonson begin with an apostrophe to the happy life, the initial words being almost the same. The chief difference follows from the fact that Ben Jonson identifies Sir Robert Wroth as the Happy Man. Hence he writes: 'How blest art thou . . .' Like Horace, Ben Jonson next proceeds to underline the absence of vice and ambition in the sort of life led by his Happy Man. Horace's Happy Man had avoided usurers and the rough alarms suffered by soldiers and sailors, and he fled 'the Barre and Courts, with the proud bords, / And waiting Chambers of great Lords.' Similarly Sir Robert, although placed close to the city and the court, is 'tane with neithers vice, nor sport'; he is no 'ambitious guest / Of Sheriffes dinner, or Maiors feast', nor does he join the crowd '(when masquing is) to haue a sight / Of the short brauerie of the night.' For this reason he is completely free 'from proud porches, or their guilded roofes' and can live at home 'with vn-bought prouision blest' (a direct rendering of Horace's *dapes inemptas*). After these initial statements both poets proceed to descriptions of rural scenes and activities, this being their chief concern. The Happy Man of both poets listens to the lowing herds and enjoys sleep in the shade of the trees and by the bank of a river:

To Sir Robert Wroth:
    [But canst . . . liue . . .]
'Mongst loughing heards, and
    solide hoofes:
Along'st the curled woods, and
    painted meades,
Through which a serpent riuer
    leades
To some coole, courteous shade
    which he calls his,
And makes sleepe softer then
    it is!

Or in the bending Vale beholds
    afarre
The lowing herds there grazing
    are:
Then now beneath some ancient
    Oke he may,
Now in the rooted Grasse him
    lay,
Whilst from the higher Bankes
    doe slide the floods;
The soft birds quarrell in the
    Woods,

> The Fountaines murmure as the
> streames doe creepe.
> And all invite to easie sleepe.

In the subsequent description of rural activities both poets proceed from daytime pursuits to those of the evening, and both
depict rural holidays and the pleasant home-life of the gentleman-farmer. Similarly both touch on the various sports of the
different seasons, Horace describing the hunting of boars, thrush,
hares and cranes, while Ben Jonson dwells on English deer and
partridge, hares, thrush, and hawking. Further echoes from Horace
are encountered in Ben Jonson's lines on rural holidays, but even
more important than these is the fact that the general mood is
exactly the same in both poems.

However, Horace's second Epode is not the only source; the
last thirty-nine lines form a free paraphrase of Virgil's *Georgics*, II,
503-512. Lines 1-67, too, can present occasional echoes from Virgil;
thus the 'proud porches' (1. 15) reflect the 'proud portals' of
Georgics, II, 461. Echoes from Martial are also heard, but more
faintly, in the concluding lines.

Since Sir Robert died in 1614, Jonson must have written his
poem before this date. It would therefore seem to be the earliest
example of the complete conversion into English terms of the
classical *beatus vir*. We have seen how Horace, Virgil, and Martial
contributed to the shaping of Ben Jonson's epode, so that it
becomes, in fact, a sort of anthology of *beatus ille* passages in
loose paraphrase. We can be sure that Sir Robert realised that
Ben Jonson had drawn him as a contemporary counterpart to the
classical *beatus vir*, and that the greatest force of the compliment
lay in exactly this circumstance. The way in which the easily
recognisable echoes were worked into an original composition
would also have provoked much admiration. One imagines that
the relevant classical passages had been conned over by every
schoolboy until he had them word-perfect; hence the clear verbal

echoes of Ben Jonson's poem would have been immediately apprehended. Despite its obvious indebtedness to classical sources, Ben
Jonson's poem is more than a mere imitation. The English poet has
succeeded in stamping this elaborate poetic compliment with his
own genius. There is fire and vigour even in the lines where the
indebtedness is most obvious:

67   Let others watch in guiltie armes, and stand
        The furie of a rash command,
     Goe enter breaches, meet the cannons rage,
70   That they may sleepe with scarres in age.
     And shew their feathers shot, and cullors torne,
        And brag, that they were therefore borne.
     Let this man sweat, and wrangle at the barre,
        For euery price, in euery iarre,
75   And change possessions, oftner with his breath,
        Then either money, warre, or death:
     Let him, then hardest sires, more disinherit,
        And each where boast it as his merit,
     To blow vp orphanes, widdowes, and their states;
80   And thinke his power doth equall *Fates.*
     Let that goe heape a masse of wretched wealth,
        Purchas'd by rapine, worse then stealth,
     And brooding o'er it sit, with broadest eyes,
        Not doing good, scarce when he dyes.
85   Let thousands more goe flatter vice, and winne,
        By being organes to great sinne,
     Get place, and honor, and be glad to keepe
        The secrets, that shall breake their sleepe:
     And, so they ride in purple, eate in plate,
90   Though poyson, thinke it a great fate.

It is, perhaps, superfluous to point out how perfectly the spirit
of the original (*Georgics*, II, 503-512) has been rendered. There

is here no unwarranted intrusion of 17th-century religious sentiment, no interest in solitude and religious contemplation of the
kind which marks the poetry of William Browne, Sir Henry
Wotton, and William Drummond.

'To Penshurst' (the second poem in *The Forrest*)[9] presents
no argument about the happiness of country life, but gives a very
pleasing portrayal of the honesty, innocence, and contentment of
rural life. The initial lines glance at the polished pillars and roofs
of gold denounced by Virgil. 'To the World' (the fourth poem
in the same collection) concludes with praise of the quiet life
spent at home:

65   Nor for my peace will I go farre,
            As wandrers doe, that still doe rome,
        But make my strengths, such as they are,
68   Here in my bosome, and at home.

'Epistle. To Katherine, Lady Avbigny'[10] gives Horatian praise
to the lady for her Stoic virtue; she has been wise enough to avoid
the vulgar crowds, living instead 'Farre from the maze of custome,
error, strife', and keeping 'an euen, and unalter'd gaite'.

The Forrest, then, presents clear evidence of the interest which
Ben Jonson took in classical *beatus ille* sentiments, one poem
being completely devoted to the motif of the Happy Man, and
three poems incorporating briefer references.

Ben Jonson's contemporary, Phineas Fletcher (1582-1650),
possessed a similar interest, but his hand was less felicitous.
Fletcher's translations were published posthumously in 1670 under
the title *A Father's Testament*. Among these is found a version
of the fourth metre from the first book of Boethius' *De Consolatione Philosophiae*, a poem often found in close juxtaposition
with translations of classical *beatus ille* passages. Boethius' denunciation of all passionate desire for wealth, rank, and influence,
and his portrayal of the ambitious man as an unhappy slave,

accord well with the basic doctrines of our tradition. Boethius
stressed the virtues of a solitary, contemplative life in a manner
which was bound to appeal to the neo-Stoic temper of the early
seventeenth century:

> If safe thou wouldst, and quiet dwell,
> Refuse a Palace, chuse a cell.
> Wouldst thou burn out thy fenced light
> In peace, when winds, storms, tempests fight?
> . . . .
> The lowly Rock make thy foundation;
> A strong, and lasting situation.
> When thundring storms with ruins fill
> The pleasant shore, and mounting hill,
> Lodgd in thy trenches, safely lying,
> Fierce winds, and foming seas defying,
> Safe maist thou mock the angry skie,
> And quiet live, and quiet dy.[11]

Fletcher's major work is the Spenserian poem, *The Purple
Island*. Fletcher's island is a symbolic representation of man and
of society, its tragedy being caused by its failure to remain content.
Fletcher carefully contrasts the woeful consequences of discontent
with the happiness inherent in a life which is contented. The
spirits of Boethius and Virgil hover over the island on more than
one occasion. Although Fletcher must have known Virgil's *o fortunatos nimium* passage, his own paraphrase of this passage[12]
seems indebted to Du Bartas' paraphrase of it as rendered by
Sylvester (*Du Bartas His Deuine Weekes and Workes Translated*).
The point is not important, except as a reminder of the undoubted
influence of Continental literature.

Two of Fletcher's minor poems deserve special mention. These
are 'To my ever honoured Cousin W. R. Esquire'[13] and 'To Mr.
Jo. Tomkins'.[14] The latter may furnish a brief quotation:

Ah! could'st thou here thy humble minde content
Lowly with me to live in countrey cell,
And learn suspect the courts proud blandishment;
Here might we safe, here might we sweetly dwell.

. . . .

 Safe in my humble cottage will I rest;
 And lifting up from my untainted breast
A quiet spirit to heav'n, securely live, and blest.

A final classical echo is found in the second act of *Sicelides*, a play performed at Cambridge in 1615. Lines 13-31 of the chorus form a conscious and readily recognised paraphrase of *Georgics*, II, 475-486.

 As far as original poetry is concerned, the first twenty-five years of the seventeenth century have yielded a very meagre harvest. Ben Jonson's epode to Sir Robert Wroth is the only convincing example of a proper *beatus ille* poem; it is the only poem completely devoted to an exposition of *beatus ille* motifs, and it is the only poem to do this in a form which comes as close as possible to the Horatian epode. Other poets touch on such motifs more or less incidentally, and in sonnets, pastorals, or simple songs — forms utterly unsuited to render the proper mood and argument of these motifs. The tendency at this early date is to veer in one of two directions: either towards the pastoral (as in the case of William Byrd, William Browne, and Phineas Fletcher), or in the direction of the religious lyric (William Drummond of Hawthornden), or again in the direction of both.

CHAPTER III

THE SERENE CONTEMPLATOR

As soon as we enter the second quarter of the seventeenth century it becomes apparent that we have reached the first decisive phase in the history of the motifs with which we are concerned. During the reign of Charles I translations and imitations of classical *beatus ille* poems were published with a frequency which suggests a decided popularity.

Translations from Horace were particularly frequent. The second Epode was singled out for translation by a number of poets. Thus Sir John Beaumont translated three Horatian poems in praise of country life for *Bosworth-Field* (1629) — the second Epode, Satire II, 6 and Ode III, 29. He also translated Claudian's epigram on the old man from Verona — altogether a significant selection. Thomas Randolph, too, translated Horace's second Epode and Claudian's epigram, as well as Martial's advice to himself (Epigram X, 47). The date of the first edition of Wye Saltonstall's *The Country Mouse, and the City Mouse* (Satire II, 6) is not known; the second edition came in 1637.

John Ashmore's *Certain Selected Odes of Horace* (1621) was the first publication completely devoted to Horatian translations. This was followed by Thomas Hawkins's translation of thirty-six odes and five epodes in 1625; enlarged and corrected editions appeared in 1631, 1635, and 1638, the last totalling sixty-four odes and eight epodes out of a total of one hundred and thirty. Henry Rider published the first complete translation of all the odes and epodes in 1638, but this was only the beginning. The enthusiasm for Horatian translations persisted throughout the century. John Smith published another version of all the odes and epodes in 1649; Sir Richard Fanshawe published a selection in

1652, Holyday more or less pirated Hawkins's earlier translations in 1653, while complete editions of Horace's works in English translation were published by Alexander Brome in 1666, by Thomas Creech in 1684, and by John Harington in the same year. To this one must add the poetic miscellanies of the Restoration, many of which published generous selections of Horatian translations. This is particularly true of Dryden's miscellanies. Dryden's version of the second Epode is especially noteworthy.

Hesiod, Virgil, and Martial also received their share of attention. Thus Hesiod's portrayal of the simple country life appealed to the serious-minded George Chapman (*The Georgicks of Hesiod*, 1618), while Thomas May focussed on Virgil's *Georgics* (1628). John Ogilby's translation of Virgil's collected works proved so popular that the first edition of 1649 was followed by re-issues in 1650, 1654, 1665, 1668, and 1684. The century terminates with Dryden's excellent translation of 1697. The first translation of all Martial's epigrams appeared in 1656 (R. Fletcher, *Ex otio Negotium*); a liberal selection had been given to the public in 1629 by Thomas May (*Select Epigrams of Martial*). However, the frequent individual translations of Epigram X, 47 are a better indication of interest in *beatus ille* sentiments. We have already quoted from Ben Jonson's translation, and we have referred to translations made by John Ashmore, Thomas Randolph, and Abraham Cowley. Further translations are found in Owen Feltham's collection of essays, *Resolves*[1] (first published in the early 'twenties and reprinted at frequent intervals in the following years), in Mildmay Fane's *Otia Sacra* (1648), Sir Edward Sherburne's *Poems and Translations* (1651), Charles Cotton's *Poems* (1689), and Thomas Heyrick's *Miscellany Poems* (1691). Most of these translated Claudian's epigram on the old man from Verona, so that the two epigrams must have been considered as companion poems. The roll-call in this case includes Sir John Beaumont, Thomas Randolph, Mildmay Fane, Abraham Cowley, and Henry Vaughan.

This sudden increase in translations after 1625 is matched by a corresponding increase in the production of original *beatus ille* poetry. Not only are more poems inspired by such motifs but their quality is such that they form an important part of the poetic heritage of the period. In the works of William Habington, John Milton, Robert Herrick, Sir John Denham, Henry Vaughan, and Andrew Marvell the motif of a happy country life found enduring and arresting poetic expression. The austerity of life depicted by Horace and Virgil, and its retired character, appealed to the rising generation of poets. This was so largely because the classical ideal with very few changes could be made to conform to the religious temper of the age.

What happened can best be shown by means of an example. In 1635 William Habington published a poem which gives moving expression to the desire so to 'controule / What-ere is earth in us, to grow all soule'.[2] The sentiment is typical of the piety of the early seventeenth century; what is new, is its presence in a Horatian epistle, and the view that the process of growing 'all soule' can only be achieved in 'the pure innocence oth' Country ayre'. In his companion poems Milton effects a similar union between the classical motif of the Happy Man and the religious motif of the ecstatic delights of solitary contemplation. Since we do not know the date of composition of Milton's poems, it is impossible to tell whether Milton or Habington was the first to add the joys of solitude so decisively to the list of virtues typical of a retired rural existence. Habington's *Castara* (published in 1634, and with additions in 1635 and 1640) may, or may not, have appeared before Milton wrote his poems. At all events, Milton did not publish till 1645, so that the honour of being first in the field must be given to the Roman Catholic, rather than the Puritan poet. However, if one considers the entire European scene, Habington must yield the place to another Roman Catholic: the Polish Jesuit Casimire Sarbiewski.[3] The Horatian odes published by the 'divine Casimire' in 1625 and 1628 gained immediate European acclaim, and earned for their author the name of *Horatius Redivivus*.

Casimire was primarily interested in Horace's Stoic motifs; several of his finest lyrics constitute a religious version of the Horatian rural ode. Like Habington and Milton, Casimire transforms the Horatian Happy Man into a pious religious contemplator who courts rural solitude because it brings him face to face with God.

There is no external evidence to show whether Habington and Milton were at all influenced by the Polish poet; whether, in fact, they took their cue from him when they turned to *beatus ille* motifs, and to the form of the Horatian ode or epistle. It seems likely in view of the fact that Casimire was the most famous neo-Latin poet of his generation. The case of William Habington is particularly interesting, since he changed in mid-stream, as it were, from sonnets and love lyrics to odes and epistles. The first edition of *Castara* (1634) is a traditional sonnet sequence; fifty-four of its eighty-nine poems are sonnets, the rest are love lyrics. Only four of the twenty-six new poems added in 1635 are sonnets, while not a single new sonnet was added to the third expanded edition of 1640. Habington had suddenly become interested in the new medium of epistles and odes, and in motifs associated with these forms. It is possible and probable that this sudden change was stimulated by perusing the work of his famous co-religionist. On reading these, Habington may have seen how Horatian forms and motifs could be made the vehicle of sentiments more closely in keeping with his own needs and with the spirit of the times.

Before we approach Habington and Milton, it will therefore be necessary to discuss Casimire's contribution to the tradition of the Happy Man. Seven of Casimire's poems can be studied in the translation of Henry Vaughan (*Olor Iscanus*, 1651), but a more representative selection is found in G. Hills's *Odes of Casimire* (1646).[4] Sir Edward Sherburne's translations (*Poems and Translations*, 1651) are not concerned with rural retirement, but are nevertheless useful in that they prove familiarity with Casimire's poetry. However, although translations are significant, it must be remembered that the Latin text was easily accessible to seventeenth-century readers and hence indubitably better known. The English translations are therefore used here largely for the convenience of readers, and because my own Latin is so scanty.

1.

The Odes of Casimire

A majority of Casimire's odes present Stoic arguments about the nature of true wisdom or nobility. The rise and fall of transitory things is movingly described; virtue only remains, and virtue consists in a mind unmoved by external circumstance and entirely focussed on eternal issues. Man must be his own chief magistrate to prevent the 'fierce Fates' from molesting the serene palace of his breast (Ode III, 4). He should spurn the 'baser path of life' pursued by the multitude, remembering that 'In highest and remotest Hills / Vertue sequesters up her selfe, and dwells' (Ode IV, 10). Odes IV, 12 and IV, 15 directly recommend rural retirement. The first confesses that 'A private fame, a meane house, where / I live conceal'd from popular ayre, / Best fits my mind, and shelters me.' The title of the second boldly states that 'nothing in humane affaires is not full of tediousnesse', and the poem itself imitates Horace's Ode II, 16 in its insistence on the uselessness of courting happiness by moving from one place to another. Happiness is in man himself, not in his external environment. Nothing on earth is exempt from decay: 'The Sun / Which bright to our forefathers shone / To us, but little healthfull, doth appeare, / And though not guilty of one spott, not cleare.' Instead of realising this, man is full of ambitious envy and tries to improve his lot by moving to another residence:

> Each yeare we change our ayre, and soyle, so light;
> Him, *Hollands* warmer Climate doth invite:
> Another differs, and doth cry

Ausonia's clearer Suns please mee.
In vain all this, if faithfull sicknesses
Wait close behind; if secret griefes ne're cease,
. . . .
Who a sure building can from vertue boast,
　To him the smoke of's father's Hall
　Doth never hurt his eyes at all.
Vertue oft-times, rich in a rustick ease,
Confines her selfe to her owne private blisse;
　And in the guiltlesse straw, her throne
　With great delight can leane upon.

Casimire's first Epode is a poetic compliment to the Duke of
Bracciano; its sub-title explains that 'Hee commends the pleasant-
nesse of the Countrey, where, in the feasts of *September,* he
retyred from Rome.' The commendation largely consists in delightful descriptions of the scenery on the estate of the Duke, descriptions which abound in 'Witt pure and quaint, with rich conceits'.
Thus the fish are referred to as 'large-fin'd Chrystall cattell', and
the fields turn into a waving sea: 'The fields with yellow waves
doe ebbe and flow, / The ripe ears swim, when winds doe blow.'
A veritable Golden Age reigns; everything is peace and quiet, and
the stars rain down their occult influences upon the earth. The
metre — pentameters alternating with tetrameters — approxi-
mates the elegiac couplets employed by Horace.

The same metre is found in the third Epode, which gives
Casimire's reply to Horace's famous second Epode. The poem
falls into two contrasting parts. The first passionately rejects all
worldly thoughts and desires and describes the religious contemplator as the only Happy Man. The second offers pleasant descriptions of rural life.

Casimire's Happy Man has abandoned, not only the fierce
wrangling lawyers and the 'sinfull gates o'th' greedy Court', but
also his father's estate or grounds. Instead of tending cows or

sheep, he 'strives to collect and find / The dispers'd flock of's wandring mind.' At evening he contemplates the sky, filled with longing for 'the open Courts of light' and for 'thy selfe, o Christ'. He is a Platonic or Hermetic exile from the stars, who lies prostrate on the ground while the stars 'with golden wheeles, are hurried by'. The contemplation leads to an extreme concentration of his mental powers: 'From depth of soule, lesse then himselfe he lies, / And bends the angry pow'rs with cryes' (*Mentis profundus, & sui totus minor / Irata flectit numina*). Next he turns his eyes on the surrounding landscape, and everywhere he finds evidence of spiritual penetration, in the manner of the Platonic and Hermetic philosopher. The vegetable world is penetrated by a desire for union with the ultimate source of life, as reflected by the stars, and the stars in their turn attract the earth. Viewing all this, the contemplator desires a similar union:

> He viewes the fields, and wondring stands to see
>   In's shade the shining Deitie.
> See how (saies he) each herb with restlesse leaves
>   To th' starres doth strive and upward heaves:
> Remov'd from heaven they weep, the field appeares
>   All o're dissolv'd in pious teares:
> The white-flowr'd Woodbine, and the blushing Rose
>   Branch into th'aire with twining boughs;
> The pale-fac'd Lilly on the bending stalke,
>   To th' starres I know not what doth talke;
> At night with fawning sighes they' expresse their fears
>   And in the morning drop down teares.
> Am I alone, wretch that I am, fast bound
>   And held with heavy weight, to th' ground?
> Thus spake he to the neighbouring trees, thus he
>   To th' Fountaines talk'd, and streames ran by,
> And after, seekes the great Creator out
>   By these faire traces of his foot.

One realises the irresistible attraction this type of poem must have held for a man like Henry Vaughan. Although Vaughan's own translation of this epode is a much finer literary effort, it fails to convey the lush atmosphere of the original. Casimire's description of the 'amorus green' is rendered in terms which are less passionate and more abstract and spiritual.

Casimire's religious sentiments are pervaded by Neoplatonic and Hermetic ideas. Thus the mutual attraction between flowers and herbs on the one hand, and the stars on the other, suggests the Hermetic account of creation.[5] Casimire's familiarity with the Hermetic writings is seen even more clearly in his Ode II, 5, which is a poetic paraphrase of the first Hermetic *Libellus*, sections 25 and 26.[6]

To summarise: Casimire's palinode to Horace's second Epode transforms the Horatian Husbandman into a solitary religious contemplator of the world, a Platonic or Hermetic exile from the stars (the world of pure mind), whose chief purpose is to achieve union with the Deity. Although his retirement is marked by an ascetic austerity, an erotic intensity is felt throughout. The religious contemplator is a passionate lover of God, like the white-flowered woodbine and the blushing rose.

The second half of the poem, however, is as Horatian as one could wish in its portrayal of the simple, but true joys of country life. Casimire dwells lovingly on the 'plaine board with country dainties set' — new bread, salt, freshly picked strawberries, 'Cheese newly press'd', a 'messe of Beanes', and 'Clusters of grapes late gathered'. Muted echoes from Horace are heard in the description of rural activities:

> Then after noone he takes a kind of pride
>   To th' Hills to walke, or River side,
> And 'midst the pleasant Okes, a shade doth find,
> . . . .
> Sometimes the sporting fish, his baite thrown in,

Hee plucks up with his trembling line.
Meanwhile the spacious woods with echoing note
    Doe answer to the Bulls wide throat,

. . . .

With's hastning pipe the sheapheard drives away
    His flocke, which through the thickets stray:
To which as from the field they passe along,
    Each mower sings by course, his song;
O're yielding furrowes, carts full press'd with corne
    Groane, and are like to break the barne.
Our worke once done, we doe not silent sit,
    When knots of our good fellowes meet;
Nor is our talke prolong'd with rude delay;
    In harmlesse jests we spend the day . . .

Marvell has been praised for introducing the mower into his
landscape; as we have just seen, this was done some twenty-five
years before by Casimire Sarbiewski.

   Although the contents of Casimire's lyrics are our prime concern, one should not underestimate the influence of his poetry as
poetry. Casimire has much in common with the English metaphysical poets; his witty conceits and lovely descriptions of rural
scenes anticipate the achievement of poets like Henry Vaughan
and Andrew Marvell. He has all their piety (tinged with Hermetic
occultism), and the same keen eye for details in a landscape.
Conceits like the one about the hours which 'drive on heav'ns
torch' represent the same kind of wit which has made Marvell
famous. Casimire's odes must therefore have exerted considerable
attraction solely on formal grounds. No history of the ode in the
seventeenth century would therefore be complete without a consideration of the pervasive influence of the 'divine Casimire'. Here
was a man who combined a complete command of classical Latin
with poetic sensitivity, with polished wit, and with a high moral
and religious intensity. No wonder, therefore, that his odes in many

European schools came to replace those of Horace. In the eyes of Casimire's century, his formal excellence equalled that of Horace, while his subject-matter placed him far above the pagan poet.

2.

Rosse, Wither, Fanshawe, Chamberlain, and Randolph

We have traced neo-Stoic as well as Platonic and Hermetic elements in Casimire's treatment of *beatus ille* motifs. The English poets now to be considered are marked almost entirely by the Stoic philosophy; the popularity of the *beatus ille* tradition in its early stages correlates exactly with the rising popularity of neo-Stoic ideas. The trend in favour of a retired, introspective existence at this time grew so strong that it almost amounted to a compulsion.

Although a preference for the *via contemplativa* can be traced through all ages, the early seventeenth century witnessed an important phase in this ancient bent of the human mind. The religious and political situation combined to stimulate the desire for solitary introspection. Solitude came to be viewed, not as an ascetic negation of life, but as a source of endless delight. A typical statement to this effect can be quoted from Herman Hugo's *Pia Desideria Emblematis*. This tremendously popular emblem book, written by a Roman Catholic, expresses the ecstatic attitude to solitary contemplation in witty, paradoxical phrases. The city is a prison, while solitude is paradise:

> Oppidum, carcer; solitudo, paradysus est.
> O solitudo beatà! ô Ereme, mors vitiorum, vita virtutum!
> te lex & Prophetae mirantur, & quicumque ad perfectionem
> venerunt, per te in Paradysum introierunt: ô beata vita solitaria
> & contemplativa...[7]

The English Roman Catholic, Walter Mountague (*Miscellanea*

Spiritualia, 1648) speaks with equal fervour about 'this holy Garden of Speculation', where one is placed 'under the shady leaves of the Tree of Life'. There one achieves complete separation from the world and passes 'away out of this life by a kind of translation to glory'.[8]

This fondness for contemplative solitude cut across all religious party lines and was by no means the expression of a peculiarly Roman Catholic tendency. The manner in which this bias tempered the traditional picture of the Happy Man is clearly seen from a number of prose character sketches written by Joseph Hall, Wye Saltonstall, and John Earle. Both Hall and Saltonstall interpret the ideal character as a serene contemplator of life, and not as an active participant. Thus Joseph Hall's sketch called 'He is an Happy Man' (strongly indebted to Seneca's Epistle CXII) insists that 'His eyes stick so fast in heaven, that no earthly object can remove them; yea, his whole selfe is there before his time'.[9] Saltonstall's *Picturae Loquentes* (1631 and 1635) presents the happy man in the following terms:

> He esteemes not the empty mirth of this world, but delights in the inward joy of his owne conscience, and through the perspective of contemplation, takes a view of Heaven. His minde is like the Halcyon smoothnesse of the Sea, which is not troubled with the least winde of passion, but rests in a quiet calmnesse.[10]

To Saltonstall happiness is the same as virtue, and virtue is the result of Stoical self-possession tempered by Christian piety. How well Casimire expressed this attitude can be seen from his Ode III, 22, here quoted in the translation of Henry Vaughan:

> Let not thy *youth* and *false delights*
> Cheat thee of *life; Those headdy flights*
> But wast thy *time,* which posts away
> Like *winds* unseen, and swift as they.
> *Beauty* is but meer *paint,* whose *die*
> With times *breath* will *dissolve* and *flye,*

'Tis *wax*, 'tis *water*, 'tis a *glasse*
It *melts*, *breaks*, and *away* doth *passe*
. . . .

   Happy the *Man*! who in this *vale*
Redeems his time, shutting out all
Thoughts of the *world*, whose *longing Eyes*
Are ever *Pilgrims* in the *skyes*,
That views his *bright home*, and desires
To *shine* amongst those *glorious fires*.[11]

Exactly similar sentiments are found in John Earle's character sketch of 'A contemplative man'. 'He scorns to mix himself in men's actions' and instead 'knits his observations together, and makes a ladder of them all to climb to God.'[12]

In times of unrest, obscurity will always be preferred by the prudent, just as the virtue of tranquil contentment will be the lesson preached by those intent on preserving the *status quo*. This was true not only of England. All Europe was in unrest; from Poland to England the years of the third, fourth, and fifth decades were spattered with blood. In England the position of the individual was precarious also in the years preceding the actual outbreak of hostilities. Dr. Bastwick's polemic against the episcopal hierarchy in 1637 cost him his ears, while John Lilburne was whipped across London, pilloried, and imprisoned for daring to withstand the authority of the Star Chamber. No wonder that Owen Feltham devoted an essay to the topic of 'How the Distempers of these Times, should affect wise Men',[13] concluding that the distempers were incurable and that he was a fool who exposed himself needlessly to danger. The popular preacher Robert Sanderson, whose sermons appeared at regular intervals in the years from 1619 to 1648, voiced the same opinion:

> It is the most proper act of fortitude to endure hardship. True: to endure it; but not to provoke it. We shall be like to find in the world hardship enough, whereon to exercize our

manhood, without seeking. It is a foolhardy madness ... to roam abroad to seek adventure ... Fortitude is an excellent virtue doubtless; but so is prudence too.[14]

It was not always possible for men of moderation to follow their own natural bent. The Earl of Clarendon describes how Lucius Cary, Lord Falkland, resolved to 'retyre to a country life, and to his bookes', and it is well known how, at Great Tew, he established as it were a 'college situated in a purer air'. Just as Nicholas Ferrar's community at Little Gidding expresses the kind of retirement favoured by pious Anglicans, Lord Falkland's circle at Great Tew represents the forces of reason and moderation, obliged to seek shelter from the threatening storm. Nevertheless, when the war finally became an open fact, Lord Falkland, very much against his wishes, was forced to take an active part in the conflict. His subsequent death in battle in 1643 was believed to be a form of suicide.

The influence of the political unrest makes itself strongly felt in the poetry of the 'thirties and 'forties. 'The Commendation of the priuate Country Life' (1630) by Alexander Rosse, the friend of John Evelyn and Edward Benlowes, associates innocence, truth, and a quiet life with the country-side, while the towns are seen to harbour envy, flattery, treason, slander, pride, and usury. George Wither (1588-1667) suffered imprisonment in 1614 and 1621 for political reasons; after 1630 he seems to have lost heart, since one of his emblems, published in 1635 and dedicated to the King, advices men to court retirement from the world in the manner of monks. The motto of this emblem (Number II, 11) reads *In silentio et spe*, and the explanatory poem places 'true Content' in the ability to 'live remote, from places of resort'. Emblem II, 24 uses the tortoise as symbol of the prudent mind which has taken refuge in a Stoical withdrawal from the world.

On the occasion of the proclamation of peace with Spain in 1630 Sir Richard Fanshawe took the opportunity to support the king by writing an ode 'Commanding the Gentry to reside upon their Estates in the Country'.[15] Parliament had been dissolved by the king in the previous year, and hence the landed gentry, in their enforced retirement from Westminster, would obviously be unable to stir up trouble against the Crown. Fanshawe's ode explicitly exploits *beatus ille* arguments in order to give political support to the king. He begins by describing how all Europe is torn by war; England alone enjoys 'White Peace (the beautiful'st of things)'. Nevertheless, the gentry 'Leave the despised Fields to clownes' 'as if some foe were here', instead seeking their pleasure in 'walled Townes'. This convergence on London is described as a fleeing 'Into the roote' of the 'sapp and bloud o'th' land' which chokes the heart. Hence the sovereign the 'growing evill doth oppose' by forcing his subjects 'to enjoy / The peace hee made'.

> To rowle themselves in envy'd leasure
> He therefore sends the Landed Heyres,
> Whilst hee proclaimes not his own pleasure
> So much as theirs.
>
> . . . .
>
> O, 'twas an act, not for my muse
> To celebrate, nor the dull Age
> Untill the country aire infuse
> A purer rage!
>
> And if the Fields as thankfull prove
> For benefits receiv'd, as seed,
> They will, to quite so great a love,
> A *Virgill* breed.
>
> A *Tityrus*, that shall not cease
> Th' *Augustus* of our world to praise
> In equall verse, author of peace
> And *Halcyon* dayes.

84

Nor let the Gentry grudge to goe
Into those places whence they grew,
But thinke them blest they may doe soe.
    Who would pursue

The smoaky glory of the Towne,
That may goe till his native earth,
And by the shining fire sit downe
    Of his owne hearth,

Free from the griping Scriveners bands,
And the more byting Mercers books;
Free from the bayt of oyled hands
    And painted looks?
. . . .
Beleeve me Ladies you will finde
In that sweet life, more solid joyes,
More true contentment to the minde
    Than all Town-toyes.

In the country love is true and chaste; one may listen to the nightingale and the 'lyricke Larke', admire the 'Commonwealth of Flowres' and plant trees that shoot up with one's children.

Fanshawe's ode is a successful lyric which merits comparison with the retirement poetry written by more famous poets. It was published in 1648 in a collection of original poems appended to the second edition of his translation of Guarini's *Il Pastor Fido*.

A passage in Robert Farley's *Kalendarivm Hvmanae Vitae* (1638) conveys a similar political lesson:

O happy mankind, if men once did know
With meane estate themselves content to show!
That life is safest which doth keepe a meane,
Free from ambition, and from falsehood cleane.

... When thunder strikes the highest hill,
More safely in a cottage you may lurke,
Then in a Pallace cursed treason worke.[16]

Robert Chamberlain's *Nocturnall Lucubrations* (1638 and 1652) occasionally depart from the expression of religious gloom to genuine appreciation of 'the sweet that dwells / In low built cottages, and country cells'. 'In praise of a Country Life' queries the value of 'Scepters, Thrones, and Crowns of Kings', these are but 'gilded burdens, and most fickle things'.

> . . . he that's contented
> Lives in a thousand times a happier man,
> . . . Th' imbroidred meadows, & the crawling streams
> Make soft and sweet his undisturbed dreams:
> . . . This harmlesse life he leads, and I dare say
> Doth neither wish, nor feare his dying day.[17]

The last line echoes the conclusion to Martial's Epigram X, 47. Chamberlain's pleasant epistle 'To his kind and loving friend, Mr. Henry Prigg, Citizen of Exeter. On the sweetnesse of Contentation'[18] declares that honour is a spur which pricks the ambitious man, but the poet knows 'A state more full of sweet security'. This is the state of the 'russet farmer'. The subsequent genre pictures are realistic in the Horatian manner, and curiously pleasant despite the amateur character of the poetry.

It has already been stated that Thomas Randolph (1605-1635) translated Horace's second Epode, Claudian's epigram on the old man from Verona, and Martial's Epigram X, 47. Randolph's own contribution to the tradition is a beautifully pliant ode.[19] Its rhythmical movement conveys a feeling of joyous impetuosity:

> Come spurre away,
> I have no patience for a longer stay;

                    But must goe downe,
    And leave the chargeable noise of this great Towne.
                    I will the country see,
                    Where old simplicity,
                        Though hid in gray
                        Doth looke more gay
    Then foppery in plush and scarlat clad.
                    Farewell you City-wits that are
                        Almost at Civil warre;
    'Tis time that I grow wise, when all the world grows mad.
    . . . .

                        There from the tree
    We'll cherries pluck, and pick the strawberry.
                        And every day
    Go see the wholesome country girls make hay,
                    Whose brown hath lovelier grace
                    Than any painted face
                        That I do know
                        Hyde Park can show;

    . . . .

                        Ours is the sky,
    Where at what fowl we please our hawk shall fly;
                        Nor will we spare
    To hunt the crafty fox or timorous hare . . .

This is the note of true rural enthusiasm; Randolph's country
pleasures are real ones, and the ode is a genuine poetic creation
despite its indebtedness to Ben Jonson (for the form) and to
Martial (for some of its ideas).

Randolph seems to have been one of the first to realise the
potentialities of the irregular ode when applied to this particular
motif; its free rhythms permit the true note of enthusiastic rapture
so proper to a poem on happiness, while its length permits a
detailed account of rural activities. After 1660 the irregular ode

came to prevail in this type of poem, largely because of the example set by Abraham Cowley.

3.

William Habington

William Habington (1605-1654), Roman Catholic poet at the court of Queen Henrietta Maria, was preoccupied with the idea of retirement to an extraordinary extent. His *Observations Vpon Historie* (1641) is nothing but a sermon, in the best manner of Lipsius or Joseph Hall, on the vanity of the world and on the necessity of withdrawing from it. Lipsius, in the manner of the Stoics, had recommended an active life unless the state 'be possessed with mischiefs', but Habington (like Owen Feltham) advised complete inaction unless specifically called upon to perform a public duty. The concluding chapter of Habington's *Observations* is one sustained panegyric of Charles V, the emperor who left his throne to embrace the solitary life. His own professed purpose in writing the book was not so much to discuss the events of the past as to create a piece of writing capable of influencing all sober spirits to seek a secure refuge from the world and their own frailties. The retired life led by Habington at Hindlip Hall shows that he knew how to follow his own advice. Habington's life and poetry are typical of a generation whose energy was largely directed to an intellectual or mystical quest for the truth which is in man: *intra te quaere Deum*. The Elizabethan spirit of adventure was definitely dead; to the translators and imitators of Claudian, Martial, Horace, and Virgil the daring sea captain could be nothing but a fool. The real wise man knew better than to risk his life and his immortal soul for the tinsel trappings of this world.

Habington's most recent biographer, Kenneth Allott, deplores the fact that we know so very little about his life. 'Habington was born, was educated, married and made friends, published a few books, and died: with certain dates, names and places attached to this statement we have almost all we know of his career.' This very obscurity is typical of the man. In contrast, the life of the father was as violent as that of the son was quiet; Thomas Habington was deeply implicated in the plots involving Mary Stuart and in the Gunpowder Plot, and Hindlip Hall was a Roman Catholic stronghold with no less than eleven hiding-places for priests and papal agents. William Habington, on the other hand, remained completely passive, even during the years of the Civil War, so that Anthony Wood, one generation later, suggested that the poet 'did run with the times, and was not unknown to Oliver, the usurper'.[20] Allott proves that this was not true, but the very fact that it was at all possible for a Restoration biographer to make such a remark proves that the poet can have made no public demonstration of his Royalist allegiance.

Thus in the contrast between the lives of Thomas and William Habington can be measured the full extent of the change which had come over the spirit of the age. To the father, public affairs were more important than considerations of his own welfare or that of his family, but the son sought the path of virtue in the secluded, introspective and inglorious air of a half scholarly, half religious retreat from the world. William Habington was himself the Serene Contemplator of his lyrics and epistles.

We know that the poet was not sent to Oxford or Cambridge because of his faith. Instead he attended the well-known Jesuit College of St. Omer in France and afterwards spent some time in Paris. By 1629 he was established in London, where he frequented the court and the theatre. The *précieuse* atmosphere of the court is clearly mirrored in Habington's love poetry, which insists on purity and innocence in erotic relations. Habington's earliest love poetry may be said to constitute a late flourishing of the Petrarchan mode; much of it is written in a form which resembles the sonnet. These are the least interesting of Habington's poems; much more powerful are those whose inspiration derived from the Horatian ode or epistle. Of these, an impressive number present a religious version of *beatus ille* sentiments.

The indebtedness to Horace is clearly felt in the masculine lines addressed 'To the Honourable Mr. Wm. E.'[21] The Stoicism of Habington's Happy Man is apparent. Like Horace, Habington denounces the ambitious or avaricious man and instead praises the man with an unmoved, quiet mind. To this Habington adds religious overtones; he is as much concerned with eternal issues as with the 'humble quiet' decreed for him by fate:

1   He who is good is happy. Let the loude
           Artillery of Heaven breake through a cloude
           And dart a thunder at him; hee'le remaine
           Vnmov'd and nobler comfort entertaine
5   In welcomming th' approach of death; then vice
           Ere found in her fictitious Paradise.
           . . . .
17   What should we covet here? Why interpose
           A cloud twixt us and heaven? Kind Nature chose
           Mans soule th' Exchecquer where she hoord her wealth,
20   And lodge all her rich secrets; but by th' stealth
           Of our owne vanity, w'are left so poore,
22   The creature meerely sensuall knowes more.

As an example of creatures 'meerely sensuall' who know more than man, Habington inserts the fabled story of the 'learn'd *Halcyon*' which knows how to find the gentlest seasons during which to breed on the otherwise tempestuous waves of the sea. Man on the other hand, is betrayed by his vanity, pride, and avarice to court the tempests of the world. The poet's denunciation of these vices follows the established pattern:

34   Merchants plough the maine
           And bring home th' Indies, yet aspire to more,

By avarice in the possession poore.
And yet that Idoll wealth we all admit
Into the soules great temple. Busie wit
39   Invents new Orgies ...
41   ... while the beast
Content with Natures courtesie doth rest.
Let man then boast no more a soule, since he
44   Hath lost that great prerogative.

'But thee', so Habington continues, 'thee ... I must commend'. The recipient of the epistle is the prototype of the Happy Man; fortune has separated him from the crowds of the vulgar, while virtue has raised him far higher than his birth.

Horatian echoes are numerous. The initial lines recall Horace's description of the unmoved mind in Ode I, 22 (*Integer vitae*). Its total effect is not dissimilar to Horace's very first ode (I, 1) written in praise of Maecenas. The paradox in line 36 is taken from Ovid's line *Desunt Luxuriae multa, Avaritiae Omnia.* Even greater similarity of mood and phrasing is found if one compares, not Horace, but Casimire's Horatian imitations. Thus the heading of Casimire's Ode III, 6 maintains that 'those are the true riches which are fetch'd from the goods of the mind', and the ode itself drives home this point in a series of witty paradoxes. Casimire, too, proclaims that his own closed mind (Habington: 'the soules great temple') is more wide and expansive than the rich Indies, to which one can sail at most only thrice a year. And if all his riches were taken from him, he would not be the poorer for it as long as his own self remained complete (*Nunquam pauperior, si meus integer*). The initial lines may have been inspired by Casimire's description of 'The Kingdome of a wise man' (Ode IV, 3). Like Habington, Casimire states that a man who has achieved a Stoic invulnerability through a victory over his own desires, will stand unmoved though the heavens should fall on his head:

> Hee, though the Sea should every where
> Hang up its waves i'th' flitting ayre;
> And the rough winds on him, should presse
> Flames mix'd with billowes, nay whole Seas,
> From the high Court of's lofty mind
> I'th' midst o'th' ruine, sport can find.

If one places Habington's epistle side by side with Horace's Ode I, 1 and I, 22 and with Casimire's Odes III, 6 and IV, 3, one realises that Casimire and Habington paraphrase Horace's Stoic ideas in exactly the same manner. Both have converted the Stoic ideal into a Christian one, and they do this by focussing on man's eternal destination, that is, on his soul rather than on his moral virtues. It is the soul of man which is betrayed by his vanity, ambition, and avarice, not just his mental serenity or worldly happiness.

At least eleven of Habington's poems are in this neo-Stoic vein. Thus some of his poetic compliments to Castara praise her for embodying the Horatian quality of contented obscurity. 'To Castara. The Vanity of Avarice' and 'The Description of Castara'[23] exploit the image of the obscure violet as a symbol of the retired life. The former denounces pride, avarice and love of glory, and thus suits the pattern of a Horatian ode well enough; the second attributes to Castara all the virtues of an obscure and pious existence:

> Like the Violet which alone
> Prospers in some happy shade;
> My *Castara* lives unknowne,
> To no looser eye betray'd.
>   For shee's to her selfe untrue
>   Who delights ith' publicke view.

She spurns the court, since 'Vertue safely cannot sit / Where vice is enthron'd for wit'. Her reason keeps her wild passions captive, and so her pure thoughts fly to heaven.

Horatian forms and ideas are encountered even more frequently in Habington's religious poetry. 'Et Exultavit Humiles'[24]
illustrates how Habington could present purely religious ideas by
means of imagery and arguments taken from the Horatian moral
and rural ode. The first stanza attributes to the sun a partiality
for the hidden brook 'which silently doth runne / Without a
name', while the broad channel of the Thames is spurned. The
second dwells on the exposed nature of life on mountain tops,
'Though they appeare / To bid defiance to the skie'. In contrast
the humble man of stanza 3 'heaves up his head / Like some
rich vale / Whose fruits nere faile'. The Almighty deals with
man in the manner of the *beatus ille* philosopher: he prefers the
humble cottager to the king.

>   ... from his ill-thatcht roofe he brings
>   The Cottager
>   And doth preferre
>   Him to th' adored state of Kings:
>   He bids that hand
>   Which labour hath made rough and tand
>   The all commanding Scepter beare.
>
>   Let then the mighty cease to boast
>   Their boundlesse sway:
>   Since in their Sea
>   Few sayle, but by some storme are lost.
>   Let them themselves
>   Beware, for they are their owne shelves.
>   Man still himselfe hath cast away.

When we turn to Sir John Denham, it will be well worth remembering that Habington, a few years before *Cooper's Hill*
(1642), had learnt to present moral lessons by means of symbolic
imagery taken from nature, and that he possibly was inspired to
do so by his perusal of Casimire's neo-Latin odes.

Habington's character sketch of a holy man, prefixed to the third part of *Castara* (published in 1640), presents the same mixture of religious piety and Stoic philosophy:

> A Holy Man is onely Happie. For infelicity and sinne were born twinnes ... In prosperity he gratefully admires the bounty of the Almighty giver, and useth, not abuseth plenty: But in adversity hee remaines unshaken, and like some eminent mountaine hath his head above the clouds. For his happinesse is not meteor-like exhaled from the vapors of this world; but shines a fixt starre ... Poverty he neither feares nor covets, but cheerefully entertaines; imagining it the fire which tries vertue ... Fame he weighes not, but esteemes a smoake ... Lust is the Basiliske he flyes, a Serpent of the most destroying venome ... He every day travailes his meditations up to heaven, and never findes himself wearied with the Journey ... Devotion is his Mistresse on which he is passionately enamord ...

Habington's most interesting *beatus ille* poems are his various epistles (or epodes) to his friends.

'To my honoured friend Sir Ed. P. Knight'[25] advises the reader to enjoy at home what's real, and to direct his eyesight inwards. The recipient of these lines evidently intended to go abroad, and the poet strongly counsels against such a hazardous venture:

> You'd leave the silence in which safe we are,
> To listen to the noyse of warre;
> And walke those rugged paths, the factious tread,
> Who by the number of the dead
> Reckon their glories ...

All this is folly and madness; it is far wiser to remain innocent, content, and secure, though humble. The metre suggests that the poem is an epode rather than an epistle; its undoubted indebtedness to Horace's Ode II, 16 and to Casimire's Ode IV, 15 would also seem to mark it as a philosophic lyric, rather than an epistle. The poem is one of Habington's most successful efforts; its pas-

sionate eloquence conveys a strong feeling of deeply held personal
convictions:

> Why doth ambition so the mind distresse
>   To make us scorne what we possesse?
> And looke so farre before us? Since all we
>   Can hope, is varied misery?
> Goe find some whispering shade neare *Arne* or *Poe*,
>   And gently 'mong their violets throw
> Your wearyed limbs, and see if all those faire
>   Enchantments can charme griefe or care?
> Our sorrowes still pursue us, and when you
>   The ruin'd Capitoll shall view
> And statues, a disorder'd heape; you can
>   Not cure yet the disease of man,
> And banish your owne thoughts. Go travaile where
>   Another Sun and Starres appeare,
> And land not toucht by any covetous fleet,
>   And yet even there your selfe youle meete.
> Stay here then, and while curious exiles find
>   New toyes for a fantastique mind;
> Enjoy at home what's reall: here the Spring
>   By her aeriall quires doth sing
> As sweetly to you as if you were laid
>   Vnder the learn'd *Thessalian* shade,
> Direct your eye-sight inward, and you'le find
>   A thousand regions in your mind
> Yet undiscover'd. Travell them, and be
>   Expert in home Cosmographie.
> This you may doe safe both from rocke and shelfe:
>   Man's a whole world within himselfe.

One notes how Habington — like Casimire — has changed the
original Stoic emphasis on a quiet mind to one on introspective

meditation: 'Direct your eye-sight inward...' It is not enough to avoid cares and to adopt the frugal life of the rural dweller, nor is it true that no perfect good exists, and that the would-be happy man therefore must learn the art of resignation. The inner life is the new *summum bonum*, and the special virtue of country life is that it permits the peaceful exploration of the thousand regions of the mind.

Habington's finest praise of a contemplative rural existence is given in the epistle 'To my noblest Friend, I. C. Esquire'.[26] The opening lines point the contrast between court and country, and after a Horatian dissection of the stupidity of court bores, Habington breaks out into fervent praise of the rural retirement of the Serene Contemplator:

> O busie folly! Why doe I my braine
> Perplex with the dull pollicies of *Spaine*,
> Or quicke designes of *France?* Why not repaire
> To the pure innocence oth' Country ayre:
> And neighbour thee, deare friend? Who so dost give
> Thy thoughts to worth and vertue, that to live
> Blest, is to trace thy wayes. There might not we
> Arme against passion with Philosophie;
> And by the aide of leisure, so controule,
> What-ere is earth in us, to grow all soule?
> Knowledge doth ignorance ingender when
> We study misteries of other men
> And forraigne plots. Doe but in thy owne shade
> (Thy head upon some flowry pillow laide,
> Kind Natures huswifery) contemplate all
> His stratagems who labors to inthrall
> The world to his great Master; and youle finde
> Ambition mocks it selfe, and grasps the wind.
> Not conquest makes us great. Blood is to deare
> A price for glory...

Th' unbusied only wise: For no respect
Indangers them to error; They affect
Truth in her naked beauty, and behold
Man with an equall eye, not bright in gold
Or tall in title; so much him they weigh
As Vertue raiseth him above his clay.
Thus let us value things: And since we find
Time bends us toward death, lets in our mind
Create new youth, and arme against the rude
Assaults of age; that no dull solitude
Oth' country dead our thoughts, nor busie care
Oth' towne make us not thinke, where now we are
And whether we are bound. Time nere forgot
His journey, though his steps we numbred not.

Habington's idea of rural retirement is that of a leisured, gentle-manly existence, devoted to philosophical introspection. A medi-tative country life is the best means of achieving true religious insight; the aim is complete self-knowledge issuing in a perfect command of reason over passion, of soul over flesh. Part of this purpose is impeccably Neoclassical, but the religious fervour and the strong stress on solitary meditation are typical of Habington's generation. Only the introvert mind can behold truth in her naked beauty. That knowledge which concerns 'misteries of other men / And forraigne plots' is only a different form for ignorance. True knowledge depends upon expert skill in 'home cosmographie'.

Perhaps nowhere else did Habington capture more completely the spirit of the Horatian epistle. For a similar achievement we must reach across the hundred years which separate Habington and Pope. Few other seventeenth-century poems present such a brilliant epitome of neo-Stoic thought, and no other Horatian epistle from this period achieved quite the same conversational and epigrammatic tone. Habington's heroic couplets possess the rhythmical and structural freedom of blank verse, while the end rhymes provide added emphasis to his statements. Many of these are pure epigrams: 'Not conquest makes us great', 'Blood is to deare / A price for glory', and 'Th' unbusied onely wise'.

Similar ideas are encountered in the poem 'To The Right Honourable *Archibald* Earle of *Ar*'[27] and the form is again that of the elegiac couplet ($A_4 A_5$). His conclusion is that 'Vertue though rugged, is the safest way'. He refuses to leave his safe status as private citizen, to 'hazard for a doubtfull smile, / My stocke of fame, and inward peace to spoile'. Instead he prefers to spend his life 'nigh some murm'ring brooke' 'with a booke / With my *Castara*, or some friend'.

'*Perdam Sapientiam Sapientum.* To the Right Honourable the Lord *Windsor*'[28] is a Horatian epistle in heroic couplets, praising the noble lord for his eschewing the 'glorious troubles of the Court.'

> For though
> The vale lyes open to each overflow,
> And in the humble shade we gather ill
> And aguish ayres: yet lightnings oftner kill
> Oth' naked heights of mountaines, whereon we
> May have more prospect, not securitie.
> For when with losse of breath, we have orecome
> Some steepe ascent of power, and forc'd a roome
> On the so envi'd hill; how doe our hearts
> Pant with the labour, and how many arts
> More subtle must we practise, to defend
> Our pride from sliding, then we did t'ascend?

However, the man to whom the poem is dedicated, refused to expose his vessel 'to the rough / Vncertaine sea of businesse', realising that 'The wealth we by our worldly traffique gaine, / Weighes light if ballanc'd with the feare or paine.'

The same Horatian denunciation of the quest for riches and

honour pervades *'Et fugit velut umbra.* IOB. To the Right Honourable the Lord Kintyre'.[29] This is the emblem of our life:

> we sayle ore broken seas
> Vnfaithfull in their rockes and tides; we dare
> All the sick humors of a forraine ayre.
> And mine so deepe in earth, as we would trie
> To unlocke hell, should gold there hoarded lie.

But our glory and our riches never survive our death — 'our un-
thankfull heire / Will scarce retaine in memory, that we were.'
In contrast to these deluded men, 'your judgement raignes / Above
all passion in you'. By means of 'that strong fence / Which Vertue
guards you with' 'you are / Triumphant in the best, the inward
warre.' Again, then, Habington insists on the importance of introspective meditation, on a virtuous rejection of the world of
sense, and on complete self-mastery.

Horace (Ode I, 22) seems to have inspired also the lines headed
'Quid gloriaris in malicia? DAVID'.[30] This is even more apparent
in the case of *'Quoniam ego in flagella paratus sum.* DAVID '.[31]
The manner in which Habington here has exploited a Horatian
ode for religious purposes is strongly reminiscent of Casimire
Sarbiewski.

Although a few Horatian echoes occur in Habington's love
lyrics, by far the largest number can be found in his epistles and
epodes to his friends, and in his religious verse. Habington's
epistles are particularly fine, and it is surely no exaggeration to
state that he did for the Horatian rural epistle what Ben Jonson
had done for the rural epode: he created an English version,
transferred into English idioms and applicable to the situation
of his own age. If the poems in elegiac couplets are true epodes —
and this they seem to be — he also carried on the tradition already
established by Ben Jonson in his lines addressed to Sir Robert
Wroth.

4.

John Milton

Milton's *L'Allegro* and *Il Penseroso* represent the finest early flowering of the *beatus ille* tradition in English poetry. Only Andrew Marvell's 'The Garden' can be said to equal, perhaps to surpass, Milton's lines on the joys of rural conviviality and of rural solitude. Both poems present pictures of the joys of life, the chief difference being that *L'Allegro* depicts the happy man as a rural gentleman-farmer in the manner of Ben Jonson's Sir Robert Wroth, while *Il Penseroso* transforms him into a solitary Serene Contemplator in the manner of Casimire and Habington. The poems, then, are complementary and not contradictory; each is concerned with a special human type and with the kind of happy life preferred by each. The one type is vigorous and extrovert, the other pensive, reflective, and introvert. Each is placed in a congenial setting and made to pursue suitable activities. Because their personalities are directly opposed, they find happiness in settings and activities which are equally opposed.

Milton's fondness for rural solitude found early expression in one of his Latin orations written at Cambridge after the Long Vacation of 1631:

> I myself invoke the glades and streams and beloved elms of the farms under which during the summer just gone by ... I recall ... that I enjoyed the highest favour of the Muses, where amid fields and remote woodlands I have even seemed to myself to have been able to grow up as it were in seclusion.32

Milton would have been thoroughly familiar with the rural passages found in Horace and Virgil, and an imitation of these would form a suitable task for a budding poet. *L'Allegro* exploits the realistic details typical of the rural ode and also the Horatian practice of pursuing the course of a single day. Thus to begin with we watch the coming of dawn, and listen to the crowing of the cock and to the cheerful sound of hounds and horn. Then we encounter the ploughman, the milkmaid, the mower, and the shepherd, and we share their 'sunshine holiday' which lasts until 'daylight fail', and ale is passed round to the telling of stories. The subsequent passage on 'towered cities' breaks the *beatus ille* pattern, but it was obviously needed to off-set the pensive man's preference for complete solitude.

L'Allegro contains no verbal *beatus ille* echoes, no tell-tale opening words patterned after Horace, Virgil, or Martial. However, the pattern of the happy day is traditional enough, and so are the various rural activities indulged in by the Happy Man and his associates. The rural and the pastoral are not kept entirely distinct; pastoral characters like Corydon and Thyrsis occur, but their activities are realistic enough. The tradition of the realistic pastoral comes quite close to the rural ode, the form or genre being the chief difference. In form, *L'Allegro* adheres to no previously established pattern; the unique character of Milton's tetrameter couplets has often been commented on. It seems nevertheless reasonable to associate the form with the ode in view of the fact that tetrameter couplets were frequently used in the translation of Horatian odes.

Although I should hesitate to describe them as a 'source', it is nevertheless interesting to note how close two of Wye Saltonstall's character sketches come to Milton's picture of the Happy Man. These are 'A Shepheard' (published in the 1631 edition of *Picturae Loquentes*) and 'A Merry Man' (published in the second edition of 1635). And just as *Il Penseroso* forms a conscious contrast with *L'Allegro*, the character sketch of 'A melancholy Man' is contrasted with that of 'A Shepheard' in the 1631 edition, while the same is true of 'A Merry Man' and 'A Happy Man' in the 1635 edition. The first edition, then, contains one set of contrasting characters, while the second edition has two sets, the contrast in each case being identical with that of Milton's companion poems.

On comparing 'A Shepheard' and 'A Merry Man' with *L'Al-*

legro, we discover that the former begins with a paraphrase of Virgil's well-known statement: 'Is a happy man, and yet knowes not of it; his cheefe unhappinesse consists in not knowing his owne happinesse.' [33] Both Milton and Saltonstall place their shepherd so that he surveys the landscape. Thus the latter's shepherd 'enthrones himself on the top of some high Mountaine, from whence his eye is entertayned with a variety of Landskips, whilst his sheep promiscuously chuse out the threepild grasse in the valley.' Milton's Happy Man observes in similar fashion:

> Straight mine eye hath caught new pleasures,
> Whilst the landskip round it measures:
> Russet lawns, and fallows grey,
> Where the nibbling flocks do stray.

'A Merry man' comes even closer to Milton's text in that both celebrate Mirth.[34] Just as Milton invokes 'heart-easing Mirth', 'Jest, and youthful Jollity, / Quips and Cranks and wanton Wiles, / Nods and Becks and wreathed Smiles', 'Sport that wrinkled Care derides, / And Laughter holding both his sides', Saltonstall describes the man whose 'heart is so light that it leapes in his breast, and daunces to the tune of his owne conceits. He is the musicke in all companies, and you cannot please him better then to laugh at his Iest... He was fram'd by nature for mirth, for when he tells some merry story... it is his Art to hide what followes, that the conclusion may make them laugh, till they cry out of their sides, and are even pain'd with pleasure.' This man is 'the glew of good company', he 'shortens the winter evenings with merry Tales'.[35]

Both Milton and Saltonstall follow Virgil in stressing the unconscious happiness of the *agricola*; this sort of life is 'fram'd by nature' and seems a direct expression of powerful natural impulses. The contrasting state is therefore an expression of man's mind; it is the result of the supreme act of man's consciousness of himself and of the world. Its classical parallel is with the happiness of the poet-philosopher as depicted by Virgil in his second *Georgic*. Virgil himself points the contrast, while Milton and Saltonstall reinforce it by interpreting the poet-philosopher in a neo-Stoic manner. The neo-Stoic, contemplative ideal of human happiness was clearly outlined by Joseph Hall in his character sketches, published in 1608 (*Characters of Virtues and Vices*). Thus his sketches of the Happy Man, the Humble Man, and the Wise Man outline several of the features attributed by Milton to his Pensive Man. The common neo-Stoic bias shared by Hall, Saltonstall, and Milton obviously makes for similarity in the treatment of the same ideal human figure or quality. Although the character sketches of Hall and Saltonstall may not have been proper sources for Milton's poem, it is difficult to believe that Milton would have been ignorant of such a popular literary genre. Milton was writing within a definite literary convention when he wrote his companion poems, and a certain amount of common ground must therefore be expected. Thus Joseph Hall's Wise Man, like his Happy Man, prefers to lead a retired existence, 'shrowded within his own wals';[36] he 'lives quietly at home, out of the noise of the world'.[37] 'He loves to be guessed at, not knowne; and to see the world unseene ... He stands like a center unmoved ...'[38] Milton's Pensive Man similarly prefers to 'walk unseen' and to hide himself from the eyes of men. Hall and Saltonstall as well as Milton praise the studious pursuits possible to such a man, and stress the fact that these studies render him 'well-neere propheticall' (Hall);[39] that he attains 'To something like Prophetic strain' (Milton), and that 'He has *Ianus* double face, the one to looke forward, the other backward, and so by time past, judges of that which is to come' (Saltonstall).[40] The most suggestive link between Milton and Saltonstall is found in the way the two contrast two types of happiness, one conscious, the other unconscious, and that the former is labelled *melancholy*. Both insist that if happiness results from solitary contemplation, then a life spent under the influence of Saturn, i.e. a melancholy existence, is a happy one. The *Picturae Loquentes* was entered in the Stationers' Register on April 20, 1631 at a time when Milton was still at Cambridge, and it seems plausible that he would have known this work by an Oxford graduate. If Milton's identification of the neo-Stoic Happy Man (i. e. the Contemplative Man or Wise Man) with the Melancholy Man was in fact prompted by his perusal of Saltonstall's volume, then the date of composition would be subsequent to the publication of Saltonstall's volume.

Saltonstall's character sketch of the Melancholy Man is a concise summary of the various characteristics of the man governed by the planet Saturn. His speech is sparing, he is 'content in the knowledge of himselfe', and he avoids company.

> If he walke and see you not, 'tis because his mind being busied in some serious contemplation, the common sense has no time to judge of any sensuall object ... His apparell is playne like himselfe, and shewes the riches of his minde, which contemnes a gaudy outside as the badge of fooles. He goes therefore commonly in blacke, his Hat unbrusht, a hasty gate with a looke fixt on the ground, as though he were looking pins there, when yet his mind is then soaring in some high contemplation; and is then alwayes most busy, when hee seemes most idle.[41]

Saltonstall's sketch of a Happy Man (1635)[42] is but a new version of the neo-Stoic ideal already presented in 'A melancholy Man'. Like the classical *beatus vir*, he 'cares not for wealth, honor, or riches; and therein resembles his maker that he hath a sufficiency of all things within himself.' His happiness consists in virtue 'which next to God is his *Summum bonum*.' 'His minde is like the Halcyon smoothnesse of the Sea', and 'he stands like the center immoveable.' By his knowledge of 'time past', he 'judges of that which is to come', and through the voyage of his life 'Religion is his compasse, faith the starre that guides him, and Heaven the Haven, where after this life ended hee arrives, and enjoyes eternall happinesse.'

The character sketches by Hall and Saltonstall give fine expression to the contemporary neo-Stoic concept of the ideal man, whether he be labelled a wise man, a happy man, or a melancholy man. The terms seem interchangeable. By comparing them with Milton's similar sketch, one realises the extent to which Milton drew upon this contemporary concept of happiness, at the same time that it also becomes apparent that his poetical treatment is quite independent. As Miss Tuve has pointed out, *Il Penseroso* is a 'demonstrative oration' or *encomium* of the great humanistic ideal of 'divinest Melancholy', according to which the Melancholy Man is 'the type par excellence of the contemplative, the intellectual genius intent upon understanding hidden wisdom'.[43] Milton refers to the same ideal in *Comus*, lines 380-384:

> He that has light within his own cleer brest
> May sit i'th' center, and enjoy bright day,
> But he that hides a dark soul, and foul thoughts
> Benighted walks under the mid-day Sun;
> Himself is his own dungeon.

It is this 'light within his own cleer brest' which makes the Pensive Man such a supremely joyful figure; the darker his surroundings are, the more clearly shines his own inner light. Milton's picture of the neo-Stoic Happy Man is unequalled in poetic beauty and sheer intellectual strength; his ideal is presented with an evocative power seldom achieved by other *beatus ille* poets. William Habington is Milton's only serious competitor, but his poetry is still too argumentative. Milton evokes a picture, he does not argue. For this reason there are few *beatus ille* phrases in his poem. However, there can be little doubt that Milton was writing within the tradition established by Virgil's praise of the *agricola* and of the poet-philosopher, whose chief quest is to know the causes of things. Milton had himself paraphrased the relevant lines (*Georgics* II, 475-482 and 490-492) in his *Seventh Academic Exercise*,[44] the corresponding passage in *Il Penseroso* being lines

105

85-94. There is this difference between the two poets that Milton's wish for knowledge is less scientific than Virgil's; he desires spiritual truth rather than to know the 'causes of things' in 'this fleshly nook' of the universe. He is concerned with the 'immortal mind', with the occult lore of a Plato and a Hermes Trismegistus, rather than with 'heaven's pathways, the stars, the sun's many lapses, the moon's labours; whence come tremblings of the earth', and so forth.

Both Virgil and Milton supplement their austere pictures of the quest for truth with appealing descriptions of the peacefulness and sensuous richness of rural scenes. Thus lines 132-154 of Milton's poem should be compared with lines 467-471 and 485-489 of the second *Georgic*.[45] Both poets prefer the dark shade, the cool glens, the secret caves, and the soft slumber beneath the trees. The humming of bees, on the other hand, and the sound of the woodman may have been fetched from Virgil's first Eclogue, lines 51-58.[46] Milton retained the bees, but he transformed the song of the woodman and the cooing of the pigeons into sweet music, sent by some unseen genius of the wood, just as he previously had transformed Virgil's reference to the howls of hungry Acheron into 'those *Daemons* that are found / In fire, air, flood, or under ground'. A further classical parallel may be located in Horace's second Epode, lines 23-28.[47] Milton's description of the 'Waters murmuring' which 'Entice the dewy-feathered Sleep' forms a fairly exact echo of Horace's fountains which 'plash with their flowing waters, a sound to invite sound sleep'. The idea, of course, is a poetic commonplace, but to a scholar like Milton an attempt to describe this particular type of scene would surely call up memories of these popular lines by Horace and Virgil. Nor must we undervalue the intellectual satisfaction which this age derived from being able to introduce a classical echo into original compositions. The ability to recognise such echoes, and perhaps perceive what unexpected twist of meaning has been created by the new context, formed part of the pleasure of reading poetry.

To summarise: *L'Allegro* and *Il Penseroso* present *picturae loquentes* of the vivacious, gregarious man whose happiness is unconscious, and of the contemplative or pensive man, whose happiness derives from that clear light which shines in his own breast. Both are songs of joy — the first of the joys of a convivial existence, the second of the more sublime joys of solitude. Both are connected with the classical tradition of the *beatus vir*, but the neo-Stoic bias of the second is the result of a completely contemporary interpretation of the idea of human happiness. We have traced the gradual development of this interpretation through the original *beatus ille* poetry of the early seventeenth century, and also through those prose character sketches which present human virtues and vices in neo-Stoic terms. Milton's companion poems therefore represent the culmination of a trend typical of the early seventeenth century and should be viewed as a contribution to an existing poetic tradition.

5.

Sir John Denham, Robert Herrick, and George Daniel

To the Restoration, Denham and Waller were the truly important poets of the preceding generation, and Denham's *Cooper's Hill* (1642) was universally acclaimed as a masterpiece. It was Denham who first gave to the heroic couplet those structural characteristics which gradually came to distinguish it from blank verse, and his diction was also that of the future. In view of its great popularity *Cooper's Hill*, therefore, must have done more to familiarise the public with the motif of 'sweet retired content' than either Milton or Habington. In the early eighteenth century, it is true, dozens of poets would imitate Milton's companion poems, but to the seventeenth century Denham seemed the finer poet.

Sir John Denham's *Cooper's Hill* is above all a fervent plea for a *via media* in religion and in politics, and it is a piece of tragic irony that it appeared in the year when civil dissent led to open war. Denham, then, is yet another of those poets in whom the spectacle of civil war conjured up a taunting vision of the 'happiness of sweet retired content'. The desire to be at once 'secure, and innocent', grew an obsession with a number of Royalist poets from Denham and the Earl of Westmoreland to Henry Vaughan and Edward Benlowes.

Cooper's Hill is one of the first poems in which the epithet *retired* is applied to country life. After 1642 the term *retirement* almost supersedes references to *country life*. Thus Mildmay Fane, Earl of Westmoreland, entitled his ode on rural life 'To Retiredness' (*Otia Sacra*, 1648), while Benlowes in 1652 devoted the last two cantos of his epic to the pleasures of retirement. Earlier poets had used titles more in keeping with the classical origin of the tradition, such as 'Of a Blessed Life', 'The Praise of a Country Life', 'The Happy Man', and so forth. The change in terminology shows that the passive, meditative aspects of country life were beginning to predominate; the Happy Husbandman was being metamorphosed into a Serene Contemplator. This development had consequences also for the treatment of the landscape of retirement. The contemplative man takes a much larger view of the scene than the more myopic tiller of the soil.

Despite these changes the underlying philosophy of life remained the same. There is still the same emphasis on the Stoic virtues of the husbandman, and Denham's Serene Contemplator moralises along lines laid down by Horace and Virgil. An analysis of the key symbols of his poem will bear this out. There are four of these key symbols. Thus the river Thames and the gentle height which carries Windsor Castle stand for the Stoic virtues of contentment and a wise *mediocritas*. In strong contrast to these, the city of London and the ruins of Chertsey Abbey serve as emblems of immoderate zeal and *luxuria*. The structure of the poem serves to point the contrast: the turmoil of London is opposed to the gentleness of the height of Windsor, and the description of the abbey ruins is followed by the panegyric on the river Thames.

Nothing was more natural than that Denham, a Royalist and a man of moderation, should feel hostile towards the city of London as a hot-bed of sedition. The innocence and quiet security of the country-side would naturally attract a man who felt that the largely town-bred Puritan factions were endangering the very foundations of State and Church. The curse of London was a double one: it derived partly from the religious enthusiasm of its inhabitants, partly from the greed and avarice of its shop-keepers. The first published version of *Cooper's Hill* is particularly forceful in its denunciation:

> I see the City in a thicker cloud
> Of businesse, then of smoake, where men like Ants
> Toyle to prevent imaginarie wants;
> Yet all in vaine, increasing with their store,
> Their vast desires ...
> Some study plots, and some those plots t' undoe,
> Others to make 'em, and undoe 'em too,
> . . . .
> Blinded with light, and sicke of being well,
> In tumults seeke their peace, their heaven in hell.[48]

It is after this Horatian denunciation of the perversity of the Londoners that Denham exclaims:

37   Oh happiness of sweet retir'd content!
38   To be at once secure, and innocent.

Then follows the antithesis to London — Windsor Castle. The presumptuous zeal of the city-dweller is contrasted to the meekness of the King, the towering ambition of the town to the gentleness of that hill whose ascent is so 'easie and unforc't'.

The second thesis-antithesis focusses on religious issues, the ruins of the Abbey suggesting extreme Protestant zeal, and the river symbolising a more rational spirit of compromise. Torn between his condemnation of the slothful lives of the monks and an equal condemnation of the havoc wrought by the zeal of the reforming Protestants, the poet exclaims in despair:

<blockquote>

139 Is there no temperate Region can be known,

140 Betwixt their Frigid, and our Torrid Zone?

</blockquote>

The subsequent famous praise of the Thames comes as a reply to this lament:

<blockquote>

189 O could I flow like thee, and make thy stream

    My great example, as it is my theme!

    Though deep, yet clear, though gentle, yet not dull,

192 Strong without rage, without ore-flowing full.

</blockquote>

Further Horatian echoes are encountered when Denham compares the towering mountains to the leaders of the state, whose fate it is to sustain the solid impact of adverse forces, while the happy life is led on the protected plain by people who are obscure and hence remain unmolested.[49]

As critics have already noted, Denham's descriptive passages are relatively unimportant in themselves; their chief interest lies in the moral lesson conveyed by the terms of description. This technique of using descriptive passages for didactic purposes was immediately perceived and imitated. Critics have tended to attribute the invention of this technique to Denham himself, but it must not be forgotten that Horace could achieve a similar effect, and that Casimire Sarbiewski had exploited the technique to the full in his Horatian imitations — and particularly in his loco-descriptive first Epode on the estate of the Duke of Bracciano. We have also found examples of the same tendency in William Habington.[50]

On comparing Casimire's first Epode with *Cooper's Hill*, similarities in theme and phrasing are sufficiently numerous and striking to suggest that the English poet had studied Casimire's poem with advantage. Thus the symbolism is the same. Casimire and Denham both allegorise the landscape by making the gentle hill and the river the symbol of an obscure and happy life, while conversely the towering mountains stand for the kind of pride and ambition which 'draw down envy from the starres' (Casimire). There is an over-riding similarity also in structure, and, finally, we find instances of verbal similarity as well. Casimire's epode begins with a description of 'A gentle Cliffe... That even to Heaven, mounts by degrees'.[51] Denham conveys the same moral in his description, in lines 39-46, of the 'easie and unforc't ascent' of Windsor. Casimire then proceeds to stress the safety of the low hill, which 'leanes upon / The solid backs, of Rocks and stone'. In *Cooper's Hill* it is the Castle which is thus carried (lines 49-52). Next both poets turn to praise of their patrons and their illustrious families. This done, Denham, after a long passage on the destruction of Chertsey Abbey, once more turns to the landscape, pointing out how much more laudable the gentle calmness of the river is than the pride of the adjoining mountains. Not only are Denham's images in this passage the same as Casimire's; they also follow in the same sequence:

Casimire:	Denham:
With rugged tops the bending mountaines round	But his proud head the aery Mountain hides
Upon the slow calme streames looke down.	Among the Clouds; his shoulders, and his sides
Romanus here his snowy back up-reares,	A shady mantle cloaths; his curled brows
And drawes down envy from the starres:	Frown on the gentle stream, which calmly flows,
The lofty head of *Cyminus* here shakes	While winds and storms his lofty forehead beat:
The Oke with trembling leaves which quakes,	The common fate of all that's high or great.

111

And holds off *Boreas,* when his
    rawer blasts
'Gainst the weake Southerne
    winds he casts,
Commands the Country farre,
    and out he sets
His Winter sides against
    Heavens threats.

Low at his foot a spacious plain
    is plac't,
Between the mountain and the
    stream embrac't:
Which shade and shelter from
    the Hill derives...
        (Lines 217-225)

Against Casimire's 'rugged tops' (*sublime caput*) and 'bending mountaines' stand Denham's 'proud head' and 'aery Mountain', and in Denham's 'gentle stream, which calmly flows', we see the reflection, as it were, of Casimire's 'slow calme streames'. Furthermore, both poets animate the mountains, making them 'looke downe' (Casimire) or 'Frown' (Denham) upon the humble river at their foot. Both interpret the mountains as grandeur which is itself exposed and vulnerable, but because of this grandeur the plain is given shade and shelter. In Casimire, the 'snowy back' of the mountain 'drawes downe envy from the starres', and the 'lofty head' 'shakes / The Oke with trembling leaves'. Similarly the 'lofty forehead' of Denham's mountain is beaten by winds and storms. The allegory is plain enough: the lofty mountain is the King in Denham's poem, the duke in Casimire's. As far as personal peace and happiness is concerned, a safe mediocrity must always be preferred.

    Both poets conclude by praising the occasional retirement enjoyed by their respective patrons on their estates, and by focussing on the pleasures of the chase. Here, too, verbal parallels are encountered. Thus Casimire's patron is exhorted to 'Withdraw thy selfe from cares, from all resort / So cloy'd with Citie, and with Court, / So full of great affairs', while Denham describes how he has seen the King, 'when great affairs / Give leave to slacken, and unbend his cares, / Attended to the Chase by all the flower / Of youth.'

As we shall see in the next chapter, Marvell's loco-descriptive poem 'Upon the Hill and Grove at Bill-borow' also repeats the pattern established by Casimire and, as it would seem, imitated by Denham. Part of the reason for the great popularity accorded to the new genre is surely found in its ingenious didacticism, and in the nature of the moral lesson so cleverly conveyed through the description of natural scenery. It must have come as a welcome relief from the pastoral tradition, while its formal elegance did much to establish a pattern for future generations of poets. The loco-descriptive poem suited the temper of the new age because of its novel presentation of well-known classical motifs; instead of being confined to the praise of a Sabine farm or its English equivalent, poets now were free to apply their descriptive powers to an entire landscape. The interpretation of this landscape, however, still followed the pattern of thought associated with the Sabine farm. The lesson taught by Casimire and Denham remained the classical one of Horace's second Epode or Virgil's second *Georgic*.

In the opening poem of *Hesperides* (1648) Robert Herrick announced that country life was the main theme of his song. Herrick's poetic praise of country life is uniquely cheerful in its mood. Like Milton, Herrick did not content himself with philosophic arguments about happiness; he preferred to describe delightful scenes of rustic merriment.

'The Country life, to the honoured M. End. Porter'[52] is an epistle comparing the life of a husbandman to that of a merchant. Herrick's conclusion is that the former is much the happier, since it is not the extent of one's property which makes one happy, but a contented mind. The pleasures of country holidays are described, and then Herrick repeats Virgil's famous lines: 'O happy life! if that their good / The Husbandmen but understood.' Echoes from Martial and Tibullus can also be traced.[53]

'A Country life: To his Brother, M. Tho: Herrick'[54] is one of Herrick's best poems on this subject. Herrick stresses the 'sweet simplicity' of the country, its Stoic virtues, and its wisdom, but its pleasures are also important: 'The Damaskt medowes, and the peebly streames / Sweeten, and make soft your dreames.' The classical ideal of the Golden Mean is the key-note of the whole epistle. If you limit your desires and keep them within their natural bounds, your rural retreat will become an Elysium. The very phrasing reveals Herrick's indebtedness to Antiquity. Thus the concluding words are taken from the last line of Martial's epigram 'Ad Seipsum', and the praise of his brother's wife derives from Horace's second Epode.[55] The opening lines are indebted to Martial,[56] and the passage on riches is taken out of Tibullus.

Like so many of his troubled contemporaries, Herrick echoes the classical wish for a private existence:

> We blesse our Fortunes, when we see
> Our own beloved privacie:
> And like our living, when w'are known
> To very few, or else to none.[57]

Herrick's appreciation of the pure joys of country life is also apparent in 'The Hock-Cart, or Harvest Home',[58] dedicated to Mildmay Fane, Earl of Westmoreland, and in the epistle on 'His age, dedicated to his peculiar friend, M. *John Wickes*, under the name of *Posthumus.*'[59]

With the advent of the Civil War and the Commonwealth, Herrick, like Habington, ceased writing poetry. Unlike his friend, the Earl of Westmoreland, he was not inspired by adversity to write poems in praise of retirement. He was a true lyric poet and the last of the Elizabethans.

George Daniel of Beswick (1616-1657), a selection of whose poetry has recently been published,[60] found his chief inspiration in the works of Horace, whom he often seems to have imitated at two removes, i.e. through the mediation of Ben Jonson, Thomas

Randolph, or William Habington. Thomas B. Stroup has described Daniel as a 'retiring gentleman of cultivated and scholarly tastes, a would-be seventeenth-century Horace', who chiefly loved 'his reading and painting, his fields and his pastures'.[61] Daniel's portrait of himself in Horatian costume, placed against a rural landscape, sufficiently illustrates his keen desire to pose as a Horatian *beatus vir*.

Although Daniel was strongly influenced by Neoplatonic ideas, his presentation of the Happy Man groups him with Ben Jonson, Thomas Randolph and William Habington, rather than with Henry More, Edward Benlowes and Andrew Marvell. This is seen from 'A Pastorall Ode',[62] which imitates similar odes by Ben Jonson and Thomas Randolph. The title reveals how the two genres of the pastoral and the rural ode tended to merge. The pastoral element, however, is inconspicuous, consisting in casual references to 'my loved Sheepe' and 'my owne Silvia'. Horace's rural philosophy pervades the ode and is fairly faithfully rendered; the poet contributes little that is new or deeply personal. He is content to echo the traditional rejection of 'the Cities Strife', of plush and 'gaudie Sattin', of wool 'in Tirian Dye' and 'Beavers Fleece'. He will shun 'Court Care', instead centering his joys 'in a poore Countrie Life'. 'An Epode',[63] written in pentameters interlaced with trimeters, again denounces 'the Cities Strife' and the 'vaine Applause' of the populace.

Beatus ille motifs are found also in Ode V (dated 1645), Ode XII and Ode LVII. Odes XII and LVII combine Horatian moral advice with Christian sentiments by stressing the importance of contemplating the works of God. In his rural retirement the poet will 'sing vast Nature, in her Store' and 'the Power / Which gives to Nature all her wealth'.

The two epistles, 'Freedome'[64] and 'The Author',[65] sound a more personal note and achieve a more pleasing poetic effect than the odes. Although they can scarcely be said to equal Habington's epistles, they compare favourably with Mildmay Fane's. 'Freedome' presents vigorous defence of rural retirement: 'I sitt retir'd, while other men are high / In State Employments.' The poet glories in his own obscurity:

> I am not in Commission, of the Peace;
> Noe Constable, the greater, nor the Lesse;
> Ide nothing Glorie, if I had ben made
> Poll' gatherer of the Groats; I should evade
> Truly, to be a Parish warden; or
> A domineering Elder; with the power
> Our well-affected Parliament can give.
> Fitt Men shall have Emploiment fitt; I live
> Obscure; Blood, Tears, nor oppression
> Burden my Soule: my Guilt is but my owne:
> . . . .
> I'me as I am, Content; and free, to pittie
> The faction of the Countrie, Fraud o' the Cittie.
> Sometime Ile take my Stone-bow, or my Gun
> With my true Servant, readie still to run,
> And fetch the Quarrie, from the Brooke or Bush,
> The Mallard, Teale, the Sparrow, or the Thrush;
> With these innocuous pleasures I can rest
> In my selfe quiet . . .

'The Author' presents a similar defence. After an introductory passage on Orpheus and Virgil Daniel considers himself and his own age. Just as civil war disrupts the nation and the church, tearing the 'seamles Coat' and dipping it in 'cisternes of Profaneness', man's passions are 'Rebells all / To Monarch Reason'. 'Each man's one Monarchie'.

> Hee who lives Innocent
> Is wise Enough: where Innocence and witt
> Combine, what wonders in that brest are mett?
> The Trumpets Clangor, nor the ratling drum,

Noises of warre; nor the more troublesome
Rage of the Souldier...
... nor all the plundge
Of Apprehension, shakes, or enters on
The temper of that true Complexion.
Vertue is ever Safe...

This is admittedly very minor poetry, but it is nevertheless interesting to observe how the pressure of the times caused men like George Daniel to seek refuge in a Horatian philosophy of happiness.[66] His preference for odes and epistles is a clear consequence of his choice of poetic motifs, a choice no doubt greatly influenced by the example set by Ben Jonson.

We have seen from the poetry discussed in this chapter how the contemplative bias of the Caroline period resulted in the adding of the motif of solitary contemplation to the *beatus ille* tradition. We have also seen how this passion for solitary meditation was directly responsible for popularising the motif of the Happy Man, since a retired rural existence obviously forms the best background for a contemplative life. This does not mean that the more joyous rural mood was abandoned; Milton wrote *L'Allegro* as well as *Il Penseroso*, and Herrick's poetry is almost entirely in the *Allegro* vein. One consequence of the adoption of the new motif can be traced in the terminology; with increasing frequency *retirement* replaces *country life* as the term best suited to the description of the Happy Man.

The Stoic austerity of the classical sources has remained unimpaired; it is often heavily underscored and elaborated in a religious direction. Herrick is the most conspicuous exception; in his poetry the Epicurean sensuousness often expressed by Horace and Tibullus found congenial expression. The new motif of religious solitude represents, of course, an ascetic impulse. It must nevertheless be stressed that the figure of the Serene Con-

117

templator — the Il Penseroso of Casimire, Habington, and Milton, — is basically a joyous one. He courts a contemplative solitude because, to him, this forms the highest bliss imaginable. We have noticed a certain amount of sensuousness in the description of this contemplative retirement, particularly in the odes and epodes of Casimire. This sensuousness was natural to a generation accustomed to using the erotic terminology of *Canticles* for the description of religious experience. When further strengthened, this half sensuous half ecstatic note was to transform the Serene Contemplator into a Hortulan Saint, as we shall see in the poetry of Edward Benlowes, Andrew Marvell, and Henry Vaughan.

We have seen how the increasing popularity of the *beatus ille* themes entailed a turning away from songs, sonnets, and pastorals towards odes, epodes, and epistles. As the chief classical exponent of these themes, Horace inevitably became the chief formative influence. William Habington's *Castara* is a particularly good illustration of the fact that the sudden interest in new poetic motifs had to lead to the adoption of new poetic forms.

Finally we have noticed a gradual and steady increase in the amount of natural description, a tendency which culminates in Milton's companion poems and Denham's *Cooper's Hill*. The strong emphasis on the delights of rural retirement caused the landscape to loom larger on the poetic horizon, while philosophic argument tended to diminish. Philosophic argument, however, could be expressed through the terms employed to describe the scene. From the days of Habington and Milton, then, a retired country life was presented, not only as pious or virtuous, but also as pleasant. In the words of the former, the *beatus vir* combines 'Honour with sweetnesse, vertue with delight'.

We shall now turn to the story of the culmination of this trend in the poetry of the Civil War and the Commonwealth.

CHAPTER IV

THE HORTULAN SAINT

The figure of the Puritan 'saint', in all his uncompromising grimness, has long been considered the typical exponent of early seventeenth-century religiosity. It is nevertheless scarcely just to the temper of the age to forget that a totally different ideal was being developed in quarters opposed to Puritan intolerance and sectarian enthusiasm. Many of the Royalists seem to have been conscious of the need for rallying around an ideal which could form a challenging contrast to that of their opponents. In his letter to Sir Thomas Browne, dated Jan. 28, 1658, John Evelyn expresses the hope that gardening, which he refers to as 'the hortulane pleasure, these innocent, pure, and vsefull diversions', might be encouraged by the defeated Royalists, 'whilst brutish and ambitious persons seeke themselues in the ruines of our miserable yet dearest country.' [1] Evelyn's sentiments are typical of the Royalists, who associated the rebellious faction with the reign of pride, ambition, and passion, while the classical virtues of contentedness and self-mastery were attributed to themselves.[2] In this manner the Horatian belief in the ability of a quiet country life to subdue the passions and ensure a proper mental serenity, was given direct political application.

Driven back upon themselves as the Royalists were after their defeat, and often exiled on their rural estates, it was only natural that they should seek to make a virtue out of necessity. Thus, after describing how 'the aire and genious of gardens operat vpon humane spirits towards virtue and sanctitie' and 'prepare them for converse with good angells', Evelyn suggests to Sir Thomas Browne that they form 'a society of the *paradisi cultores*, persons of antient simplicity, Paradisean and Hortulan saints'. Evelyn's phrasing is felicitous; his 'Paradisean and Hortulan saints' already were a reality. What are poets like Mildmay Fane, Henry Vaughan, Henry More, Andrew Marvell, and Thomas Traherne but *paradisi cultores?* Instead of pining for the pleasures of the life to come, they tasted the delights of eternity within the limits of time. Instead of sighing for the imaginary happiness of a Golden Age, they found their *hortus conclusus* on English soil. Thus Henry More described himself as '*Incola coeli in Terra* — an Inhabitant of Paradise and Heaven upon Earth — I sport with the Beasts of the Earth; the Lion licks my hand like a Spaniel; and the Serpent sleeps upon my Lap and stings me not.'[3]

The landscape, then, became of extraordinary importance to the new type of *beatus vir;* trees, fields, and fountains seemed charged with a secret life which, if he could share it, would bring him into direct contact with God. If his piety were of a more orthodox type, he would look upon natural scenes and objects as vehicles of allegorical truth. The river would become an emblem of human life, the fountain of spiritual power and grace. The orthodox approach can be illustrated by a quotation from the preface to Ralph Austen's *A Treatise of Fruit-Trees... Togeather with The Spirituall use of an Orchard* (1653). Like his Renaissance and medieval predecessors, Austen looks upon the world as a great library, '*and Fruit-trees* are some of the *Bookes* wherein we may read & see plainly the *Attributes of God* his *Power, Wisdome, Goodnesse,* &c. and be instructed and taught our duty towards him in many things even from Fruit-trees.' For the occult view we may turn to the *Signatura Rerum* by Jacob Boehme, a translation of which appeared in 1651. The purpose of this book was to prove 'the manifestation of the Deity through Nature'. Its title suggests the method: everything which exists is interpreted as having a secret correspondence, or commerce, with the invisible world. Indeed, the outward, visible world is 'a Signature, or Figure of the inward spiritual World'. The decades of the Civil War and the Commonwealth are marked by the publication of numerous works of a similar kind. No period before or since has witnessed a greater religious intensity, or a greater preoccupation with occult lore. Religious publications outnumbered every other type, sects flourished as never before, and the occult exerted an irresistible attraction on large numbers. As the influence of this interest in the occult was brought to bear on the classical motif of the *beatus vir*, his rural retirement was seen as a secret pathway to God. And if he believed, with Jacob Boehme, that the Deity manifests itself through Nature, his attention would be largely focussed on the landscape. The most typical feature of the *beatus vir* as Hortulan Saint is therefore his almost sensuous enjoyment of the landscape of retirement. He abandons himself to it with an enthusiasm oddly at variance with the austerity of the classical Happy Man. This is done, not only because God is there, but because the rural scene turns into an Earthly Paradise.

This development raises the question of the justification of sense experience. While the Puritans tolerated no compromise with the world of the fallen Adam, Anglican theology found no evil in the world itself, except what had been introduced through the Fall. Many of our poets tended to limit this corruption to man himself, and to his social sphere (particularly the sphere of the town), while rural scenes were invested with almost prelapsarian perfection. In so doing, they were often influenced by Platonic or Hermetic thought, and so it will be useful to outline the position of these schools with regard to the world of matter and more particularly to sense experience.

It is confusing to find that Hermetic and Platonic writings both contain passages which condemn the world as evil, and passages which praise it as good. The poets, then, can scarcely be blamed if they exhibit the same uncertainty. In his fourth *Ennead* (VIII, 1) Plotinus thus draws attention to the fact that Plato sometimes expressed contempt for the world of sense, sometimes the directly opposite view. In the *Phaedrus*, for example, Plato attributes the entry of the soul into the realm of matter to a failing of its powers, referring somewhat obscurely to 'fates' and 'necessities' which drive souls down into this lower order of being. In the *Timaeus*, however, he exalts the Cosmos and calls it a blessed good, stating that 'the Soul was given by the goodness of the Creator to the end that the total of things might be possessed of intellect.' Plotinus himself explicitly rejects the idea that matter is evil, instead maintaining that God is present in the universe. 'If He is absent from the Universe, He is absent from yourselves' (Second *Ennead*, VIII, 4). The contemplation of the world of sense hence becomes one of the accepted paths to true knowledge:

> Admiring the world of sense as we look out upon its vastness and beauty and the order of its eternal march, thinking of the gods within it, seen and hidden, and the celestial spirits and all the life of animal and plant, let us mount to its archetype, to the yet more authentic sphere...
> That archetypal world is the true Golden Age, age of Kronos ... For here is contained all that is immortal: nothing here but is Divine Mind; all is God; this is the place of every soul. Here is rest unbroken ... what increase can that desire, which stands utterly achieved?[4]

In other words, the world of sense is first studied and admired, then abandoned as a lesser good in order to reach the 'yet more authentic sphere'. Much in Hermetic thought corresponds to this Plotinian position, but the attacks on the world of matter are stronger and more sustained. For this reason Ross Garner, in his recent study of Henry Vaughan, has gone so far as to equal Hermeticism with a dualistic position. It is his contention that the mystical strain in Hermetic thought springs from the dualistic current, not from the monistic. In other words, the ecstatic experience is reached through escape from matter, and not through the love of God's creatures.[5]

The poetry with which we are concerned in this chapter will reflect orthodox Anglican views, as well as Platonic and Hermetic ideas. The attitude towards the Creation is usually one of approval, the approval being bestowed upon a regenerated Nature, or upon Nature as viewed through the eyes of him who courts a vision of true reality, and not of mere outward show. It has been maintained that Marvell never accepted 'any criticism of the pure delight of his senses in the beauty of the creatures'.[6] There is nevertheless a certain dualistic tendency in Marvell's insistence on the necessity of a retreat into the realm of pure mind; his comments on the relationship between mind and body or mind and matter are not at all clear.

The importance attributed to the Hermetic writings by the Renaissance can be understood only when we realise that they were believed to contain divine revelation. The *Corpus Hermeticum* became easily accessible to the Western world when Ficino published his Latin translation of it. Ficino's comments on the text reveal that he invested the visions of Hermes with divine authority: that which Moses conveyed to the Israelites, Hermes gave to the Egyptians. Hermes was one of the so-called ancient theologians or prophets who predicted the coming of Christ; he 'prophecied the decay of the ancient religions and the birth of the true faith, the coming of Christ, future judgment, the resurrection, the glory of those who have achieved beatitude, and the supplication of sinners.'[7] Ficino therefore never thought of Hermes as a pagan, and the same is true of seventeenth-century translators like Dr. Everard and Thomas, Lord Fairfax.

It is interesting to find a modern historian emphasising the importance of the *Corpus Hermeticum* 'for understanding the thought-world in which Christianity took its rise and formed its fundamental doctrines'.[8] The same historian assigns some of the Hermetic books to an earlier period than the one usually given (i.e. A.D. 100 to 300), maintaining that some of the documents 'incorporate much older traditions'. This is said to be particularly true of the account of creation given in *Libellus I*, which would seem to antedate the rise of Christianity. If this is so, if the 'formative thinking of Christianity' was actually done in 'an atmosphere greatly influenced by the type of thought that finds expression in the Hermetic and Gnostic writings', and if the nature of Gnostic thought has been largely misrepresented (because transmitted to us only by its opponents), then the Renaissance view may not be so wide of the mark after all. However this may be, one thing seems certain: if we are to look upon the Hermetic books with the eyes of a Marvell or a Fairfax, we should not consider them as a pagan work, marked by an un-Christian dualism. They should appear, instead, as important religious documents incorporating divine revelation.

Our first examples showing how *beatus ille* motifs were modified by mystic, or occult, tendencies, will be taken from the odes of Casimire Sarbiewski. It will be remembered that his version of Horace's second Epode (i.e. his own third Epode) places the happiness of the *beatus vir* in his passionate yearning for union with God. Casimire's third Epode combines the tradition of the Horatian rural ode with the classical eclogue (particularly Virgil's fourth) and with *Canticles.* The indebtedness to the latter two traditions, as interpreted by Renaissance poets and theologians, helps to explain the lushness of the rural scene, and the innocent eroticism which pervades the *res creatae.* Religious fervour is conveyed through sensuous description of rural scenes. However, since we know that Casimire exploited the Hermetic writings for poetic purposes, these must be considered partly responsible for the manner in which the landscape is portrayed. This point is illustrated also by Ode IV, 21 ('Ex sacro Salomonis Epithalamio'), which tells how the earth prepares to receive Christ, having reverted to its original uncorrupted state. Nature woos man, just as Christ woos man. Nature, in this fashion, becomes Christ. The entire poem, bar the first two lines, is spoken by Christ to his beloved (the soul of man). He calls to her to arise and enter his Earthly Paradise: '... in the sacred Green, a bow're we see, / Doth spread it selfe for thee. / The Earth new Turff's it selfe for thee to tread, / The straying starrs fresh fields make glad.' The Latin text has *Sidera pascit ager*, thus suggesting that there is a mutual bond of love between the field and the stars — a typically Hermetic idea. The wild beasts, too, are pacified, and Nature offers all her riches voluntarily to all. These riches appear spontaneously, and not as the result of the work of man:

> No want appeares; th' officious Vine doth stand
> With bending clusters to our hand.
> Here, thou shalt pick sweet Violets, and there
> Fresh Lillyes all the yeare:
> The Apple ripe drops from its stalke to thee,
> From tast of death made free.
> The luscious fruit from the full Figtree shall
> Into thy bosome fall.
> Meane while, the Vine no pruning knife doth know,
> The wounded earth no plow.
> The Corne growes green alone, and th' unhurt land
> Doth white with harvest stand.
> The grasse affords a stately bed, the Plane
> Spreads thee to entertaine.
> Arabian mists sweat from the gummy tree
> Of Balme, and all for thee;
> Which through the ayre, a rich perfume doe throw,
> Fann'd with each neighb'ring bough.

Echoes from Virgil and *Canticles* are easily recognised; behind both is the same traditional religious symbolism. The ripe apple which has been made free of the taste of death is particularly suggestive. It recalls the fatal apple of the Garden of Eden, and the fatal tree. Casimire's apple, however, conveys life, not death, and hence recalls the fruit of the Tree of the Cross, that second tree which annulled the effect of the first.[9] Similarly the 'officious Vine' which offers its 'bending clusters' and the corn which grows

127

green alone, are allusions to the Holy Sacraments, and to Christ himself.[10] Through Casimire's Earthly Paradise, therefore, Christ offers himself to man.

Casimire's version of the classical motif of the return of the Golden Age (*redeunt Saturni reges*) is given similar religious overtones. The Golden Age returns, not only because peace has been re-established in the nation, but because there is peace between God and man:

> Faith joyn'd with Truth, and Plenty too
> O're pleasant fields doe nimbly goe;
> The precious Ages past, doe flow
>   With liberall streames againe.
> . . . .
> The streams which Milk and Honey yeild,
> Their passage cut through open field,
> And the full banks with Nectar swell'd
>   Doe drowne the flowrie plaine.
> The glad Corne in the restles stalke
> Waves, and the fields as wee doe walke,
>   So fruitfull reele ...
> The Herdsman's Pipe to's wandring Goats,
> Provokes the Grashoppers hoarse notes;
> The tyred Herd with strayned throats,
>   Makes Hills and Woods to low.
> The Mountaines leape, and rough Rocks smile
> For gentle Peace rejoiceth still ...
> *Ceres* with yellow Chaplet, and
> The Summer rich with eares doth stand,
> Great Prince of our appeased Land,
>   Thee to encompasse round.
> The Myrtle begs with humble shade
> To serve thee, and the Laurel's glade ...
> Hee that o're Starrs and earth hath powre,

Beholding us, from his bright Towre,
Calms all, and sets thee father o're
The covetous world below.   (Ode I, 1)

Among the English poets, Edward Benlowes was much taken with
these and similar passages, so that he would reproduce them almost
verbatim in his own lines on the delights of rural retirement.

Casimire's many descriptions of mystic ecstasies or raptures
would sometimes be given a Horatian cast. Thus his Ode IV, 32
is a free version of Horace's Ode II, 20 on the poet as *vates*. On
other occasions he was inspired by Hermetic descriptions of ecstatic visions, as in his finest mystic ode, 'E Rebus Humanis Excessus' (II, 5). As already stated, this ode is, in fact, a poetic
rendering of sections 25 and 26 of the first Hermetic *Libellus*;
these describe how the soul of man ascends through the seven
planetary spheres to the eighth sphere of the divine powers, and
from there to the sphere of the Divinity.

Casimire's poetry was, of course, easily accessible in its Latin
form, to the English poets now to be considered. Moreover, all of
them — Edward Benlowes, Mildmay Fane, Andrew Marvell, Henry
More, and Henry Vaughan — wrote Latin poetry themselves. It is
my belief that they were all familiar with the odes of Casimire;
in the case of Benlowes and Vaughan we know that this was so.

1.

Henry More, Mildmay Fane, and Edward Benlowes

Henry More (1614-1687) has been called the 'singing Cambridge
Platonist'. As this term suggests, the dominating motif in his
poetry concerns the achievement of the true Neoplatonic vision
of ultimate truth, goodness, and beauty. Like so many of his contemporaries, More, in his own life, testified to a genuine love of
rural retirement. This love was a direct expression of his religious
philosophy. Thus one early eighteenth-century biographer stressed

the point that a passionate love of nature made More wish 'to be always *sub dio*, if it were possible',[11] while a recent editor of More's poems is of opinion that 'sunlight and scenery were the most potent external objects exciting his mystical fervour'.[12] More's attitude to the world of sense is as ambiguous as that of Plato or Hermes Trismegistus. Thus he would praise solitude as an escape from 'this worlds Magick' which chokes the soul 'with foul smothering mists and stench',[13] while, on the other hand, he would approve of the scenes of nature as a bridge leading to God, and of sense perception as one of the means employed in crossing this bridge.

The two positions are less contradictory when one realises that More's joyous acceptance of the life of the senses presupposes a purification of sense experience, while his denunciation of the world is a denunciation of a way of life in which sense dominates the mind. This Platonic position is the distinguishing feature of the *beatus vir* as Hortulan Saint. Passages from four different poems will serve to illustrate the point.

'Insomnium Philosophicum' depicts the world as a reflection of the divinity. To the man of pure vision the creatures are essentially good; hence he does not flee from the world in hate or contempt, but because he aspires to the greater good: the fountain of all life.[14] Stanza I, 32 of *Psychozoia, Or the life of the Soul* (1642) similarly approves of the 'gladsome life of sense that doth adore / The outward shape of the Worlds curious frame'. The external appearance of things forms the 'lowest hem' of the 'stole of Uranore', and so the man of pure vision kisses this hem, refusing to let it be dragged 'in dirty earth'. And why should he be blamed for his love of the external world? 'How sweet it is to live! what joy to see the Sunne!' *Psychozoia* contrasts the garden of heavenly love or *caritas* with the garden of carnal love or libido.[15] Before man can enter the former, he must leave all physical passion behind — as Marvell was to insist in 'The Garden'. 'Cupid's Conflict', first published in the *Democritus Platonissans* (1646)

and then in the *Philosophicall Poems* (1647), is More's most interesting garden poem. Its setting is a secret grove with a crystal
spring, the traditional symbol of the moving spirit of God. When
immersed in the waters of this spring, profane love loses its fiery
influence, and hence when Cupid appears to attack the poet, the
river becomes his best defence. In the subsequent debate between
the two, the poet places true pleasure or happiness in the pursuit
of heavenly joys. Through this pursuit he becomes 'half equall
to All-seeing Jove', and his mighty wings 'brush the starres'. True
happiness is possessed only by him who has purged himself, in
neo-Stoic fashion, of all vain fears and desires, instead esteeming
'virtuous life his treasure'. In this fashion More rejects all worldly
ambition, and invokes the aid of solitude to effect an ascent into
the 'hid paths of heavenly Love' through contemplation of 'all
the works of God'.

Religious ecstasy is the key-note also of 'Resolution', a poem
very much in the tradition stemming from Boethius and Horace
and re-inforced by Casimire.[16] Thus lines 85-102 are a direct
paraphrase of Horace's Ode I, 22 and were surely intended to
appear as such. The point of More's paraphrase is to show that
man may become invulnerable, not through mere moral strength
alone, but through a purified love of God. Through this love he
also achieves moments of religious ecstasy. As far as I have been
able to ascertain, this poem offers the first English example
of the new type of Happy Man who is a Hortulan Saint rather
than a Happy Husbandman. Virgil's praise of the philosopher-
poet in the second *Georgic* forms the closest classical analogue,
but, as one might say somewhat facetiously, the balance of his
mind has been upset. The desire for ecstatic union with God has
ousted the classical insistence on an 'equal mind'.

Although More never achieved the lyric grace of a Casimire
or a Marvell, his poetry commanded widespread interest and exerted a not inconsiderable influence. His fame as a philosopher
caused his poetry to be read with close attention, and among

his readers must surely have been our next poet, Mildmay Fane, second Earl of Westmoreland.

Mildmay Fane's volume of poetry, published privately in 1648, is important to this study for several reasons. Like More and Casimire, Fane combined Platonic ideas with classical *beatus ille* motifs, and, secondly, Fane is the first English poet to write about *retirement* rather than country life. Fane's *Otia Sacra* is the first publication to contain an ode dedicated 'To Retiredness' and devoted to an exposition of the joys that can be experienced only in a rural retirement marked by religious fervour. The motivation for seeking retirement is still Horatian (in sentiment, if not in phrasing), but the keenest happiness of Fane's *beatus vir* is derived from tracing the footsteps of God through His creation.

Fane is an important figure also because of his connection with other poets of interest to this study. Thus we know that he was acquainted with Edward Benlowes, from whom he received a presentation copy of *Theophila*,[17] an acquaintance which may date back to the time when both were at Cambridge, or, subsequently, when both stayed at Lincoln's Inn. Benlowes was admitted to Lincoln's Inn on January 30th, 1622, Fane on August 7th. Through his friendship with Robert Herrick, Fane was connected with yet another poet who habitually praised the happiness of country life. Herrick paid many compliments to the noble Earl in his verse, and he dedicated his 'Hock-cart, or Harvest home' to him. Fane's most important connection was with his brother-in-law, Lord Fairfax, through whose agency Marvell may have had access to the *Otia Sacra*. Like Fane and Benlowes, Marvell transformed his *beatus vir* into a Hortulan Saint, and he did so in poetry curiously reminiscent of Fane's ode 'To Retiredness'.

A strong supporter of the Royalist cause, Fane spent some time as a prisoner in the Tower. In 1644, however, he took the covenant and was able to return to his estate. Like so many Royalists, he then proceeded to write poetry in praise of retirement and in disparagement of the age in general and of town life in particular. The *Otia Sacra*, which contains some poetry in Latin, is divided into a religious and a secular part. The two are nevertheless closely connected in mood and theme. While his sacred poetry discusses the nature of the *summum bonum*, his secular poetry shows how this highest good may be achieved in daily life. The chief means is rural retirement. Each section has its own title-page, and these, too, are complementary. The first shows the pillar of faith upon which shines the all-seeing eye of the purified human heart. The Virgilian motto attached (*Deus nobis haec otia fecit*) suggests that the pillar of faith can be raised only by the retired contemplator. The second title-page presents a solitary rural scene with a tree, twin hills, and a fountain, and the Virgilian motto (*tutus in Umbra Silvestram tenui Musam meditatus avena*) again praises the virtue of a meditative rural retirement.

Fane's poetic exposition of the meaning of the first title-page stresses the problem of sense perception. Whereas the senses should be a means of elevating the soul, they are only too often used to drag the soul through the mire. Like More, then, Fane insists that the retired life, the life of leisure provided for men by God, has as its end the purification of the senses and the vision of ultimate reality. As Fane phrases it in his lines on 'The Fallacy of the outward Man',[18] 'whilst alone with th' outward sence / We doe behold, and not with th' Minde, / We are asleep, or we are blinde', a sentiment which we also find expressed, again and again, in the odes of Casimire.

Fane's paraphrase of Psalm 19 ('Coeli enarrant Gloriam Dei')[19] expresses belief in the purifying effect of solitary contemplation, asserting that such a process turns men into 'Saints and Kings'. Suitable objects for contemplation are found in God's creation; suns, comets, meteors, and rainbows are sent here on purpose by God, who thus offers a 'Lecture in Divinity'. The proper technique is taught in the 'Contemplatio Diurna':[20]

When we behold the Morning Dew
Dissolve ith' rising Sun: What would it shew?
    But that a Sun to us did rise,
Our Fathers hoary sin to Atomise.
    And when the Flowers display'd appear,
To entertain the mounting Charettier:
    What would they speak in that fair dress?
But Man's redemption out of wretchedness.

There is nothing subtle about this allegorical interpretation of
natural scenes. There is no inner connection or correspondence
between the morning dew and 'Our Fathers hoary sin', nor between the flowers and man's redemption. This is the most serious
limitation of Fane's poetry; the better poets knew how to invest
the rural scene with a secret life of its own; they were not content
to superimpose a more or less vicarious allegory.

A Neoplatonic bias pervades also Fane's secular poems. His
two outstanding *beatus ille* poems — 'To Retiredness' and 'My
happy life, to a Friend' — express a desire not only for the traditional Stoic invulnerability of the classical *beatus vir*, but, above
all, for the transforming glory of the contemplative ecstasy.

'My happy Life, to a Friend'21 opens with the well-known
defence of country retirement. In his 'sweet retirement' the poet
banishes fear, and arms himself with innocence. After he has
worshipped God, he devotes the rest of his day 'to some choice
Book or Friend' in order to enrich his mind. He may also indulge
in the beneficial exercise afforded by hunting and hawking, but
the crowning moment occurs underneath a 'well-grown Tree',

Under whose Shades I may reherse
The holy Layes of Sacred Verse;
Whilst in the Branches pearched higher,
The wing'd Crew sit as in a quier.

After a long passage where the allegorical interpretation of the landscape is political rather than religious, Fane returns to the ecstatic note. The 'cool delights' of his garden tie 'enchantments' to 'every senses facultie' and every drop of the fountain where 'Crystall is limbeckt all the yeere' conveys an 'Ocean of Felicities' and provides 'musick like the Sphere'. The epistle ends with pleasant genre pictures of the singing milkmaid and of the happy family life of the poet.

'To Retiredness' has for some time been seen to anticipate Andrew Marvell's 'The Garden', and the similarity is indeed striking. [22] Since Fane's poetry is inaccessible to most readers, it may be useful to quote the entire poem:

To Retiredness

1

Next unto GOD, to whom I owe
What e're I here enjoy below,
I must indebted stand to Thee,
Great Patron of my Libertie;
For in the Cluster of affaires,
Whence there are dealing severall shares;
As in a Trick thou hast conveigh'd
Into my hand what can be said;
Whilst He who doth himself possess,
Makes all things pass him seem farr less.

2

Riches and Honors that appear
Rewards to the Adventurer,
On Either tide of Court or Seas,
Are not attain'd nor held with ease;
But as unconstancy bears sway,
Quickly will fleet and Ebb away:
And oft when Fortune those Confers,
She gives them but for Torturers:

When with a Minde Ambition-free,
These, and much more come home to Me.

3

Here I can sit, and sitting under
Some portions of His works of wonder,
Whose all are such, observe by reason,
Why every Plant obeys its season;
How the Sap rises, and the Fall,
Wherein They shake off Leafs and all:
Then how again They bud and spring,
Are laden for an Offering:
Which whilst my Contemplation sees,
I am taught Thankfulness from trees.

4

Then turning over Natures leaf,
I mark the Glory of the Sheaf,
For every Field's a severall page,
Disciphering the Golden Age:
So that without a Miners pains,
Or *Indie*'s reach, here plenty raigns;
Which watred from above, implies,
That our acknowledgements should rise
To Him, that thus creates a birth
Of Mercies for us out of Earth.

5

Here, is no other Case in law,
But what the Sun-burnt Hat of Straw,
With crooked Sickle reaps and bindes-
Up into Sheaves to help the hindes;
Whose arguing alon's in this,
Which Cop lies well, and which amiss,

How the Hock-Cart with all its gear
Should be trick'd up, and what good chear,
Bacon with *Cook's* reports express,
And how to make the Tenth goe less.

6

There, are no other Warrs, or Strife's-
Encouragers, shrill Trumpets, Fyfes,
Or horrid Drumms; but what Excels
All Musick, Nature's Minstrels
Piping and Chirping, as they sit
Embowr'd in branches, dance to it:
And if at all Those doe contest,
It is in this, but, which sings best:
And when they have contended long,
I (though unseen) must judg the Song.

7

Thus out of fears, or noise of Warr,
Crowds, and the clamourings at Barr;
The Merchant's dread, th' unconstant tides,
With all Vexations besides;
I hugg my Quiet, and alone
Take thee for my Companion,
And deem in doing so, I've all
I can True Conversation call:
For so my Thoughts by this retreat
Grow stronger, like contracted heat.

8

Whether on Natures Book I muse,
Or else some other writes on't, use
To spend the time in, every line,
Is not excentrick but Divine:

And though all others downward tend,
These look to heaven, and ascend
From whence they came; where pointed hie,
They ravish into Mysterie,
To see the footsteps here are trod
Of mercy by a Gracious God.

Fane's ode is dedicated to retirement as the one agency which, next to God, is responsible for his liberty and for the happiness resulting from this liberty. The poet's ideal is that of the self-possessed Stoic Wise Man. In traditional *beatus ille* fashion Fane stresses the contrast between the rewards of the adventurer, intent on the pursuit of riches and honour, and the rewards of the mind which is totally without worldly ambition. Fane's classical *beatus vir* is next turned into a Serene Contemplator of the world; through his observation of the *res creatae* he learns to be grateful to God for His infinite mercies. The Hortulan Saint appears in stanza four, where Fane observes that the Golden Age prevails in his rural retirement; 'plenty raigns' through the liberal gifts of the Creator, and not because miners and merchants have scoured the earth and the seas for worldly riches. Here everyone is honest, kindly, and innocent; no one is disturbed by legal suits or by war, and instead of the martial sound of drums, the sweet music of the birds prevails. The ecstasy so typical of the Hortulan Saint is achieved in the concluding two stanzas. Underneath his tree, the poet 'hugs' his quiet, by means of which he enjoys the only 'True Conversation', i. e. the colloquy between the soul and God. Society is therefore scorned by implication. The poet's colloquy with God is made possible by the strong concentration of his mental powers, contracted like the rays of the sun when they pass through the lens of a magnifying glass. By observing the 'footsteps' 'here are trod / Of mercy by a Gracious God' the poet finally is ravished 'into Mysterie'.

Love is the key-note of this poem: love of God and love of

His creation in so far as it reflects the divinity of God. One notes that the sensuous appreciation of the landscape as a Golden Age occurs after the contemplative exercise has revealed the true nature of things. While Fane is less fervent than Casimire, and completely orthodox in his approach to God and His creation, his poem nevertheless repeats all the points stressed by the Polish Jesuit in his third Epode. Fane's presentation of these points is sufficiently independent to mark him as an original poet; he was no mere imitator, nor did he borrow words and phrases and entire lines from Casimire in the manner of his friend, Edward Benlowes. The question of indebtedness is not important; what matters is the fact that there was a certain tradition within which poets like Fane were writing, and that their poetry for this reason should be appraised in the context of this tradition. When this is done, Fane's finest achievement is seen to be a formal one. Fane's tetrameter couplets are extraordinarily pleasing and well suited to present philosophical ideas in lyric form. Fane employed the same metre for his epistle, but the mood and diction of this poem sustain the epistolary impression with sufficient emphasis to prevent generic confusion. Fane's formal elegance is perhaps his main achievement. Marvell and Dyer, exploiting the same formal pattern, were to write the finest retirement odes of their respective generations. G. Hills had employed this metre for some of his translations of Casimire's odes, and Dryden adopted it later on for his spirited rendering of Horace's second Epode. Tetrameter couplets therefore became one of the acknowledged English equivalents of Horatian asclepiads.

Edward Benlowes was an ardent Royalist and an Anglican convert from Roman Catholicism. No wonder, therefore, that he looked upon the Puritan victory as a catastrophe and a sign of the general decay of the world. Like so many of our poets, he concluded that salvation could be achieved only by retiring into rural shades for the purpose of pious meditation. *Theophila* (1652) is the record of such a quest, the ultimate purpose of which is the achievement of the mystic union between the soul and God.

Although published in 1652, we have evidence that manuscript versions of Benlowes' epic circulated among his friends and acquaintances before 1650.[23] The views expressed by Benlowes on God, man, Nature, and the religious quest are usually completely orthodox. His strong denunciation of the sins of the flesh is in the Christian tradition entirely. Matter is not evil; evil was introduced through man's apostate will, and it is this will which must be purged and re-activated. Benlowes, it is true, describes mystic raptures, but I hesitate to call him a mystic in the sense that he writes about personal religious experience. He seems, instead, to be writing within a literary convention to which he gives his own fervent assent. The literary character of his inspiration is apparent from the frequent use which he makes of phrases and lines taken from poets like Du Bartas, Shakespeare, Donne, Francis Quarles, Owen Feltham, Crashaw, Cleveland, and John Ogilby.[24] Borrowings from Milton are particularly frequent in the two concluding cantos on 'The Sweetness of Retirement or the Happiness of a Private Life' and on 'The Pleasure of Retirement'.[25]

The poet to whom Benlowes turned more than anyone else was Casimire Sarbiewski, an indebtedness which so far has gone unnoticed. Thus the ecstatic vision presented in Canto III, stanzas 14-20, is a loose paraphrase of Casimire's Ode II, 5, while Canto XIII abounds with borrowings from Casimire's Odes I, 1, IV, 21, IV, 44 and his Epodes 1 and 3. Benlowes leans heavily upon the Polish Jesuit in his sustained portrayal of rural retirement. Thus he shares the latter's fervent sensuousness, transforming the landscape of retirement into an Earthly Paradise and into a symbol of the union between the soul and God. Few English poets combined the *beatus ille* themes more persistently with the ecstatic strains of *Canticles* than Edward Benlowes, and he clearly learnt this method from the *Odes of Casimire* (1646) into which he so frequently dipped for images, phrases, and entire lines.

Benlowes seems to have been thoroughly familiar with Latin; he wrote parts of *Theophila* in Latin as well as English, while many introductory and concluding passages are given in Latin only. It is therefore puzzling to find that he borrowed so extensively from G. Hills's translation of Casimire's odes, rather than from the Latin original. However, it is fortunate for us that he preferred the English translation, since this serves to establish his indebtedness beyond a doubt. In one respect Benlowes goes beyond the Polish Jesuit; his mystic raptures are far more sustained and elaborated, and his interest in occult lore led him to compose an epic whose very structure reflects the mystic insights conveyed by the contents. Benlowes persistently exploits that mystique of numbers which conditioned the structure of Dante's *Divina Commedia*.[26] Thus, like Dante, he based his poem on a three-line stanza with a triple rhyme scheme (aaa). Three and ten are particularly sacred numbers representing the nature of God. For this reason there are thirteen cantos, while each of the first eleven cantos consists of 100 stanzas, 300 lines and 3,000 syllables (30 syllables in each stanza). Since the square of a number denotes the result of its creative action, each canto can be said to represent the creative activity of God (10^2). The cantos with which we are primarily concerned, XII and XIII, form an exception in that they consist of no less than 120 stanzas, a number which suggests 10 stanzas for each of the 12 months in the year, or signs of the zodiac. The total number of lines is 360, the number of degrees in the cosmic circle. However, if one adds the concluding four lines in Latin, one obtains the actual number of days in a year — 364. The symbolism would therefore seem to be partly temporal, partly cosmic, implying that the contents of these cantos are relevant to the world of time and space, as indeed they are. The text itself refers to the science of numbers. Thus Canto VIII is devoted to an exposition of the nature of God, and in so doing exploits largely Platonic concepts. The initial Latin argument discusses the relationship between One and Three. God is one as the waters of the sea, the river, and the fountain form one, and as the sun, heat, and light form one. This oneness (or elixir) 'centuplies itself' (i.e. multiplies itself by a hundred or the second power of ten) in order 'T'express GOD's Essence'. The Latin motto — *Omnia in uno et in omnibus unus* — may be a reference to the holy 'tetraktys' of Pythagorean lore, according to which the holy number 10 includes within itself those numbers which signify all aspects of creation: 1, 2, 3, and 4.[27] This preoccupation with occult insights marks the entire poem and explains why Benlowes presents his Happy Man as a Hortulan Saint.

Theophila is an epic about the voyage of the soul to God. To begin with, the soul is taken through a process of purgation whereby she learns to denounce the false joys of the world. By nature, man is 'Deprav'd by vice, depriv'd of grace' (II, 57), but as soon as 'Nature is kept down' 'The seed of grace sprouts up' (II, 75). During the stage of illumination the soul fervently embraces true heavenly joys, and under the influence of the Holy Ghost man is transformed from a brute into an angel (IV, 75). This influence is assiduously courted in Canto XII, where segregation from the world leads to the enjoyment of 'The Sweetnesse of Retirement or the Happiness of a Private Life'. Canto XIII, 'The Pleasure of Retirement', describes the mystic banquet of the soul. Despite their strong religious bias, both cantos exploit *beatus ille* arguments persistently, and the landscape of retirement is full of realistic detail — of milkmaids, mowers, anglers, and cattle.

The Latin argument of Canto XII states its theme: *Tu, mihi Thema, Quies Animae, sanctusque Recessus.* The poet prays for God's spirit to saturate him, and states his policy of avoiding the many in favour of the holy temple of the forest: *Hoc Nemus est Templum.* This comparison between the forest and a temple is elaborated: the wide branches of the trees form the fretted ceiling, the trunks are the sacred pillars, the open forest offers a host of doors, the birds provide the music, and the echo acts *quasi clericus,* offering the proper responses.

The Canto distinguishes between six stages on the road towards the achievement of the garden ecstasy. First comes the Horatian apostrophe to rural retirement and the corresponding denunciation of the false desires and ambitions of the world; second, a neo-Stoic dedication to contemplative solitude; third, a Neoplatonic process of purification of the senses; fourth, the revelation of the Earthly Paradise within the rural retreat; fifth, a moment of meditative concentration when the mind focusses on the spiritual reality behind external appearances; and, sixth, the final ecstasy when the soul is set free and tastes the joys of eternal life. This is the sequence described by Casimire, Henry More and Mildmay Fane; it is also the sequence of Andrew Marvell's 'The Garden'.

Canto XII, then, opens with the traditional exhortation to leave the city and instead court rural retirement: 'Waste not another word on fools', exchange nonsense conversations for 'pure notions', abandon all frivolities, and be content to tell the time of day by observing the progress of the sun. The richer mind spurns 'cumbrous gain' and instead courts guileless solitude:

> More than high greatness humble goodness draws;
> Elm rafters, mantled o'er with straws,
> Outbless Escurial tow'rs that seem Heav'n's cupolas.
>
> Each city-shop's a trap; each toy, a yoke;
> What wise man willingly would choke
> Himself in thicker clouds of griping care, than smoke?
>
> (XII,5-6)

Like Denham, Benlowes denounces London, comparing its smoky atmosphere to the 'clouds of griping care' which beset its inhabitants. And like so many Royalist poets, he associates city life with sedition and with perverted religion. Because city, church, and state have become defiled, the pious man must flee from 'publick roads, to private joy':

143

Thus go we, like the heroes of old Greece,
In quest of more than golden fleece,
Retreating to sweet shades, our shatter'd thoughts we piece.
(XII, 21)

Charles V sought retirement, and so did Moses, 'That sea-dividing Prince', John the Baptist and Christ. Those who, in similar manner, 'eclipse' themselves, are 'to Heav'n's court more dear'. The retired life leads to hope, virtue, and a good conscience; fear itself is overcome, and, more importantly, 'by Thee/ We conquer lusts: each sense wears Reason's livery.' In contrast to the world which 'Suffers by rage of war, and dearth', the retired man is 'Seated in safe repose'. 'The low-built fortune harbours Peace', while the mighty are exposed to storms; 'content with thankfulness each blessing has.'

So fragrant vi'lets, blushing strawberries,
Close-shrouded lurk from lofty eyes,
The emblem of sweet bliss, which low and hidden lies.

No maskèd fraud, no tempest of black woes,
No flaunting pride, no rage of foes,
Bends hitherward, but soon is laid, or overblows.

We rule our conquer'd selves; what need we more?
To gadding Sense we shut the door;
Rich in our mind alone. Who wants himself, is poor.
(XII, 36-38)

In stanzas like these Benlowes achieves a fine poetic effect; had he written always thus, no critic would have hesitated to place him among the better known lesser poets of his century.

After this classical exposition of *beatus ille* sentiments, Benlowes transforms the landscape into a Golden Age, the transforming agent being the re-birth of true religion:

Faith link'd with Truth, and Love with Quiet too,
O'er pleasant lawns securely go;
The Golden Age, like Jordan's stream, does here reflow.

For fields of combat, fields of corn are here,
For trooping ranks, tree-ranks appear;
War steels the heart, but here we melt heart, eye, and ear.

(XII, 40-41)

These lines offer a typical example of the manner in which Benlowes would borrow entire passages from Casimire. Compare the following lines from Casimire's Ode I, 1:

Faith joyn'd with Truth, and Plenty too
O're pleasant fields doe nimbly goe;
The precious Ages past, doe flow
With liberall streames againe.

One sees how few changes Benlowes made, and how obvious his borrowing is, and again one wonders why he did not bother to cover up his traces more carefully. Could it have been that he was so taken with Casimire's poetry that he wished to proclaim his indebtedness? Did he, perhaps, write the last two cantos as a free paraphrase of Casimire — throughout following the spirit of the latter's retirement poems, and occasionally embodying direct quotations? This as we know, was the habit of translators; each took what he considered best and most apt in the work of his predecessors, as Dryden did when he translated Virgil.

After a few additional stanzas on the true joys of rural life ('Our roof is neat, and sweet our fare'), Benlowes returns to the motif of the Golden Age or Earthly Paradise. 'When early Phosphor lights from eastern bed / The grey-eyed morn',

Then walk we forth, where twinkling spangles shew,
Entinselling like stars the dew,
Where buds, like pearls, and where we leaves, like em'ralds view.

(XII, 51)

145

Like Casimire's *beatus vir*, Benlowes dissolves in tears, 'the pious convert's sweetest sport'. And again like Casimire, Benlowes describes how the earth itself woos the Hortulan Saint:

> Earth's flow'r-wov'n damask doth us gently woo,
>   On her embroider'd mantle to
> Repose, where various gems, like constellations, shew.
>
>   Ourselves here steal we from ourselves, by qualms
>   Of pleasure, rais'd from new-coin'd Psalms,
> When skies are blue, earth green, and meadows flow with balms.
>   (XII, 70-71)

After this ecstatic moment, the poet contemplates the landscape, drawing spiritual allegories and emphasising the wonders of creation. It is interesting to observe that Benlowes was familiar with the microscopic examination of nature's wonders:

> More than at tusks of boars we wonder at
>   This moth's strange teeth! Legs of this gnat
> Pass large-limb'd gryphons; then, on bees we musing sat.
>   (XII, 73)
>
>   Abstruser depths! here Aristotle's eye
>   (That Ipse of philosophy,
> Nature's professor) purblind was, to search so high.
>   (XII, 78)

Stanzas 93-99 reverse the process by showing the littleness of the earth, and even of the heavens. To God 'all nature is as wither'd leaves that fall', and 'Heav'n was his watch, whose starry circles wind / All ages up'. In between these meditations on the tiny and the great is placed a passage on the Creation as the book of God's works. 'By observation GOD is seen in all we see':

> Our books are Heav'n above us, air and sea
>   Around, earth under; Faith's our stay,
> And Grace our guide, the Word our light, and CHRIST our way.

Friend, view that rock, and think from rock's green Wound
How thirst-expelling streams did bound:
View streams, and think how Jordan did become dry ground.

View Seas, and think how waves, like walls of glass,
Stood fix'd, while Hebrew troops did pass;
But clos'd the Pharian host in one confusèd mass.

(XII, 80-82)

To the contemplative mind various features of the landscape
provoke associations with crucial events in the universal history
of man as recorded in the Bible (see *Exodus* 14 and 17 and
Joshua 3). To understand the lesson properly, one must call
to mind the typological interpretation usually given to Moses
striking the rock, and to the crossing of the Israelites through
the Red Sea. These and similar Old Testament events were seen
to foreshadow the events of the New Testament, to predict them,
as it were. Thus Moses striking the rock foreshadowed the crucial
moment on the cross when Christ's side was pierced so that blood
and water gushed out. To think of Moses striking the rock was
therefore tantamount to thinking of Christ on the cross. Similarly
the crossing of the Red Sea was taken to foreshadow the baptism
of the Christian and his redemption from sin (represented by
the 'Pharian host'). To this traditional allegorical method of interpretation Benlowes seems to add the anagogical when in the next
Canto the landscape becomes a type of the heavenly bride, and
the poet re-enacts the crucifixion.[28] As Benlowes phrased it, 'Such
mental buds we from each object take, / And, for CHRIST'S
Spouse, of them we make / Spiritual wreaths...' (XII, 100).

Canto XII ends with a return to the mood of the initial stanzas.
The simplicity and strict temperance of rural life is praised: 'Next
fountain has / Bath, drink, and glass', and 'Our meal's as short
as grace'.

Canto XIII opens with a Latin argument, stressing the Stoic

position that the wise man is he who conquers himself: *Felix qui Suus est*, and *Rex est quem Ratio regit, & quem ducit Honestum*. The Canto itself begins with a fine description of the morning. Stanzas 1-15 present a pleasant rural scene; for a poet who habitually escapes into abstract thought, Benlowes possessed a curiously felicitous ability to focus on realistic and concrete detail. His landscape is alive with the activity of men and animals:

> ... view the mower, who with big-swoln veins,
>   Wieldeth the crookèd scythe, and strains
> To barb the flow'ry tresses of the verdant plains.

The river contains 'bright-scal'd gliding fish' caught on a 'trembling line', and the fields abound with 'nibbling ewes' and 'frisking lambs', 'wide-horn'd oxen' and 'many a strutting-udder'd cow'. Nor is sound absent; 'all the merry hamlet bells chime holy day', the 'hoarse note' of the 'skipping grasshopper' is heard, and so is the song of the 'aery choristers'. The description is replete with echoes from Casimire. To facilitate comparison, the passages in question will be quoted in opposite columns.

Benlowes, Canto XIII:

6

With them [shepherds], we strive to recollect, and find Dispers'd flocks of our rambling mind ...

Casimire, tr. Hills:

Or else retyr'd, strives to collect and find The dispers'd flock of's wandring mind. (Third Epode)

10

Hard by, tir'd cattle draw the plough, Whose galled necks with toil and languishments do bow.

The tyred Herd with strayned throats, Makes Hills and Woods to low. (Ode I, 1)

11	The glad Corne in the restles

11
Near which, in restless stalks,
  wav'd grain promotes
The skipping grasshopper's
  hoarse notes ...

The glad Corne in the restles
  stalke Waves, ...
The Herdsmans Pipe to's
  wandring Goats,
Provokes the Grashoppers
  hoarse notes. (Ode I, 1)

12
Dry seas, with golden surges,
  ebb and flow;
The ripening ears smile as we
  go ...

The fields with yellow waves
  doe ebbe and flow,
The ripe eares swim, when
  winds doe blow ... (Epode 1)

15
Their orchards with ripe fruit
  impregned be,
Fruit that from taste of
  death is free ...

The Apple ripe drops from its
  stalke to thee,
From tast of death made free ...
  (Ode IV, 21)

No less than three different poems by Casimire furnish passages that have been woven into the fabric of Benlowes' stanzas. The Polish Jesuit's conceits seem to have exerted particular attraction. Since so many of the concrete details in Benlowes' landscape are fetched straight out of Casimire, I suppose that the former's eye for detail is largely a result of his literary imitation. However, I have been unable to find a previous example of Benlowes' picture of the mower with his 'big-swoln veins' who barbs 'the flow'ry tresses of the verdant plains', and also other details seem original.

Benlowes interrupts his description of the rural scene to insert a digression on the nobility of the Stoic *beatus vir*. This man 'shuns prolixer law-suits', refuses to court personal advancement from those in power, and neither alarming trumpets nor 'drowning storms' have power to disturb his mind. 'He in himself, himself to rule, retires ... All blessings up are bound in bounding up desires.' While London gallants proudly display themselves and their coaches through Hyde Park, this man retires to groves where 'flow'rs of Grace, / And fruits of Glory bud'. This is the 'Spring-Garden to spiritual eyes', and Christ alone is the end of his walk.

Stanzas 23-50 describe the rapture of the soul who partakes of the mystic banquet. His joy is such that he becomes totally invulnerable to all external circumstances:

68
Then let fierce Goths their
    strongest chains prepare;
Grim Scythians me their slave
    declare;
My soul being free, those
    tyrants in the face I'll stare.

Let th' *Goth* his strongest chaines
    prepare,
The *Scythians* hence mee captive
    teare,
My mind being free with you, I'le
    stare
The Tyrants in the face.
                    (Casimire, Epode 3)

A culmination is reached in stanzas which render the familiar Renaissance motif of Cupid on the cross in religious terms.

73
Here wound, here lance me, LORD, thy Austin cries,
    Dissect me here for Paradise!
The Cross the altar be, so Love be sacrifice!

77
Who makes th' Almighty his delight, he goes
    To martyrdom, as to repose;
The Red Sea leads to Palestine, where all joy flows.

Three levels of meaning merge in the last line: (1) the literal, geographical sense, (2) the typological meaning of the crossing of the Red Sea into the Promised Land, and (3) the sense in which the Red Sea stands for the streaming blood of the martyr.

The Canto ends with a return to the evening scene; 'the whistlers knock from plough', 'Maids have their curtsies made to th'

spongy-teated cow', 'Larks roosted are, the folded flocks are pent'
and 'the tir'd ox sent / In loose trace home'. 'When dark'ning
mists our hemisphere invade' so that mortals are 'immantled in
their silent gloomy shade', prayers are offered: 'Saints fight on
bended knees.' This is the time when the soul is lifted to God in
prayer, like Moses descrying 'Fair Canaan, type o'th' Heav'nly
Bride'.

Benlowes' retirement cantos, viewed as poetry, are neither
particularly obscure nor clumsy. Certain passages even achieve a
definite grandeur, while the various genre pictures have undoubted
charm. When one has accustomed oneself to the stanza form, and
to the manner in which conceit follows conceit scarcely without
a pause, it is possible to enjoy the poem on its own merits, and
not merely as an interesting fossil dating from a previous era.

A second aspect of Benlowes' epic deserves even more attention. This is the question of the poem's impact on other poets.
Gunnar Qvarnström has argued that the structure of *Theophila*,
based as it is on the science of numbers, bears such a close resemblance to the structure of Milton's *Paradise Lost*, that it seems
more reasonable to credit Milton with acquaintance of *Theophila*,
than to postulate his ignorance of it.[29] Similarly, on comparing
Theophila and Marvell's 'Upon Appleton House', one is struck by
the frequency with which Benlowes' retirement cantos anticipate
descriptions, images, and sentiments encountered in Marvell's homage to Lord Fairfax. Thus both poems praise the purifying effect
of retirement, both compare the forest to a temple, and contrast
the peace and innocence of rural life with the massacres of civil
war. Both describe how the earth woos man to court repose, both
comment on the wonders of creation, and in both various features
in the landscape recall the exodus of the Hebrew tribes under the
leadership of Moses, thus providing what Benlowes calls *animi
pabulum*. The landscapes, too, have many points in common. Both
stress the action of the mower, both convert the waving grain into
dry seas with 'golden surges', from which sound the hoarse notes

of grasshoppers, and both stress the fertility of the scene which abounds in fruit (free from 'taste of death'), and in quails and manna. Finally, in both the sacrifice of the body in a voluntary symbolic crucifixion leads to ecstatic joy. On turning to the poet in whose work the motif of rural retirement found its finest and most intriguing expression, it will therefore be wise first to submit the last cantos of *Theophila* to a close scrutiny.

2.

Andrew Marvell

Although very little is known about Marvell's career in those crucial years when he wrote his finest lyrics, it is possible to deduce a few important points from his connection with Thomas, Lord Fairfax.

Fairfax was a man with wide literary interests, who himself composed poetry which he copied into a manuscript volume entitled *The Recreations of My Solitude*. It is therefore highly unlikely that his library would not have included a copy of the *Otia Sacra* written by his own brother-in-law. Whether *Theophila* also found its way to Nun-Appleton, must remain conjectural, but it seems highly probable in view of Fairfax's pronounced interest in theology and in religious poetry. Surely there must have been some table-talk at Nun-Appleton, some poring over recent poetic publications, some encouragement on the part of Fairfax, or some ambition on the part of Marvell to equal or surpass this fashionable philosophic poetry on the happiness of rural retirement. To assume that both were ignorant not only of the retirement poetry of Casimire,[30] but also of Fane and Benlowes, would surely be absurd. Also Milton's 1645 poems would have been sure to stir their interest; Marvell was bound to know the poetry of the man who, in February 1653, wrote a letter recommending his application for government service. Fairfax may even have been personally acquainted with Cromwell's Latin secretary, whose appointment occurred in March 1649 more than a year before Fairfax's retirement from active service. Finally it may be mentioned that Milton, Fairfax, Fane, Benlowes, and Marvell were all Cambridge men. Milton and Fairfax were contemporaries at Cambridge, and so were Fane and Benlowes, who also entered Lincoln's Inn at roughly the same time. Finally Gunnar Qvarnström has traced a possible connection between Benlowes and Milton through the men who set some of their poetry to music.[31]

So much for the literary milieu. In discussing the intellectual milieu of Nun-Appleton we are on safer ground, since Fairfax's manuscript translation of a French commentary on *Mercurius Trismegistus Pimander* can still be consulted in the British Museum Library. The British Museum Catalogue of Manuscripts lists this work as a translation of the *Pimander*, but this is not quite correct. Such a translation had already been published in 1650 by a certain Dr. Everard, and so there was scarcely need for yet another effort. Nor was this Fairfax's aim. His purpose was, instead, to translate the learned French commentary published by François de Foix in 1579.

De Foix' attitude to the Hermetic *corpus* is typical of his age. His commentary persistently adduces parallels between the Hermetic text and the Bible. Like Ficino and Dr. Everard, de Foix believed that the two were in complete accord.[32] This view was not quite without foundation. Thus when Hermes insists that there is nothing in the universe which is not the image of God, and that the operations of Nature are 'Streams running from the Fountain of Good, which is God',[33] no Christian would hesitate to give his assent, and similarly with respect to a statement like the following: 'For therefore hath he [God] made all things, that thou by all things mayest see him. This is the Good of God, this is his Virtue, to appear, and to be seen in all things.' [34] This insistence on Nature being the Book of God's work through which He reveals Himself, is one of the most powerful impulses of the seventeenth century, and the fact that the *Corpus Hermeticum* so strongly supports this position surely partly explains why Marvell's generation was so attracted by it.

As professional linguist and man of letters, Marvell must have been frequently consulted by Fairfax and would surely also have read the book that Fairfax laboured to translate. We may therefore safely assume that Marvell's knowledge of Hermetic doctrines was detailed and exact. I believe we may also assume that Marvell, like his age, viewed these doctrines as part of the Christian tradition. It is, of course, true that Marvell's position in Fairfax's household partly explains why his poetic compliments to his employer should contain so many overt allusions to Hermetic lore. No flattery is more subtle than the intellectual kind. However, neither 'The Garden' nor 'Upon Appleton House' can be adequately explained merely as poetic compliments. It would be more just to state that the milieu which Marvell entered on becoming a member of Fairfax's household, activated his poetic powers by providing direct inspiration. The poetry dedicated to Fairfax could only have been written by a man who shared the latter's passionate interest in the occult aspects of the Christian faith.

(a) 'The Garden'

Although 'The Garden' is not dedicated to Fairfax, it obviously belongs to the period which produced 'Upon Appleton House', just as its contents may be viewed as a condensed version of the longer poem.

It may be as well to begin with the most difficult of Marvell's retirement poems. No other seventeenth-century lyric has provoked more interpretative ingenuity on the part of contemporary critics. Mr. Empson's discussion, in *Seven Types of Ambiguity*, springs readily to mind, and among his followers interpretations have been produced with a fertility little short of amazing. Among literary historians Miss Wallerstein's contribution is perhaps the most monumental.[35] The chief difficulty of a study like hers is the gap between the text of Marvell's poem and the philosophic or theological works that are brought to bear upon it. This gap may be bridged by showing that Marvell's poem is part of a definite literary tradition inspired by particular religious or philosophical trends, a task which is the purpose of this study.

The tone of Marvell's poem is one of its major problems. The tone seems almost disassociated from the subject-matter, at times even in direct opposition to it, so that a subtle contrapuntal effect is achieved. The various statements are serious enough, but the voice is curiously tinged with irony or mockery. Consider, as an example, the opening proposition. In what sense can non-doing lead to greater rewards than the persistent pursuit of one's objective? In a spiritual sense, of course, but one hesitates to offer this solution. Can a serious defence of the contemplative, religious life be expressed in such ironical phrases? 'Your sacred Plants, if here below, / Only among the Plants will grow.' 'Society is all but rude, / To this delicious Solitude.' The epithets *rude* and *delicious* must have been consciously chosen for their paradoxical contrast to the words they qualify, but their implication is such that both society and solitude seem invested with a faintly ludicrous air. The mockery is even more apparent in the third stanza, where the beauty of trees is praised at the expense of mere mortal woman. Surely it is the height of absurdity to associate 'this lovely green' with amorousness, and to proclaim that this amorousness exceeds that of women? A garden enthusiast might prefer his garden to the company of women, but why attribute amorousness to it? The seeming topsy-turviness of the argument reaches a climax in the fourth stanza, where the pursuit of Apollo for Daphne and Pan for Syrinx is entirely deprived of its customary motivation: '*Apollo* hunted *Daphne* so, / Only that she might Laurel grow.' The hot pursuit, so Marvell insists, was prompted by the desire to turn a woman into a tree. Surely this can be nothing more than a piece of metaphysical cleverness, a series of

155

witty paradoxes designed to provoke laughter and admiration rather than philosophic or religious insight?

Stanza five has been variously described by different critics. Its purpose is clearly to explain the thesis concerning the amorousness of 'this lovely green'. The spectacle of the poet ensnared with flowers, drinking in the juice of grapes which crush themselves against his lips, and stumbling over melons, seems a caricature of the traditional picture of the Golden Age. The lushness of the scene is overwhelming. However, on turning to stanzas six and seven a mystic fervour suddenly pervades the narrative; even paradox itself disappears from the lines describing the release of the soul. It reappears in stanza eight, where Marvell denounces the creation of Eve, instead praising the time when Adam was completely alone. The comparison, in the concluding stanza, between the sun and the stars on the one hand, and, on the other, the 'fragrant zodiac' created by the skilful gardener, is similarly paradoxical. The infinite has been made finite; the grandeur of the zodiac has been reduced to 'herbs and flow'rs'. This is the reverse of the technique in the initial stanzas, where the tiny and the inanimate (plants and trees) were enlarged by being invested with transcendent beauty and transcendent powers of love.

Is it possible that this series of paradoxical propositions was designed to convey, not detached irony, but esoteric insight? That, by turning every commonplace, accepted notion on its head, the poet is trying to establish a truer perspective? If paradox can be used as an arresting medium for the conveyance of truth (as G. K. Chesterton certainly believed), then Marvell's poem must be viewed as serious. Perhaps Marvell intended his lines to convey two kinds of meaning to two kinds of people: to the worldly they would appear as nothing but a witty version of the traditional retirement ode, but to the initiated the esoteric message would stand clearly revealed. The esoteric poem has ancient roots in the history of the Western world. Thus the editor of the works of Plotinus, Porphyry, relates the following anecdote:

Once on Plato's feast I read a poem, 'The Sacred Marriage';
my piece abounded in mystic doctrine conveyed in veiled words
and was couched in terms of enthusiasm; someone exclaimed:
'Porphyry has gone mad'; Plotinus said to me so that all might
hear: 'You have shown yourself at once poet, philosopher, and
hierophant.' [36]

In the fourth decade of the seventeenth century strong
support of this point of view was given by Henry Reynolds in
Mythomystes (1633?). 'In this perverse work', remarks J. E.
Spingarn, 'Henry Reynolds ... has given us the chief example
in English of the systematic application of Neoplatonism to the
interpretation of poetry.' [37] Modern readers who, in Reynolds's
phrase, 'scarce suffer themselves to looke beyond the dimension
of their owne braine', may, perhaps, agree with J. E. Spingarn
when he calls the treatise 'a tropical forest of strange fancies',
but one should not fail to observe that this 'perverse work' provides an exact theoretical basis for the poetry considered in this
chapter. Since most of Reynolds's observations are applicable to
'The Garden', it may be well to summarise what he says.

Reynolds distinguishes sharply between the common reader
and the initiate few. While the former never would look 'farther
into those their golden fictions for any higher sence, or any thing
diuiner in them infoulded & hid from the vulgar', the latter would
read with the eye of the mind, refusing to be 'lulled with the
meruellous expression & artfull contexture of their fables.' Thus
when the poet describes how Tyresias saw Pallas naked, this 'signifies no other then that Ideall beauty, whence proceeds all sincere
wisdome, and not cloathed or couered with corporall matter ...
so as that which blinded his corporall eyes opened to him the
eyes of his understanding.' Among the secret lore once possessed
by the ancients and since lost, Reynolds emphasises particularly
'the mysteries and hidden properties of Nature'. After 'our first
fathers disobedience' both man and Nature became as it were
poisoned. Hence man's chief task must be the attempt to refine

157

and advance what Reynolds calls his 'rational part', 'to the purchase & regaining his first lost felicity'. Two means are available to him: (1) to trust in Christ and in the Book of God's Word, and (2) to study the 'Misteries of Nature' in the Book of God's Work. This *Magia naturalis* is best taught by the most ancient prophets and poets, chief among whom are Orpheus, Musaeus, Moses, Zoroaster, Mercurius (or Hermes) Trismegistus, Pythagoras, Socrates, and Plato. No distinction is made between pagan and Christian, the former having possessed 'the entire Secret of our great God of Nature, in his miraculous fabrick of this World.' Indeed, Nature herself is the best teacher, if properly understood: 'The hidden workings of which wise Mistresse could we fully in her wayes comprehend, how much would it cleare, and how infinitely ennoble our blind and groueling conditions, by exalting our vnderstandings to the sight... of God...'

I shall now try to show that this is exactly what Marvell does: that he re-interprets ancient fable in the manner suggested by Reynolds, and that he submits Nature, or the Book of God's Works, to a similar scrutiny, the purpose of which is to exalt his understanding to the sight of God. In following him, we, too, must try to look beyond the dimension of our own brain.

Reynolds, in his turn, clearly took his cue from the Florentine Neoplatonists. Thus Edgar Wind informs us, in his study *Pagan Mysteries in the Renaissance*, that Pico della Mirandola had defined the Orphic tradition as the art of interweaving the divine secrets with the fabric of fables, so that anyone reading those hymns would think they contained nothing but the sheerest tales and trifles. Wind also mentions that Plato had taught that the deepest things are best spoken of in a tone of irony, and that *Serio ludere* was a methodical maxim of Cusanus, Ficino, Pico, Calcagnini, and Bocchi. Is it possible that Marvell's poem belongs in the same tradition? That he, too, was protecting himself by conveying his ideas in a deceptively facetious manner?

Let us, however, first consider the formal aspect of Marvell's poem. The 'numbers' are highly suggestive in their regularity: the poem consists of nine stanzas, each stanza in its turn containing eight lines of eight syllables each. It is possible that numerical significance was intended, particularly since Reynolds makes such a great issue of the *Secreta de numeris doctrina*, but the form is too common to lead to any but the most tentative hypothesis. The tetrameter couplets are admirably suited to the formal elegance and relative brevity demanded by the lyric ode. The poem, of course, is a rural ode, and not a pastoral, although pastoral elements can be identified in the fifth stanza. Marvell's initial denunciation of the 'uncessant Labours' of men is entirely in keeping with the *beatus ille* tradition, and so is his praise of 'Fair quiet'. Even more conclusive is the fact that Marvell's poem develops like a Horatian ode. It proceeds from image to aphorism. 'In the place of propositions, there are pictures, in the place of arguments, illustrations.'[38] And, again like Horace, Marvell draws his illustrating examples from mythology, every-day life, and nature. Through these illustrations he then conveys his argument. We also recognise the initial address typical of the ode, and the concluding picture which drives home the point of the poem.[39]

Marvell's treatment of the Horatian philosophy places him directly in line with the poets included in this chapter. It is highly instructive to place Marvell's poem next to, not only Fane's 'Ode to Retiredness', but also to *Theophila* XII-XIII, and to Casimire's third Epode and his Odes IV, 32 and IV, 21. By so doing one gains a better understanding of the general tradition within which all these poets were writing, and in some cases Marvell's ambiguous phrases can be resolved by comparison with similar, but plainer statements in the retirement poetry of Fane, Benlowes, or Casimire. Thus Casimire's phrase: 'From depth of soule, lesse then himselfe he lies' (third Epode) furnishes an interesting analogue to Marvell's much-debated description of the mind, which 'from pleasure less, / Withdraws into its happiness'. In Casimire the lessening of the mind is directly caused by his absolute concentration on God in the act of prayer. When thus focussed, the soul obviously no longer reflects the *res creatae*; the mirror of the mind has been converted into a burning-glass for the purpose of focussing the rays issuing from the divinity. Fane and Benlowes had written in similar fashion: 'For so my Thoughts by this retreat / Grow stronger, like contracted heat' (Fane), and: 'Rays drawn in to a point, more vig'rous beam' (*Theophila*, XIII, 70). Marvell's phrase 'from pleasure less' would therefore seem to mean 'made less by virtue of its concentration on its true pleasure or happiness'. A second instance is afforded by Marvell's gods who 'still in a Tree did end their race'. Casimire similarly sees 'the shining Deitie' in the shadow of the green fields (third Epode), while Fane admires 'the footsteps here are trod / Of mercy by a Gracious God.' Thirdly, Marvell's 'amorous green' is paralleled by Casimire's description of 'each herb' which 'with restlesse leaves / To th' starres doth strive and upwards heaves' (third Epode), and by Fane's concept of the *liber creaturarum* in which 'every line' is focussed on the Divinity: 'And though all others downward tend, / These look to heaven, and ascend / From whence they came.' By choosing the epithet *amorous*, Marvell implies that which is directly stated by Casimire and Fane. Analogues to Marvell's bird which 'Waves in its Plumes the various Light' can be found in Henry More, Casimire, and Benlowes. Thus Henry More, in *Psychozoia*, lets the soul enter a garden to stand beside a 'good lucid spring of living blisse' (I, 17), and, once there, it dons an iridescent robe around which play the Iris and the halo (I, 22). Benlowes also invests the soul with an iridescent garment, borrowing his phrasing directly from More (see *Theophila*, V, 38 and *Psychozoia*, I, 22). In More's poem the function of the robe is to reflect the whole world: 'Nothing in Nature did you ever spy, / But there's pourtraid' (I, 41). However, since the robe may be donned only beside the symbolic fountain, the inference must be that the mind then has been purified and hence is capable of reflecting reality clearly and truly. The iridescence, in other words, symbolises the Platonic penetration behind the outer surface of things into true reality. Casimire's Ode IV, 32 in the same manner surrounds the soaring mind of the poet with the Iris: 'Iris about my neck hangs round, / And with her divers colour'd bow, I'me bound.' In this state the poet has shed everything which is mortal; in other words, he is pure mind ('nought to my dull bulke I owe') and therefore capable of true vision.

An overall indebtedness to the same Neoplatonic tradition is clearly indicated by these similar phrasings, and even more so by the fact that the process leading to illumination in each case is the same. The most striking difference between Marvell and the others is found in the circumstance that the former leans more heavily on Hermetic ideas, and that his lines therefore carry a much greater weight of that which Reynolds called 'higher sence'.

To the majority of Marvell's interpreters, the prime puzzle of 'The Garden' is found in the seeming crass contradiction between the stanzas that offer a vision of life which is both austere and ascetic, and those that err in the direction of a voluptuous abandonment to the world of sense. Thus Marvell begins with an impassioned apostrophe to solitude, next he denounces mere mortal lovers as stupid, and finally he condemns erotic love utterly in favour of a different kind of love. Logically enough, the reader expects that the next stanza will give him a picture of purified, spiritual love, and he is much confused when instead he is confronted with the poet's pursuit of sensual pleasure: 'Ripe Apples drop about my head; / The Luscious Clusters of the Vine / Upon my Mouth do crush their Wine.' This, surely, is no ascetic existence; the amorous behaviour of the vegetable world merely seems to copy the erotic abandon of earthly lovers. Hence to one critic, writing for *Scrutiny*, Marvell's garden seemed 'a sort of giant fleshy orchid, deliciously hostile and unbridled by any rational end or discipline, which closes around the man and devours him.' And a curious kind of sexual experience is hinted at when he adds that there is 'an ominous air of uncontrol about this picture of sensory pleasure, in which man becomes not agent but victim.'[40] In a fairly recent article Lawrence W. Hyman puts the following, highly relevant question: 'What kind of garden is this where all the pleasures of passion can be enjoyed among trees and flowers, where plants are sexual and man is not? Despite the efforts of the critics, this central contradiction remains.'[41] In an attempt to solve this contradiction, L. W. Hyman applies the legend of the androgynous — or bi-sexual — Adam, and this legend admittedly does solve part of the puzzle. If one assumes that Marvell was thinking of the time, before Eve was created, when Adam was supposed to have been bi-sexual, one can understand why he describes this kind of solitude as 'delicious' and why he rejects the presence of Eve. In offering this solution Hyman does not claim originality, since Ruth Wallerstein had already referred to the same legend as a possible strand in the intellectual pattern of the poem. My main objection to it is that it does not go far enough. Thus a convincing explanation of the amorous behaviour of the vegetable world is still missing. The circumstance that plants represent the androgynous state desired by the poet does not explain why *they* should pursue *him* so persistently with their love. This problem must still be solved, and it would also be desirable to discover whether Marvell could have been familiar with a specific literary source for the legend.

References to an androgynous Adam are found in *Genesis*, in Plato, and in Robert Burton, but the Hermetic books are a far likelier source. As we have seen, Marvell spent nearly two years in the household of a man who was translating a theological commentary on the Hermetic books. The passage which helps to explain Marvell's poem occurs at the beginning of the very first *Libellus*. The passage in question explains the creation of the world in terms indebted to Plato, and the context in which the legend of the androgynous Adam is placed, provides a highly satisfactory explanation of the amorous behaviour of 'this lovely green'. Moreover, the bi-sexual state itself is there given a spiritual explanation which leads up to the ecstatic experience in which the mysteries of the universe are revealed. As one studies this particular account of creation, one's conviction deepens that Marvell must have been writing within a Hermetic, rather than a Mosaic or Platonic convention. The following analysis should make this clear.

As our point of departure let us take the strong contrast drawn in stanzas 1 and 2 between the 'uncessant Labours' of men in society on the one hand, and, on the other, 'delicious Solitude', 'Fair quiet', and the 'Garlands of repose'.

This contrast between a meditative, introvert existence and a worldly, busy life is, of course, frequently enough encountered in contexts that are purely Christian or neo-Stoic, and also Epicurean philosophers placed the pleasures of rest above those of motion. This contrast, however, is also a basic part of the Hermetic philosophy, and is there given a much deeper significance. The establishment of complete silence and bodily repose is there seen as the first step towards establishing the reign of mind over matter, and hence towards union with God. The vision of God, so one reads in Dr. Everard's translation, induces 'a Divine Silence, and the rest of all the Senses: For neither can he that understands that, understand any thing else, nor he that sees that, see any thing else, nor hear any other thing, nor in sum, move the Body'.[42] This was a point that stirred de Foix' interest deeply and, one presumes, that of Fairfax, too. The first Hermetic *Libellus* begins with the description of a vision experienced by Hermes, and in his extensive comments on this passage de Foix again and again underlines the fact that while the vision lasts, the body no longer functions but is, as it were, completely paralysed. Furthermore, he compares the ecstatic experience of Hermes with that of the prophet Daniel, and again to that of St. Paul on his way to Damascus, 'where by a vision he was cast to the ground, deprived of all strength & corporal facultys, nothing remaining in him but the use of reason, understanding, & other intellectual powers'.[43] And on another occasion Fairfax writes that silence is important, since by its means the intelligible powers peculiar to man 'are maintained in their vigour, & garded from all hindrences and perturbation of speech'. Man's intelligible powers are diverted from their proper function by 'extravagant words unprofitable, or vitious'. And before sin was introduced, God 'was knowne, praised, and reverenced' by silence.[44]

The concepts that we are discussing — 'Fair quiet', 'repose', and 'delicious Solitude' — should therefore be related to the Hermetic view of the dual nature of man. Since man is compounded both of matter and mind, he is mortal and immortal at the same time. It is the mortal part that insists on the pursuit of inferior pleasures ('the Palm, the Oke, or Bayes'); the immortal part reveals itself only 'While all Flow'rs and all Trees do close / To weave the Garlands of repose'.

To understand the curious relationship between the poet and 'this lovely green' (stanzas 3, 4, and 5), it is necessary to give a brief summary of the Hermetic account of the creation of man.

During the first stage in his development man was mind only, like God. However, soon after his creation man penetrated downwards through the seven planetary spheres until he reached the earth. There he sees reflected 'the fair and beautiful Shape or Form of God' and falls in love with it. This reflection is that of his own mind, which is immortal and divine and part of God. On seeing 'a shape like unto himself' reflected in the watery element, man 'loved it, and would cohabit with it; and immediately upon the resolution, ensued the Operation.'[45] As a result of this union was created man's 'unreasonable Image or Shape', that is an image devoid of reason because composed of matter only. The interesting fact at this point is this: not only is man in love with Nature, because Nature reflects the image of God and hence also of his own mind, but Nature itself loves man when it sees the reflection of God in him: 'Nature presently laying hold of what it so much loved, did wholly wrap her self about it, and they were mingled, for they loved one another.' [46] One now sees exactly why 'No white nor red was ever seen / So am'rous as this lovely green', and why the poet submits to the passionate embrace. As in the Hermetic account, the sexual embrace reflects a union between the images of God in man and in Nature.

It is at this early stage in the history of the creation of man that it is explicitly stated that man is a Hermaphrodite. In the words of Fairfax, he is 'male & female, in the same body as the Scriptures said of the first man before he siñed & before god took the woman out of the side of man'.[47] Moreover, all creatures shared this bi-sexual structure and retained it for a certain un-specified period. During this period they were tied, as it were, in a bond or knot which, in the words of Fairfax, 'held all things from action, poyse or motion'.[48] The bi-sexual stage which pre-vents all beings from indulging in action (forcing them to enjoy the garlands of repose) therefore possesses a profound spiritual significance. While it is the property of matter to move, the mind is utterly quiescent. The androgynous state, therefore, is one in which matter is subordinated to pure mind. When Marvell ex-plicitly rejects motion, or physical pursuit (whether of honour or of women), in favour first of repose and then of a state 'with-out a Mate', we can be sure that Fairfax would have grasped the Hermetic context immediately. He would at once have seen that the Earthly Paradise visualised by Marvell reflects the androgyn-ous period during which the divine element in the Creation reigned supreme, and when this element was mutually recognised and loved on all levels, whether animate or inanimate.

The androgynous period, however, was destined to come to an end, and so in due course 'the bond of all things was loosed and untied by the Will of God . . . and so the Males were apart by themselves, and the Females likewise'.[49] Subsequently God com-mands all creatures to increase and to multiply (i. e. to engage in action or motion), but with this important caution attached:

'... let him that is endued with Minde, know himself to be immortal; and that the cause of death is the love of the body.'[50]

If one returns to Marvell's poem with these passages in mind, one sees at once how pregnant with meaning his lines are. The usual type of mortal lover is 'fond' or stupid because he permits his soul to be engrossed by the vastly inferior love of the body, which is the cause of death. He is ignorant and cruel because he does not know himself or the true character of that which he sees. As Sir John Davies had observed in stanza 109 of *Nosce Teipsum*: 'Sense outsides knows: the Soul through all things sees ... Sense sees the bark, but she the life of trees.' He sees neither his own divinity nor that of the trees. Only the man who sharpens his intellectual powers through silence and bodily repose sees how far the beauty of 'this lovely green' exceeds that of women. Man, to him, stands revealed as a 'mortal God',[51] just as Nature becomes a 'material God'.[52] Unlike woman, the amorous green never tempts man to lose his true identity as a mortal God by causing him to succumb to the world of sense. Man's erotic or sexual passion, he realises, is nothing but a thoroughly undesirable preoccupation with the world of sense and motion. Indeed, the act of generation is evil in its effect on man: 'For all things that are made or generated, are full of Passion; ... and where Passion is there is not the Good; where the Good is, there is no Passion.'[53] Hence Marvell writes with admirable Hermetic logic: 'When we have run our Passions heat, / Love hither makes his best retreat.' The true good, in other words, is in the garden, in silence, physical repose, and in loving communion with the 'sacred green'.[54]

It should now be possible to conclude that the purpose of Marvell's re-enactment, in stanza 5, of that first passionate embrace between mind and matter, seems to be to receive a taste of that pure love or *communion* which can be experienced only when the passions of the body have been stilled. Such communion is possible between superior and inferior parts of the Creation. 'But there is a communion of Souls', so Hermes says, 'and those of God, communicate with those [of] men; and those of men, with those of Beasts ... Therefore is the World subject unto God, Man unto the World, and unreasonable things to Man.'[55] And after having received mental illumination Tat, the son of Hermes, discovers that he is one with the entire Creation: 'I am in living Creatures, in Plants, in the Womb, every where.'[56] This is so because man's mind is part of the divine mind, and mind penetrates the entire Creation in diminishing degrees. It has been observed that Marvell is curiously preoccupied with the *greenness* of things. Thus in 'The Garden' Marvell, in his well-known phrase, annihilates 'all that's made / To a green Thought in a green Shade', while 'Upon Appleton House' places the poet inside 'this yet green, yet growing Ark' (1. 484). Vaughan, too, was fond of the same word, as E. C. Pettet points out,[57] and surely for the same reason. According to Hermetic alchemy, the very essence of the vegetable world consisted in the so-called *benedicta viriditas*. The creative spirit descended into the vegetable world in the form of greenness. Hence a concentration on greenness itself, and a rejection of all other aspects of the vegetable world, leads to union with (or at least perception of) the creative spirit. 'This lovely green', then, stands for the visible manifestation of the divinity in Nature, which is why its beauty must far exceed that of the mere fleshly beauty of women, and why its powers of love must be so vastly superior.

The process of purification or illumination through silence, repose, and communion with the creative principle, leads logically to the climactic experience when the mind succeeds in 'Casting the Bodies Vest aside'.

The relationship between mind and body is clearly stated by Hermes. The Hermetic philosopher distinguishes between mind, soul, spirit, and body — the soul and the spirit forming intermediate stages between pure mind and pure matter. The mind informs the soul, and the soul is connected with the body through the spirit, which in its turn is diffused and passes through the veins and arteries of the body.[58] The mind, it must be remembered, 'is of the very Essence of God' and hence 'is not cut off, or divided from the essentiality of God, but united as the light of the Sun'.[59] Since each mind thus is part of God, it may be said to form an ocean reflecting everything created by God. God, as pure mind, contains within Himself the ideas, or archetypal patterns, of all created things, and in this manner 'each kind' will there find 'its own resemblance'.

To summarise: Once the proper degree of bodily repose has been achieved, pure mind reasserts its superiority over matter, and it becomes possible for it to 'Withdraw into its happiness', that is, to withdraw into that part of the Creation which is God by dismissing 'the bodies Vest'. Since God is present everywhere, union with God (pure mind) entails a union with all the creatures, and even with the vegetable world (through its 'greenness', i. e. through the creative principle as manifested in the vegetable world). However, the creative principle which is God is not exhausted with the creation of man and the earth; it comprises 'Far other Worlds, and other Seas', areas which the mind of man may penetrate if it achieves complete release from the body and union with the creative principle.

Union with the creative principle is also aimed at in the desire for bi-sexuality, a state attributed to God. In his translation of the commentary on *Libellus* I, section 12, Fairfax, referring to God, adds: 'which was sayd before to have in him selfe both sexes) that is to say all power of production without any succour, or exteriour ayde.'[60] By thus associating bi-sexuality not only with the reign of mind over matter, but also with the creative principle, the legend of the androgynous Adam is made the vehicle of profound spiritual insight.

But to return to the garden ecstasy. One notices that Marvell explicitly states that it is the *soul* which glides into the boughs. The implication must be that the mind is not released in its naked and divine state; it is still dressed in the soul as in a 'Covering or a Cloathing'.[61] As every student of Hermes would have known, the mind can be completely released only by the death of the body. The ecstasy experienced while in the body, yet out of it, must consist in a release of the *soul*. After death, the mind puts on a *fiery coat*, fire being its proper element. Pure mind 'hath the fire for its Body'.[62] In this Hermetic concept one may possibly find an explanation of the 'various Light' which Marvell's bird 'Waves in its Plumes'. The fiery body of pure mind shines through the outer garment of the soul, waiting for death, or 'longer flight', before it can be released.[63] Marvell's use of the words *mind* and *soul* is precise and clearly indicates complete awareness of their Hermetic connotation.

It is significant that Marvell directly associates 'that happy Garden-state' with the ecstatic experience by writing, in the next stanza: 'Such was that happy Garden-state...' The implication is clearly that both consist in the reign of mind over matter. That the religious ecstasy consists in a release of the soul from the body is a traditional idea, but that the Earthly Paradise should symbolise a similar state is a concept directly derived from Hermetic doctrines. When one adds the concept of the first, androgynous character of the Creation to this idea — as Marvell does in stanza 8 — the identification becomes complete. As far as I know, this particular juxtaposition of ideas can be found in no other context. The rejection of Eve, then, is no mere rejection of female companionship in favour of masculine solitude. It is a rejection of the reign of matter, symbolised by the act of generation, and an acceptance, instead, of that bi-sexual structure which man and the *res creatae* originally shared with God, but which God alone retained together with the vegetable world.[64] As soon as man became mortal he could no longer remain solitary, since his mortality was the result of the division into two sexes. Hence it was 'beyond a Mortal's share / To wander solitary there'. However, unlike man, the 'fragrant Zodiac' of the final stanza has retained its androgynous structure and hence also its ability to commune with God and with the image of God in man. The world of flowers

and herbs therefore forms the only suitable focussing-point for
the concluding lines, just as it formed the point of departure for
the opening stanza. The 'sweet and wholesome Hours' are those
in which 'all flow'rs and all Trees do close / To weave the Garlands of repose'.

When thus related to that Hermetic philosophy which Fairfax
laboured to elucidate, Marvell's lines fall into a coherent and
fascinating pattern. His rejection of women and of the passions
of the body has now been placed in a context which explains why
it is possible to turn from a rejection of sex and the world of sense
in one moment, to a frankly erotic intercourse with the 'lovely
green' in the next. This 'central contradiction' now has completely
vanished. It is important to realise that Hermetic ideas do not
occur here and there in isolated lines; they carry the entire poem.
On the esoteric level, the poem explains quite clearly how to
achieve the reign of mind over matter in this life. For a man like
Fairfax (and, one imagines, Henry Vaughan) it would have been
mere child's play to catch the various allusions. He would at once
have seen that the ulterior purpose of Marvell's retirement was
to effect a process of regeneration whereby the mind is released
from its subjection to the body.

The final emblematic picture of the garden with its fragrant
zodiac drives home the point of the entire poem with concrete
forcefulness. In these lines Marvell may be glancing at Claudian's
well-known and popular epigram on the old man from Verona:
'Happy the Man, who his whole time doth bound / Within th'en-
closure of his little ground.' [65] This man refuses to embark on
foolish wanderings, and is content to observe the passing of the
seasons and the time of day in the surrounding landscape rather
than by means of calendars or dials: 'He measures time by Land-
marks, and has found / For the whole day the Dial of his ground.'
Benlowes, too, had made this point.[66] However, in Marvell's poem
the sundial and the fragrant zodiac are made to convey a profound
religious lesson. Thus the 'skilful Gardner' and his plot of ground

become a type of God and the Creation, while the bee (by virtue of its lack of procreative ability) symbolises that state of innocence which once had marked 'that happy Garden-state'. Similarly the visible sun becomes a symbol of the invisible Deity of a spiritual universe. Just as man's physical eye looks to the sun and stars to compute the time, his mind looks to the Divine Mind to trace the progress of the invisible angelic world. In this manner the visible shadows forth the invisible. The world of bees and flowers is equally governed by the sun; in other words, even the lower level of intelligence assigned to the animal and vegetable worlds is capable of communion with the stars. The importance of rightly computing time by studying the heavenly bodies is stressed by Plato, who maintains that the result of this process will be to reproduce the same ordered motion in the mind of him who computes. The 'milder Sun' is a pregnant phrase. The disciples of Plato and Hermes looked upon the visible sun as the shadow of God,[67] as God's physical counterpart in the realm of matter. During his ecstasy, the poet has for a while contemplated the Sun of the sun and been one with it, sharing its creative power. Hence his attitude of benign approval in the concluding stanza, so reminiscent of the attitude of God on the seventh day of creation, and hence also his allusion to the physical sun as necessarily 'milder'.

So far, I have almost completely overlooked the more orthodox religious ideas, although the similarity between stanza 5 and the traditional paraphrase of *Canticles* has been pointed out. For this reason the traditional theological interpretation of *Canticles* must be taken into account. Marvell's ripe apples recall the Earthly Paradise described by Casimire and Benlowes, whose apples were free from the taste of death by virtue of the fruit of the tree of the cross, that fruit which set at nought the effect of the fatal apple eaten by Adam and Eve. The luscious clusters of the vine may be interpreted as a reference to Christ, while the embrace between the poet and the *res creatae* shadows forth the mystic

171

marriage between the soul and Christ. The fruit tree at whose foot the poet is placed, would in this case be the tree of the cross (Christ being its 'fruit'), the fountain the baptismal waters or the waters of redemption. If this is true, Marvell would seem to be contemplating the deepest mystery of the Christian faith, the mystery of Christ on the cross, the moment of that supreme sacrifice when the Saviour divested Himself of the 'Bodies Vest'. It is a commonplace of the Neoplatonic tradition that the contemplated object and the contemplating mind become one.[68] This enables the poet's mind to ascend the tree, where 'Like a Bird, it sits and sings'.

A parallel may be intended between the idea of the *felix culpa* and the hot pursuit of Apollo for Daphne, and of Pan for Syrinx. Just as Adam and Eve may be said to have eaten the fatal apple only in order to bring about the supreme event of Christ's sacrifice, the pagan gods may have pursued their unwilling mistresses only to bring about their metamorphosis from a lower state to a higher.

There is no contradiction or incongruity between these more orthodox religious ideas and those that are patently Hermetic. This was only to be expected, since the French commentary partly translated by Fairfax aimed at proving that Hermes and Moses shared the same divine revelation. Marvell, therefore, in combining Biblical and Hermetic traditions, followed the pattern set by Italian and French Neoplatonists. The same combination will be found in 'Upon Appleton House' as well, the chief difference being that traditional religious symbolism is much more to the fore in this lengthy poetic compliment to Lord Fairfax.

b. *'Upon Appleton House'*

The entire design of Marvell's poem seems grounded on a single theological or religious concept, to wit the contrast between innocence and corruption. The quest for moral and spiritual regeneration is pursued through regional history (the history of the religious establishment at Nun-Appleton), the history of England (in the allusions to the civil war), and universal history (the allusions to the major events of the Old and the New Testament).[69]

Biblical allusions are particularly important. On viewing the landscape both Benlowes and Marvell are reminded of the crossing of the Red Sea and the river Jordan, of the miraculous provision of manna and quails in the desert, of Christ's love sacrifice on the cross, and of the religious devotee's union with Christ in a holy death which murders sense. To this Marvell adds references to the building of the tower of Babel and to Noah and the Ark. The ancient Church fathers had given these Biblical events quite specific typological meanings, and unless we are familiar with their interpretations, we shall fail to realise the implications clearly intended by Benlowes and Marvell. We must therefore study the symbolical value of these events, remembering that medieval and Renaissance theologians submitted both books of revelation (the Book of God's Word and the book of God's Work) to a searching, multi-levelled technique of interpretation. A deeper, spiritual sense was sought behind the historical events and behind the surface of things. It can scarcely be doubted that this habitual quest for various levels of meaning exerted the strongest influence on the type of poetry considered here.

In his study of *Symbolism in Medieval Thought* H. Flanders Dunbar explains how the rock might have three levels of meaning beyond its literal use as descriptive symbol:

> It may stand for Christ, . . . or it may exemplify that which each soul should be to its fellows . . . or finally the rock may mean the foundation of the heavenly kingdom. In other words, every natural object may be taken allegorically as telling of the life of the Logos; tropologically, as conveying teaching as to the inner life of man; and anagogically as containing revelation of the life in glory. Every symbol should be understood at one and the same time in all of these significations . . . Each natural object, whether animate or inanimate, had its particular meaning on each of these levels.[70]

173

Marvell's poem displays a similar semantic complexity. Behind the literal, surface meaning lie both political allegory and a deeper, more spiritual sense. The political allegory has been ably explained by Don Cameron Allen.[71] I shall therefore focus on the purely religious or philosophical aspects. In the course of his exposition D. C. Allen takes notice of certain parts which may be interpreted typologically or anagogically,[72] but this type of insight symbol is not pursued systematically.

An excellent survey of the traditional interpretation of the main events of the Old Testament is given by Jean Daniélou, S. J., in his book *From Shadows to Reality. Studies in the Typology of the Fathers.*[73] I have also found Rosemond Tuve's book on George Herbert very useful.[74] The following exposition of some main points in the typology of the Church Fathers is based on the former.

The basic principle of typology is found in the belief that human existence constitutes an imperfect order which prepares for and prefigures an order of perfection. This perfection is achieved when natural man turns into spiritual man. The achievement of this process is the purpose of all the events in the Old Testament and the New. God's scheme for the redemption of the fallen Adam stands reflected in the four fundamental types of the Old Testament: the ark of Noah, the crossing of the Red Sea, the Mosaic Law, and the entry into the promised land. In the words of Jean Daniélou: 'All the outstanding persons and leading events of Scripture are both stages and rough outlines to prepare and prefigure the mystery which is one day to be fulfilled in Christ.' [75] Thus paradise lies in the future as well as in the past; the New Paradise was realised with the coming of Christ, and each Christian becomes a New Adam in his turn through Holy Baptism, 'which is thus revealed as a new creation and a return to Paradise.' [76] Paradise may therefore be realised in the Christian life, as Marvell suggests in his homage to Fairfax, whose garden is a literal Paradise. The ark of Noah is particularly rich in typological

significance. The deliverance of Noah and the deliverance of Moses
are the two main works of God in the Old Testament, and they
are often associated together. Noah and Moses are types of Christ,
their actions foreshadowing his. With the Flood is associated the
sea beast Leviathan, a type of wickedness, just as in the crossing
of the Red Sea Pharaoh and his horsemen represent the devil,
or sin. Both are overcome by Christ. The Flood is

> the figure of Christ's triumph over the sea dragon through his
> descent into Hell: he is the true Noah who has experienced the
> swelling of the waters of death, and has been delivered by God
> to be the beginning of a new world; it represents also Baptism
> wherein the Christian is buried with Christ in the water of death
> through the symbol of the baptismal waters, figuratively under-
> going the punishment due to sin and being free with Christ and
> henceforth belonging to the new creation . . .[77]

Baptism therefore is a spiritual version of Noah's deliverance from
the Flood, and also of the deliverance wrought by God through
Moses when he commanded the Red Sea to divide.

A further turn of the interpretative screw is achieved on considering the interpretation submitted by Philo, whose influence on
Origen and St. Ambrose was profound. Philo interpreted *Genesis*
as a Platonic myth. Thus the creation of Adam represented the
creation of mind, while the creation of Eve represented the creation of sensation, or the life of the senses. As St. Ambrose commented: 'Very rightly is mind represented by the symbol of man,
and feeling by that of woman.' [78] Marvell's rejection of women
therefore signifies a rejection of mere sense; at this point the
teachings of Hermes and the Church Fathers coincide. Similarly
Philo interprets the rescue of the Israelites from the Egyptians
as a transition from a state dominated by the body (the Egyptians
representing the bodily passions) to a state dominated by mind.
As we shall soon see, Marvell, too, associates Pharaoh's horsemen
with the physical passions, from which he seeks, and finds, deliver-

ance in his 'yet green, yet growing Ark'. In this manner the journey through the desert becomes a type of the soul's passage through life. The passions must be overcome, and this is achieved through the progressive enlightenment afforded by the Logos. Both Benlowes and Marvell are intent on depicting such a spiritual journey. Both refer to the act of retirement as a retreat into a fortress, from which the soul wages a pious war against the world, the flesh, and the devil. And, in so doing, both refer to the five senses as the *Cinque-Ports* over which the strictest guard must be kept.[79]

We can now turn to the poem itself. As already stated, its main motif is the quest for redemption and innocence regained, a quest closely associated with the fortunes of the Fairfax family. Thus the rescue of the 'Virgin *Thwates*' from her gloomy nunnery was a rescue from a state dominated by Evil ('I know what Fruit their Gardens yield, / When they it think by Night conceal'd') to the holy state of matrimony. In the same manner the retirement of the Lord General was prompted by the wish to avoid the depravity inherent in the world; it represents the triumph of conscience over ambition, of mind over the world of sense. Fairfax's environment reflects the same contrast between innocence and corruption. Over against his modest house appears 'proud *Cawood Castle*' as a visual manifestation of the ambition of its *'Prelate* great' (stanza 46). The beauty and sweetness of his garden makes the poet bewail that 'luckless Apple' which made man mortal and laid waste 'The Garden of the World' (stanza 41). The corruption which thus gained entrance into man, Nature, and the body politic is allegorised in the stanzas describing how the *'Traitor-worm'* destroys the oak so that it may be felled by the lightest stroke. The cruel massacres of the mowers (types of soldiers engaged in civil war) provide a graphic illustration of that state of war which marks the postlapsarian state.[79a] The chaotic state of the world is again strongly stressed in the concluding stanzas which denounce it as 'a rude heap together hurl'd; / All negligently overthrown, /

Gulfes, Deserts, Precipices, Stones'. The lesser world of the garden contains the same elements, but in 'more decent Order tame'.

The forces of innocence form a strong contrast to the forces of evil. In attacking the Nunnery and exposing the *'Wooden Saints'* and *'Relicks False'* the first Fairfax becomes a type of the Protestant hero, 'whose Offspring fierce / Shall fight through all the *Universe'*. On a smaller scale he imitates the redemptive action of Christ by rescuing a human soul from corruption to sanctity. A second strong contrast is that between the cruel massacres of the mowers and the spiritual warfare conducted by the Lord General against the world and his own five senses. The concluding section focusses on Maria Fairfax as the symbol of innocence. She is seen as the archetype of that beauty and innocence which marks the garden of Nun-Appleton. By virtue of the sanctity of its residents, Fairfax's estate becomes *'Heaven's Center, Nature's Lap, / And Paradice's only Map'.* The internal and external worlds are interdependent in the familiar manner of the Renaissance. When redeemed from vice, pride, and ambition, man bestows the same redemption upon Nature, just as conversely the corruption of Adam and Eve once had brought death and decay into the world.

Once it is seen that Marvell's poem is organised in this manner, its unity becomes apparent. The historical episode concerning the abduction from the Nunnery becomes relevant, and so does the political allegory, and the various compliments to Fairfax and his daughter. The individual, the church, the body politic, and Nature must undergo the same process of purgation. As in 'The Garden' the method employed involves a contemplative retirement into rural scenes and a focussing of all the powers of the mind on God. To the contemplating mind the chief events in the universal history of man yield up their inner, spiritual significance, at the same time that deeper insights are gained from a close study of the Book of God's Work.

After these preliminary remarks we can now examine the poem more in detail.

Stanzas 1-9 describe Fairfax and his house. The building is a reflection of the man who lives in it, and accommodates itself to him, like a living organism. While the more extravagant buildings of the age reflect the vanity which once spurred on the builders of Babel (the 'first Builders' of 1. 24), Fairfax's house is composed 'Like Nature, orderly and near', thus reflecting a more 'sober Age and Mind'. The fact that a man like Fairfax is content to live in 'dwarfish Confines' proves that 'Things greater are in less contained' (1. 44). Indeed, so dwarfish is the house that it is compared to '*Romulus* his Bee-like Cell' (1. 40). (While considering the 'body politic' of bees Benlowes had commented that 'Great souls' may be confined 'in small breasts'. *Theophila*, XII, 76.) Because of this disproportion between the outer structure and its inhabitant, the house 'scarce indures the *Master* great' (1. 50), and sweats and swells to accommodate him. It takes but little effort to realise that the description forms a conscious analogue to the soul-body relationship. The body labours to support the heavy weight of the mind. The statement that 'the *Square* grows *Spherical*' (1. 52) is a piece of literal description, since the great hall was topped by a dome, but the spiritual sense is the most important one. Both the house and man's body are mortal, temporal and imperfect and hence associated with that well-known symbol of the world, the square. Man's soul or mind, however, is divine, immortal and perfect and hence symbolised by the circle. These are the '*holy Mathematics*' that can turn a square into a circle.[80] One may in this manner trace no less than four levels of meaning: Marvell's description of the house conveys literal truth, moral truth (the importance of humility), allegorical truth (the house is but an inn, a temporary dwelling-place in the long pilgrimage of the soul), and ultimate truth (the house-master relationship is a type of the soul-body relationship).

Stanzas 11-35 trace the progress of 'this Houses Fate'. It is a neat paradox that the Nunnery stands for a corrupt worldliness, while, after the Protestant reform, it turns into a proper religious

178

house: ''Twas no Religious House till now' (1. 280). The Nunnery
was like an enchanted castle; the 'glad Youth' acts to break the
evil spell, and so the 'Castle vanishes or rends' (1. 270).

Fairfax's career clearly prompted the use of military terms
employed in the subsequent description of Fairfax himself and
his estate (stanzas 36-46). However, these terms were also surely
intended to provoke associations with the traditional picture of
the true Christian as a soldier armed with the weapons of his
faith.[81] Fairfax's garden reflects his own innocence and piety, and
thus forms a suitable setting, like the house. The very stars, flowers, and bees combine to form vigilant patrols to protect this New
Paradise. The poet's complaint that man lost his 'Garden of the
World' through the 'luckless Apple' carries the argument one step
further. After the Fall, man did indeed turn into a soldier, but in
a different sense, since war is a symptom of the fallen state. For
this reason war and the implements of war have overgrown the
innocent magazines and forts of Nature. Instead of flowers, man
'plants' ordinance (artillery)[82] and 'sows' powder. Therefore,
what the world (and particularly England) needs more than anything else, is the cultivation of 'that Heaven-nursed Plant', conscience. Its flowers are eternal and shine in 'the Crowns of Saints'.

Stanza 47 opens that long mid-section where the poet traces
the universal history of man in the surrounding landscape. Can
it be mere coincidence that this landscape possesses all the features
subsequently attributed to the world in the last stanza but one,
to wit 'Gulfes, Deserts, Precipices, Stones'? Thus Marvell discovers
veritable gulfs in the 'abyss' of the 'unfathomable Grass'; when
the mowers cross the field, they remind him of the Israelites in
the desert; the green 'spires' of the grass resemble 'Precipices
tall' from which giant grasshoppers squeak out their contempt for
man, while the haystacks on the level meadow appear like rocks
above a calm sea. The poetic vision seems to transform the landscape into a complete map of the world against which all major
events in the history of man are acted out.

Marvell has already alluded to the Garden of Eden and the Fall, and to the tower of Babel. The giant grasshoppers of stanza 47 may therefore be an allusion to that race of giants which peopled the earth between the expulsion from the garden and the Flood. If so, they represent forces of evil. A similar interpretation follows, if one associates the grasshoppers with the events narrated in *Numbers* 13 : 33 or *Nahum* 3 : 17, passages which provide useful clues to an understanding of the political allegory.[83] According to the former passage spies sent by the Israelites to investigate Canaan bring back false reports which cause the chosen people to lose confidence in God and in Moses. The spies allege that the Promised Land is peopled by giants, 'and we were in our own sight as grasshoppers, and so we were in their sight.' In theological expositions the seven hostile tribes of Canaan were taken to represent the Seven Deadly Sins. Just as Israel, after crossing the Red Sea, had to overcome these tribes in battle, the Christian, after Baptism, must rout the forces of evil. For the time being the giants seem the superior force, pouring out their contempt on men 'as we walk more low then them'. They cannot be overcome until after Baptism, i. e. after the crossing of the Red Sea. This event follows in stanza 49. It is possible that the reference to the 'green Sea' may bear a Hermetic connotation; the subsequent reference, in line 484, to the 'yet green, yet growing Ark' undoubtedly does. Since the *benedicta viriditas* was seen to represent the spiritual essence of the vegetable world, the crossing of the green sea may suggest a penetration into the creative essence of God. Baptism, then, would consist in a spiritual penetration into the sphere of the divinity as manifested in the Creation. A further Hermetic concept is encountered in stanza 63, where Marvell emphasises the darkness and closeness of the forest by stating: 'There the huge Bulk takes place, as ment / To thrust up a *Fifth Element*.' An exposition of this concept is given in *The Book of Quinte Essence*,[84] a manuscript treatise dating from 1460-1470, professing to be a summary of 'the book of quintis essenciis in latyn, that hermys the prophete and kyng of Egipt, after the flood of Noe fadir of philosophris, had by reuelacioun of an aungel of god to him sende'. The effect of this fifth element or essence is to purify or preserve that which otherwise would have been subject to corruption, and in its working the heaven and the sun combine to influence man 'in as miche as it is possible in deedly nature'. When Marvell therefore retreats into the forest, 'this yet green, yet growing Ark', he enters as it were a Holy Temple penetrated by forces which preserve from corruption.

The retreat into the forest is an escape from the flood. On the political level the flood undoubtedly symbolises civil war, as suggested by D. C. Allen. On the spiritual level, it stands for the kind of confusion which existed in Chaos. Sea monsters were popularly supposed to usurp the dwellings of men at the time of the Deluge,[85] just as a serpent was believed to inhabit the primeval sea of Chaos. The Ark itself was given varying interpretations. It stood for the Church (the saving agency), or it was viewed as a type of the tomb of Christ. Christ stayed in the tomb, as Noah did in the Ark, to put an end to the deluge of foulness.[86] According to St. Justin the mystery of man's salvation is implicit in the Flood. Noah once marked a new era in the history of man, thus foreshadowing the new era brought by Christ. 'Now Christ . . . is become the head . . . of a new race, which has been regenerated by him through water, faith and wood, which embraces the mystery of the cross, as Noah, together with his family, was saved by the wood of the ark carried on the waters.' [87] Marvell's reference to Noah as the 'first Carpenter' may be an allusion to the typological significance of Noah as a type of Christ, the 'second carpenter.' Just as Noah constructed his Ark to serve as an instrument for the deliverance of mankind, Christ saved mankind through the agency of the wood of the cross.

Marvell's flood is caused by the river Denton, and in the Bible it is the Holy Ark of the Tabernacle which is associated with flooded rivers, since it was this holy vessel which, when carried in front of the Israelites, caused the river Jordan to dry out (*Joshua*, 3 : 13). The river Denton, like the Jordan, was apt to overflow at harvest-time, and the Jordan was so flooded at the time of the crossing into Canaan. The statement that in the Ark 'all Creatures might have shares, / Although in Armies, not in Paires' can be interpreted on two levels. As applied to the Ark of Noah, the couplet suggests that vast numbers are capable of finding accommodation there. However, since the creatures taken aboard by Noah notoriously arrived in pairs, the negation seems curious. The paradox is explained if we apply the phrase, not to the Ark of Noah, but to the Ark of the Tabernacle as a symbol of God. It is also explained if we interpret the Ark of Noah as the typological symbol of Christ. In Platonic and Hermetic philosophy, God, as pure mind, contains within Himself the archetypes of all created things and of everything yet to be created. Hence 'all Creatures' are encompassed by the sphere of the divinity. The rejection of creatures 'in Paires' is most likely yet another reference to the Hermetic doctrine of the androgynous creation as one in which mind has complete control of matter. After the division into two sexes, man lost this complete command and became mortal and subject to the reign of brute matter unless he succeeded in subjecting his body to his mind. Both 'The Garden' and 'Upon Appleton House' are, in effect, sermons on the necessity of liberating the mind, couched in language understood only by the initiated; the square must be transformed into a circle. If, then, it is the mortal aspect of creatures which is reflected by their living together in pairs, they shed their sexuality together with their mortality on entering the Ark, i. e. the sphere of Christ, or the divinity, which is pure mind.

The attribution, to the forest, of a Fifth Element, serves to stress the purity and immortality of the place. Its holy associations are further strengthened by the subsequent comparison, in stanza 64, between the forest and the Holy Temple. At this point Marvell again shares a poetical motif with Benlowes.[88] The trunks form

182

'*Corinthean Porticoes*', the arching boughs the 'columnes of the Temple green', while the birds act as 'winged Quires' which 'echo about their tuned Fires'. Stanzas 68-71 focus attention on the single tree. If the Holy Temple of the forest represents the Church, each individual tree would represent one member of this spiritual body. The 'inverted Tree' of line 568 recalls Plato, who compares man both to an inverted plant and an inverted tree. Thus the *Phaedrus* states that man is a tree 'whose nervie root Springs in his top'. And *Timaeus*, section 9, places 'the most sovereign form of soul in us' in 'the summit of our body'. This soul 'lifts us from earth towards our celestial affinity, like a plant whose roots are not in earth, but in the heavens. And this is most true, for it is to the heavens whence the soul first came to birth, that the divine part attaches the head or root of us and keeps the whole body upright.'

The manner in which Marvell, in stanzas 71-76, identifies himself with his environment, merging his own identity with trees and birds, suggests the contemplative technique of Plotinus, according to which the advanced stages of contemplation are marked by an intimate union between the contemplator and the object of his contemplation.[89] A similar intimate union had marked the prelapsarian relationship between God and man, and man and the *res creatae*. The statement that the poet begins to understand the language of the birds therefore suggests that his contemplation is leading to a re-establishment of man's ancient innocence and of his effortless communion with all created things. According to *Genesis* 2 : 20 the first man had control over the animals, while *Ezekiel* 34 : 28 prophesies that in the Messianic era he will have such dominion again. This era will also be marked by complete harmony and peace (*Isaiah* 11 : 6). In other words, the effect of the Fall is annulled when the poet begins to speak in the language of the birds; the Messianic era is at hand. Marvell is in complete accordance with Biblical tradition when he proceeds to describe this new creation in terms of a new Paradise. Ezekiel describes the new Jerusalem in terms of a new Paradise, and so do the non-canonical Jewish apocalypses.[90] Christ is the New Adam, but so is each Christian. This New Adam is born through Holy Baptism (the entry into the Ark of Noah) which is, in fact, a return to Paradise and a new creation. The poet's communion with all created things is so intimate that he begins to grasp the occult significance of that which he reads in *'Natures mystick Book'*. He reads all secrets of life in a *'light Mosaic'*. The literal sense (that the light, falling through the branches and the leaves, forms a design in mosaic) should be supplemented by interpreting the phrase as a reference to 'the Light that Moses, also brooding in the wilderness, saw in the blazing bush'.[91] *Mosaic* may also be taken in a wider sense as referring to all occult accounts of the mysteries of creation. Thus Ficino refers to the Hermetic account of creation as *Mosaica mysteria*.

Stanzas 74-78 form the central part of the poem. Marvell begins by depicting himself as a priest whose 'antick Cope' consists of oak leaves, caterpillars, and the 'familiar trails of ivy' which enclose him like a mistress. The breezes and the mossy banks similarly court the poet, offering soft beds and cooling air. Stanzas 74-75 recall the fifth stanza of 'The Garden' and indubitably have the same background in Hermetic lore. The vegetable part of creation loves man for the sake of the image of God in man, and so man becomes a lover-priest, mediating between the *res creatae* and God. Stanza 76 may refer to the apocalyptic horsemen, as suggested by D. C. Allen, but it seems to me to make better sense to associate the horsemen with Pharaoh and his hosts, in theological exposition the traditional symbol of the devil and his forces, or, according to Philo, of the bodily desires. *Exodus* 14 refers so frequently to 'Pharaoh's horses, his chariots, and his horsemen' that the phrase is hammered home like a refrain. The poet, then, has 'incamp'd' his mind behind the trees (the symbol of the Ark and of spiritual baptism) so that he is as invulnerable in relation to 'the World' as the encamped Israelites were in relation to Pharaoh and his horsemen.[92] When attacked, the Israelites are rescued when Moses, lifting up his rod, divides the Red Sea. An allusion to this action also occurs in stanza 78, where the *trees* are said to *divide* before their Lord. The Lord in question is Fairfax who is thus presented as a new Moses, leading a recalcitrant nation through the desert. It is in this lane, protected by the rod of Moses-Fairfax that Marvell wishes to remain fixed or staked down.

Stanzas 77-78 employ phrases which suggest that the lover-priest turns into a sacrifice in imitation of the Passion of Christ. It has already been stated that Christ on the Cross was viewed as the New Adam, bringing about a return to a New Paradise, and that each Christian, through Baptism, similarly became a New Adam. St. Paul's Epistle to the Romans, chapter 6, is the best possible commentary on stanzas 77-78, the gist of this chapter being that the old Adam must be crucified with Christ; 'we are buried with him by baptism into death', so that similarly 'we also should walk in newness of life.' I take stanza 78 to mean that through baptism (i. e. by being placed in the lane which divides before its Lord) the poet in the words of St. Paul, is baptised 'into his [Christ's] death' so that his 'old man' is 'crucified with him, that the body of sin might be destroyed.' It will easily be seen how this spiritual baptism closely parallels that release of the mind from the passions of the body which forms the core of Platonic and Hermetic doctrines. Benlowes, too, describes Christ's entrance into man as a crucifixion of the old man and the birth of a totally new being. Thus he states that Christ 'binds when he embraceth us', he 'kills us into life'. That which dies on the cross are our carnal affections, and as soon as this has been achieved, 'the soul becomes a living sacrifice, holy and acceptable unto God'.[93] Stanza 77 reads like a paraphrase of Benlowes' statement: 'In the cords of love he leads us captives.' The woodbines and the vines are traditional symbols of love, the twining vine often symbolising the mystic wedding of the soul to Christ. Benlowes frequently refers to Christ as the vine,[94] and he describes the mystic union in those sexual terms which derive from the accepted spiritual interpretation of *Canticles*. Thus he exclaims: 'Loving, I'm lov'd! While with my Spouse I twine!' [95]

Several points support the theory that the purpose of the sacrifice described in stanzas 77-78 is to establish the reign of mind over body. The initial description of Fairfax and his house had stressed the view that the mind should command the body, that the mind should turn the square of the body into a circle, i. e. into that which is eternal and immortal. And in the stanza just preceding the symbolical crucifixion, Marvell had stressed how completely his *mind* has encamped itself behind the trees, and how securely he 'gauls' the horsemen of the world. My interpretation therefore depends not only upon the descriptive terms ('brambles chain me too', 'courteous briars nail me through', and 'stake me down'), but upon the entire context. While 'stake me down' and 'tye my Chain' might be taken as simply suggesting that Marvell is comparing himself to an animal chained to a stake, I cannot see that 'nail me through' fits into such a context. Surely the briars are chosen for their resemblance to the crown of thorns? And when one considers the sequence of events leading up to this stanza — the reference to the first Garden of Eden, the tower of Babel, the Fall, the race of giants begotten by devils on the descendants of Cain, the Flood, the exodus from Egypt, the crossing of the Red Sea and the defeat of Pharaoh and his horsemen — when one considers this sequence of events and their typological or anagogical significances, one is led to conclude that stanzas 77-78 must present an imitation of the crucial moment in the universal history of man — the crucifixion — as symbolically imitated by each Christian.

The lane where Marvell desires to be staked down is compared not only to the crossing of the Red Sea, but also to 'a long and equal Thread' leading 'Betwixt two *Labyrinths*'. The lane in other words represents that narrow path on which the Christian must pass through the wilderness of this world. The final staking down must occur 'where the Floods did lately drown'. The next stanza (79) explains the reason why. Now that the Flood has receded, 'No Serpent new nor *Crocodile* / Remains behind our little *Nile*'. The reference must be to *Ezekiel* 29 : 3. In chapter 28 God promises deliverance to the 'house of Israel' while chapter 29 denounces the king of Egypt (referring to him as 'the great dragon that lieth in the midst of his rivers...'). This must be the basis for the typological interpretation of Pharaoh as sin, or the devil, an interpretation followed by Milton in *Paradise Lost*, XII, 190-196. Milton is also clearly following the typological technique when, in lines 312-314, he concludes that on the killing of 'the adversarie Serpent' 'long wandered man' is finally brought 'Safe to eternal Paradise of rest'. This is also what happens in Marvell's poem. The serpent of the Nile has been killed, Chaos has been overcome, and the result is a new creation and a new Paradise, whose grass 'Seems as green Silke but newly washt'.

The most conspicuous feature of the new creation is the '*Chrystal Mirrour* slick' of the river, 'Where all things gaze themselves, and doubt / If they be in it or without' (stanza 80). And, like Narcissus, the sun pines for its own reflection in the water. These lines are clearly charged with allusions to Platonic and Hermetic ideas. Ficino states flatly that the mind is the mirror of God: *Mens est Dei speculum.* [96] If the river, then, symbolises the mind of man (that which reflects God), the purity of the river suggests a corresponding purity in the mind of man. The crucifixion of the old Adam has brought about a purification of the mind so that it reflects things truly. Lines 636-638 should be compared to lines 43-44 of 'The Garden', where Marvell compares the mind to an ocean where each kind 'Does streight its own resemblance find'. As an emanation of the Divinity, the mind must — like the river — reflect all things within itself. Which is true reality — the *res creatae*, or their archetypal forms in the mind of God? The fact that the river now holds the meadow in

187

'wanton harmless folds', licking 'its yet muddy back', suggests a new relationship between all created things in general and perhaps between mind and matter in particular. Conflict has been superseded by mutual love and harmony.

The comparison between the sun and Narcissus becomes meaningful when interpreted in the light of the Hermetic account of creation. It will be recalled that pure mind, on seeing its own reflection in the waters of the earth, falls in love with it and desires to cohabit with it, and that man's physical body is created in the course of this process. In Marvell's lines it is the sun which views its own reflection in the waters, yearning for it like Narcissus for his own image. The physical sun was usually viewed as the shadow of God, and Marvell refers to it in this manner in 'The Garden', when he characterises our great luminary as that 'milder sun'. Ficino had written: 'By what means, then, exists the light of the sun? As the shadow of God. What, then, is God? God is the sun of the sun, the light of the sun is God in earthly form.'[97] If God, then, is the sun of the sun, we get a series of diminishing reflections of the divine mind: in the visible sun, and in the reflection of the visible sun in the river. Although the image of the sun in the river is a reflection of a reflection, the reflecting medium is so pure that there is little loss in power or quality. This then, is what happens when the serpent is expelled and the world made over anew. The image of God (the sun) is reflected in the mind of man (the river) without distortion and is attracted to it.

The descriptive terms of stanza 81 further underline the identification between the mind and the river, the body and the muddy bank. Thus the poet's temples are said to be 'hedged' with 'heavy sedge', while his 'lazy Side' is 'Stretcht as a Bank unto the Tide'. Similarly his 'sliding Foot' is suspended (temporarily comes to a stop) against the roots of trees. In 'The Garden', too, Marvell employs the term 'sliding foot' about the stream issuing out of the fountain.

The concluding homage to Maria Fairfax underlines the basic

idea of the poem by presenting her as a true reflection of purity and innocence. She is herself the archetypal pattern of beauty responsible for each separate manifestation of beauty in her own environment. As the exponent of peace, beauty, and innocence, she serves as the great counterfoil to 'bloody Thestylis' (1. 401), the cruel goddess of war, *sanguinea Bellona*. D. C. Allen associates Maria Fairfax with heavenly wisdom, with the goddess Athena as explained by Plato, and with the heroine of the Christian poem, *Sophia Salomonos*. As the former she represents what Plato calls 'the mind of God', an interpretation which fits nicely into the context which I have tried to establish. As the latter, in the words of D. C. Allen, she is an emanation rather than a creation of God. She is 'the vapor of the power of God', a 'reflection of eternal light', a 'spotless mirror'.[98]

If the purpose of man's quest be the subjugation of the body to the mind in a spiritual baptism resulting in purification and illumination, then what could be more suitable than a concluding apostrophe to that wisdom which issues from the mind of God?

This reading of Marvell's poem has revealed an undoubted unity of theme and purpose. As in 'The Garden', literal description is made the vehicle of insights into various kinds of truth. Various levels of meaning merge at all important points. The mowers are actual labourers, at the same time that they stand for soldiers engaged in a bitter and devastating civil war. On a third level — as Israelites crossing the Red Sea — they symbolise the ancient quest for purification through baptism. This baptism is then achieved through an *imitatio Christi*, that is, by a crucifixion of all carnal desires so that the divine principle in man, his mind, may regain its ancient purity and supremacy. Just as the fallen state implies the dominion of body over mind (a state of affairs which leads to war both in the body politic and in the microcosmos of man), the regenerated state is marked by a supremacy of mind over body (a state reflected in the relationship between Fairfax and his house), and by mutual love not only

189

between mind and body, but also between man and the *res creatae*, and man and God. This is the ultimate truth revealed by Marvell's poem, and one which Fairfax was likely to interpret as an acknowledgement of his own professional concern with the theological exposition of the Hermetic *corpus*. Writing for such a patron, Marvell could safely include philosophical or theological allusions of such a subtlety that they would be beyond the range of the uninitiated. In this circumstance lies perhaps his subtlest compliment to his noble employer.

c. *'Upon the Hill and Grove at Bill-borow'*

It is useful to study Marvell's loco-descriptive poem in the context of previous poems along the same lines, particularly Denham's *Cooper's Hill* (1642) and Casimire Sarbiewski's first Epode on the estate of the Duke of Bracciano. The following points apply to all three poems: (1) The chief purpose is to drive home a moral lesson concerning the desirability of keeping a Horatian Golden Mean; (2) this message is conveyed through the very terms in which the local scene is described, and (3) the proud, towering mountains are contrasted with the gentle hill where 'no horror turns away our eyes' (Denham). Other points are common only to Marvell and Casimire. Thus it seems to me that Marvell's poem forms the same compromise between lyric and epistolary verse associated with the Horatian epode exploited by the Polish Jesuit; both poets also praise the military exploits of their respective patrons. The Duke of Bracciano, it seems, was a terror to the Imperial force, throwing his 'fearfull thunder-bolts' through the 'brasen troops' of his foes, just as Fairfax is said to have 'thundered' through 'Groves of Pikes'. Both furthermore conclude with a homage to the retired life.

The first stanza of Marvell's poem commences with an apostrophe to the 'arched Earth' which rises from the ground in a 'perfect Hemisphere':

> The stiffest Compass could not strike
> Rise in a perfect Hemisphere!
> See how the arched Earth does here
> A line more circular and like.

Casimire exploits much the same image and conveys the same moral lesson when he writes: 'A gentle Cliffe from a steep Hill doth rise / That even to Heaven, mounts by degrees.' The second stanza addresses 'ye Mountains more unjust' which, unlike the low hills, dare challenge the skies:

> Here learn ye Mountains more unjust,
> Which to abrupter greatness thrust,
>
> . . . .
>
> Learn here those humble steps to tread,
> Which to securer Glory lead.

Sarbiewski, too, had stressed the folly of the towering mountain which 'drawes down envy from the starres', and whose lofty head is buffeted by storms. Stanzas 3 and 4 praise the hill for its unselfish courtesy to the surrounding country-side:

> See then how courteous it ascends,
> And all the way it rises bends;
> Nor for it self the height does gain,
> But only strives to raise the Plain.
>
> Yet thus it all the field commands,
> And in unenvy'd Greatness stands.

Sarbiewski had written similarly about his hill, which

> holds off *Boreas*, when his rawer blasts
> 'Gainst the weake Southerne winds he casts,
> Commands the Country farre, and out he sets
> His Winter sides against Heavens threats.

Having thus exhausted the symbolic aspects of the hill, Marvell turns to the grove which decorates its crest:

Marvell:	Sarbiewski:
Upon its crest this Mountain grave	A Bow're growes green, set round with trembling Okes
A Plump of aged Trees does wave.	Which fanns the Heavens with gentle strokes.
	. . . .
No hostile hand durst ere invade	Whence 'mid'st the Bulwark'd Forts, we may descry
With impious Steel the sacred Shade.	A displayd Banner from on hye,
For something alwaies did appear	Which to th' Imperiall force a terrour was,
Of the *great Masters* terrour there.	A terror to great *Borgias*...

Both poets finally recommend retirement from public affairs:

Marvell:	Sarbiewski:
Therefore to your obscurer Seats	*Jordanus* here, hither thy selfe command,...
From his own Brightness he retreats:	Withdraw thy selfe from cares, from all resort
Nor he the Hills without the Groves,	So cloy'd with' Citie, and with Court,
Nor Height but with Retirement loves.	So full of great affaires, at length thy breast
	Convey to thy domestick rest.

Our comparison has revealed a recurring parallelism in themes and descriptive technique, and a few verbal resemblances. Thus Marvell's line, 'Yet thus it all the field commands' comes fairly close to the Polish poet's *Terrisque late regnat* (Hills: 'Commands

192

the Country farre'). Similarly the *'Great Masters* terrour' (Marvell) echoes Casimire's homage to the Duke of Bracciano as 'A terrour to great *Borgias*'. Editors of Marvell have been puzzled by the poet's claim that a hill which is only 145 feet high could be said to dominate the country-side and to serve as a landmark for ships at sea. Marvell obviously sacrificed descriptive accuracy in the interests of a crucial poetic comparison. If the hill were to symbolise its noble owner (as in the poems of Sarbiewski and Denham), it must be said to command the surrounding landscape.

Marvell's Latin 'Epigramma in Duos montes, Amosclivium et Bilboreum. Farfacio' points exactly the same moral by stressing the contrast between the humble and the proud hills:

> Erectus, praeceps, salebrosus, & arduus ille:
> Acclivis, placidus, mollis, amoenus hic est.

> (The steep, the rough, the difficult, are there;
> Here all is sloping, gentle, soft and fair.)

The descriptive technique adopted by Sarbiewski, Denham, and Marvell in their respective hill poems is worth noticing. Although the moral lesson conveyed is Horatian, Horace had never used nature imagery in this particular fashion. He might advise men, not to venture too far out on the deep nor to hug the shore too closely, or again he might point out that it is the top of the mountain which is struck by lightning,[99] but he never invested the landscape itself with symbolic overtones. This new descriptive technique serves to animate the landscape. In their excessive pride, the towering mountains of Sarbiewski's first Epode seem to flaunt their peaks in the face of the sky, while conversely the gentle hill is invested with courtesy and humility.

It can scarcely be the result of chance that this technique should develop at a time when the religious impulse was so strong. To the Neoplatonic or Hermetic philosopher even inanimate objects possessed a life of their own and were connected with the 'widely wandering stars' by means of a net-work of magnetic influences between the earth and the sky. We have also seen how the tendency to interpret the Book of God's Works on several levels led to a similar animation of the scene; the concept of the 'amorous green' served the poets well. This particular generation of poets constantly traced correspondences between the landscape on the one hand and, on the other, spiritual or moral values. Since the classical *beatus ille* philosophy was given a prominent place among these moral values, Nature itself was made to reflect the central concepts of this philosophy. This is true of both types of poetry discussed in this chapter, i. e. the loco-descriptive poem in which Nature is invested with *moral* qualities, and the more mystic garden poem in which Nature is pervaded by spiritual impulses. Neither type of poem could have been conceived if the attitude towards Nature had remained uninfluenced by the strong Stoic and Neoplatonic trends of the first half of the seventeenth century. The rural retirement-poetry of Marvell's generation combines a Horatian rationalism with a curious moral and spiritual fervour, so that even a simple description of the rural scene becomes charged with metaphysical overtones.

Of Marvell's three retirement poems 'The Garden' is obviously the finest, largely because of its compactness. As E. M. W. Tillyard has stated, its speed and concentration separate it from all other poems of the same kind.[100] 'The Garden' is no doubt the supreme poetic expression of the poetic motif or myth which forms the subject of this study. Many would say that few other poems equal it in stylistic achievement or in depth of thought and feeling. It is nevertheless not unique; Marvell must have been completely aware of the fact that he was contributing to a specific poetic tradition. In his treatment of this tradition Marvell avoided both the extreme Stoic austerity of the theme of the Serene Contemplator, and the extreme sensuality of the French 'Libertins'. His affinities are not so much with Théophile de Viaud or St. Amant as with

Casimire Sarbiewski and Edward Benlowes — poets who success-fully combined the austerity of the *beatus ille* motifs with the sensuousness of the man who sees the landscape turning into an Earthly Paradise. Marvell's feeling for nature, although sensuous enough, was Neoplatonic or Hermetic rather than libertine. Like More, Fane, and Benlowes, Marvell distinguished between the lesser joys of the 'Outworld' and the supreme joys of purified sense experience. His enjoyment of the landscape of retirement was based on this distinction, and a failure to realise this leads to the kind of critical dilemma illustrated by those who recognise the mystic implications of Marvell's garden experience, and yet feel compelled to believe that a libertine abandonment to the life of the senses was part of the ritual.

3.

Henry Vaughan

Like William Habington, Henry Vaughan adhered so closely to the classical doctrine of the happiness of obscurity that only few details of his life are known. He spent two years at Oxford, and two subsequent years in London (*circa* 1640-1642),[101] and would therefore have been acquainted with the triple sphere of uni-versity, court, and town. F. E. Hutchinson has presented evidence for Vaughan's active support of the royal cause during the Civil War;[102] certainly the many references which Vaughan makes to the troubled nature of his times bespeak some degree of first-hand experience of contemporary events. Like so many Royalists, Vaughan viewed the civil and religious dissent of his generation as evidence of the decay of the world. As early as 1646, before the time of his supposed religious conversion, Vaughan was full of despair at 'these dull times' and '*Dregs* of an Age'.[103] And in a dedicatory epistle to Sir Charles Egerton, dated 1653 and pre-faced to the *Flores Solitudinis* (1654), Vaughan stated that the idea of retirement came to him and his generation as a natural

195

consequence of the turbulence of the period in which they lived: 'even *meane witts* begin to like it; the *wiser sort* alwaies did, for what (I beseech you,) hath this world, that should make a wise man in love with it?'

Vaughan's early work as a translator, published in 1651 in the *Olor Iscanus,* shows that he made a conscious selection of *beatus ille* passages in poetry and prose. Thus the title-page quotes from Virgil's second *Georgic (Flumina amo, Sylvasque Inglorius),* while its *verso* paraphrases Virgil, substituting the name of the river Isca (*O quis me gelidis in vallibus* ISCAE / *Sistat, & Ingenti ramorum protegat umbra!*). The translations which concern us, are taken from Boethius, Casimire, and Don Antonio de Guevara. Vaughan, in other words, turned primarily to Renaissance versions of the classical tradition. Guevara's prose treatise, 'The Praise and Happiness of the Countrie-Life', is, in fact, a detailed elaboration of Virgil's praise of the happy husbandman, from which he quotes the initial phrases (*O fortunatos nimium, bona si sua norint, / Agricolas!*). The happy husbandman is contrasted throughout with the courtier and the citizen: their lives are compared from every possible point of view. A few quotations will show the main drift of the argument and the tone of voice in which it is conducted:

> He [i. e. 'Whoever Loves the *Country'*] fears no *discontents* to disturbe his *Peace,* but lives well-pleased with what *providence* gives him though never so little. He is free from all fretting *cares,* and is fed with no mans *provision* but his own ...
> *Pietie* and *Religion* may be better Cherish'd and preserved in the Country than any where else ...
> He that lives in his own *fields* and *habitation,* which God hath given him, enjoys true Peace; for no Phantastick, Impudent *Companion* turns in thither to disturbe him, and to seek after a sumptuous entertainment, or to corrupt his family in his absence ...
> ... Nothing will hinder him from the pleasure of *books,* from *devotion,* or the fruition of his *friends* ... Whereas those that are *tyed* to businesse, whose *profession* makes their *life*

a meer *slaverie*, are alwaies imprison'd (as it were) and barr'd from *recreation* . . .

More happy then, yea by much more happy than any *King*, if not nearer to a *divine felicitie* is that person who lives and dwels in the Country upon the Rents and profits of his own grounds. There without danger he may act and speake as it becomes *simplicity* and naked truth; he hath liberty and choice in all his imployments . . .

The day it self (in my opinion) seems of more *length* and *beauty* in the Country, and can be better enjoyed than any where else . . .

. . . O who can ever fully expresse the pleasures and happinesse of the Country-life! with the various and delightful sports of *fishing, hunting* and *fowling* . . . what oblectation and refreshment it is, to behold the *green shades*, the beauty and Majestie of the tall and antient *groves*, . . . to ascend sometimes to the *fresh* and *healthfull hils*, to descend into the *bosome* of the *valleys*, and the fragrant, deawy *meadows*, to heare the *musick* of *birds* . . .

The Inhabitants of the Country meet with nothing all the *week* that can make them miserable, and when the *Sabbath day* comes, or other *festivall solemnities*, they enjoy a more sincere and heavenly comfort, than those that live in *Cities* and *Courts* . . . The chiefest *Citizens* aswell as the *Courtiers* spend those blessed days in pampering themselves, and obeying their own lusts and devices . . .

How happy then is the Countrey-man which moves only in the Circuite of his own grounds, that is absolute master of his time, and is not compelled to waite at the litigious *bars*, and *Courts* of *Law* by a set houre! that goes not capping from Lawier to Lawier for their opinion, and then payes for it, before he hath it . . . That is not driven to make humble requests to ev'ry rotten *Sycophant* and *favourite*, which yet in vaine he often solliciteth, and prostrates himselfe to the *Corrupt Magistrates*, for feare of being devoured by such *Cyclops* and *harpyes*. Happy I say is the Husband-man, who lives a stranger to all these miseries, and in the shadow of some faire *wood* with unspeakable delight contemplates the beauty of the *fields, meadows, fountaines*, and *rivers* of *water*. He admires and adores the only wise, and almightie god, who first *created*, and still *preserves* all things in a flourishing and fruitfull condition.

197

Just as Vaughan, by translating Guevara's treatise, transmits the Virgilian philosophy of human happiness as enriched by a genuine religious piety, his translations from Casimire Sarbiewski perform the same office for Horace. These are well done, and much superior to the translations of G. Hills and Sir Edward Sherburne. Among the odes selected are numbers IV, 15 and III, 23, both directly concerned with *beatus ille* sentiments. The first proceeds from a general feeling of despair at the decay of the world to a Claudian conclusion by way of a graphic description of the inconstancy of man's desires:

> 27   But he, whose *Constancie* makes sure
> His *mind* and *mansion*, lives secure
> From such *vain tasks*, can *dine* and *sup*
> Where his *old parents* bred him up.
> *Content* (no doubt!) most times doth dwell
> In *Countrey-shades*, or to some *Cell*
> Confines it selfe, and can alone
> 34   Make simple *straw*, a Royall *Throne*.[104]

Ode III, 23 exposes the artificiality of rich dwellings, instead praising the rare beauty of nature and that virtue which alone 'Can purchase stars, and buy the *skies*'.[105]

From our point of view the most important of Vaughan's translations from Casimire is his version of the latter's third Epode, 'The Praise of a Religious Life'.[106] Like Milton, Fane, and Marvell, Vaughan preferred the short octosyllabic line for this type of philosophic ode. Casimire's poem is in the form of a reply to Horace's second Epode:

> 1   *Flaccus* not so: That worldly *He*
> Whom in the Countreys *shade* we see
> Ploughing his own *fields*, seldome can
> Be justly stil'd *The Blessed man*.
> 5   That title only fits a *Saint*,

198

Whose free thoughts far above restraint
And weighty Cares, can gladly part
With *house* and *lands,* and leave the smart
Litigious troubles, and lowd strife
10   Of this world for a better life.

This Happy Man yearns for the sky 'Where with his *Saviour* he
would be / Lifted above mortalitie', but he also finds evidence
of the presence of God in his environment. On contemplating 'the
green fields, and *Bowres*' with eyes 'accustom'd to the *skyes*' he
discovers the '*back Parts* of the *Deitye*' in '*Veyles,* and *shades*'.
The passage which describes the yearning of the *res creatae* for
God reveals that Vaughan fetched one of his most typical motifs
from Casimire:

47   *"O how*
         "These flowres With hasty, stretch'd heads grow
         "And strive for heav'n, but rooted here
50   *"Lament the distance with a teare!*
         "The Honey-suckles Clad in white,
         "The Rose in Red point to the light,
         "And the Lilies hollow and bleak
         "Look, as if they would something speak,
55   *"They sigh at night to each soft gale,*
         "And at the day-spring weep it all.
         "Shall I then only (wretched I!)
58   *"Opprest with Earth, on Earth still lye?*

Lines 63-118 are devoted to a loving description of the joys, the
work and recreations of country life. In this section Casimire is
in complete accord with the sentiments expressed by the pagan
poet and hence follows his lead fairly closely. The poem is important because it shows how consciously the Horatian *beatus vir*
was transformed into a Hortulan Saint. It is important also because
it demonstrates how the retired *beatus vir* interprets the land-

14   199

scape in Hermetic fashion, tracing a 'league of love' between the *res creatae* and God. We have traced the same double tendency in the poetry of Benlowes and Marvell; it remains to observe how it influenced the original work of Casimire's most gifted translator. However, before we do so, it will be necessary to discuss Vaughan's translations from Boethius.

There are several points of agreement between Sarbiewski and Boethius. Both combined Platonic ideas with Stoic thought. Vaughan's selection seems based on a conscious recognition of this similarity; the mood of many of the eighteen metres translated by Vaughan comes close to Casimire's third Epode.

Metre II, 4 describes the happiness of the retired man who leads 'a life serene and faire', while II, 5 praises the rural simplicity of 'that first white age! when wee / Lived by the Earths meere Charitie, / No soft luxurious Diet then / Had Effeminated men . . .' Metre III, 12 places happiness in the ability to penetrate the external appearance of things to that 'Fountain of all goodness' which lies beyond. Boethius also touched upon the theme of the 'amorous green', or the *liber creaturarum:*

> That Plant, which of it self doth grow
> Upwards, if forc'd, will downwards bow;
> But give it freedom, and it will
> Get up, and grow erectly still.[107]

> Who would unclouded see the Laws
> Of the supreme, eternal *Cause,*
> Let him with careful thoughts and eyes
> Observe the high and spatious Skyes.
> There in one league of Love the *Stars*
> Keep their old peace, and shew our wars.[108]

Vaughan's interest in *beatus ille* themes is finally demonstrated by his translation of Claudian's epigram on the old man from Verona.[109]

200

Vaughan's translations from Guevara, Casimire, Boethius, and Claudian were obviously prompted by his interest in the philosophy of life expressed by them. In tracing the same motifs in Vaughan's original compositions, a chronological sequence will be followed.

The *Poems* of 1646 reveal clearly enough that Vaughan's grief at the events of the Civil War made him seek comfort in a conscious withdrawal from the world. 'Upon the Priorie Grove, His usuall Retyrement' [110] describes an Earthly Paradise reminiscent of Habington's 'To Zephyrus'.[111] Both poets associate the grove with innocence and chaste love. Conversely, Vaughan attributed vice and corruption to town life. 'A Rhapsodis' [112] condemns London in the harsh tones of the satirist, and the epistle 'To my Ingenuous Friend, *R.W.*' [113] expresses a strong distaste for city life and 'the loath'd noise / Of Drawers, Prentises, and boyes'.

Although not published till 1651, the majority of the poems included in the *Olor Iscanus* were finished within a year after the appearance of *Poems*, 1646.[114] The opening poem, 'To the River Isca',[115] describes the Welsh scene as a land 'redeem'd from all disorders', and as a veritable Earthly Paradise. The epistle 'To the most Excellently accomplish'd, Mrs. *K. Philips*' [116] proves that Vaughan had read her poetry thirteen years before it was published (in 1664). Mrs. Philips, too, favoured the theme of rural retirement and this must be one reason why Vaughan was so taken with her work that he proclaimed himself a 'weaker Genius'. Apart from the translations from Guevara, Casimire, and Boethius there is little more of interest to this study.

Vaughan's best retirement poems are religious ones, and both *Silex Scintillans* (1651 and 1655) and *Thalia Rediviva* (1678) contain fine examples of a religious application of *beatus ille* motifs.

One common religious motif in Vaughan is that of the divine influence which can be traced throughout the Creation, causing the lower levels to yearn for union with the higher. We have observed how this Hermetic or Neoplatonic concept coloured Casimire's description of the landscape surrounding his retired contemplator, and hence it becomes almost superfluous to hunt for evidence that Vaughan had studied the Hermetic treatises of his brother or any one else.[117] The literary source is quite adequate.

'And do they so?'[118] compares man unfavourably with the plants, that never cease to yearn for God:

21   Sometimes I sit with thee, and tarry
     An hour, or so, then vary.
   Thy other Creatures in this Scene
     Thee only aym, and mean;
   Some rise to seek thee, and with heads
26   Erect peep from their beds...

Because nature in this fashion is seen to be pervaded by a longing for God, the retired contemplator is in his turn led to God when he contemplates the scene. Vaughan's *beatus vir* who views 'Each *tree, herb, flowre*' as 'shadows of his *wisdome,* and his Pow'r,[119] is the blood brother of Sarbiewski's, who 'To th' Fountaines talk'd, and streames ran by, / And after, seekes the great Creator out / By these faire traces of his foot'.[120] Mildmay Fane, too, had fastened on this idea. The purpose of his Hortulan Saint had been 'To see the footsteps here are trod / Of mercy by a Gracious God'.[121] Vaughan's 'I walkt the other day' expresses the same desire:

48   Grant I may so
   Thy steps track here below,
   That in these Masques and shadows I may see
     Thy sacred way,
   And by those hid ascents climb to that day
53   Which breaks from thee...[122]

This quest for God through the contemplation of the landscape is a main theme in Vaughan's religious lyrics. It is given fine expression in the poem which opens the first volume of *Silex Scintillans* (1651), 'Regeneration'. [123] Following the tradition of medieval garden allegories, Vaughan distinguishes between the two gardens of false show and true reality. To the first belongs the 'Meere stage, and show' of spring; the true garden is the *hortus conclusus* of the saint. Vaughan's poem may profitably be compared with Casimire's Ode IV, 24 ('Ad Auram'). The setting in both is similar — the scented grove, the fountain, the sun which plays on the flowers, and the breeze which stirs the leaves of the trees — and both poets desire to be penetrated by this breeze.[124]

'Religion'[125] again describes the vision of the Hortulan Saint inside the mystic grove:

> My God, when I walke in those groves,
> And leaves thy spirit doth still fan,
> I see in each shade that there growes
> An Angell talking with a man.

'Corruption'[126] attributes this purity of vision to earlier ages. In those days God was directly visible to all men everywhere:

> ... each day
> The vally, or the Mountain
> Afforded visits, and still *Paradise* lay
> In some green shade, or fountain.
> Angels lay *Leiger* here; Each Bush, and Cel,
> Each Oke, and high-way knew them,
> Walk but the fields, or sit down at some *wel*
> And he was sure to view them.

The same purity of vision may be found in early childhood,

> When on some *gilded Cloud*, or *flowre*
> My gazing soul would dwell an houre,
> And in those weaker glories spy
> Some shadows of eternity.[127]

'Righteousness'[128] describes the *beatus vir* as a solitary contemplator who has recovered the innocence of past ages, and whose greatest joy therefore derives from being able to see *'Invisibles'*:

> Fair, solitary path! Whose blessed shades
> The old, white Prophets planted first and drest:
> Leaving for us (whose goodness quickly fades,)
> A shelter all the way, and bowers to rest.
>
> Who is the man that walks in thee? who loves
> Heav'ns secret solitude, those fair abodes
> Where turtles build, and carelesse sparrows move
> Without to morrows evil and future loads?
>
> Who hath the upright heart, the single eye,
> The clean, pure hand, which never meddled pitch?
> Who sees *Invisibles*, and doth comply
> With hidden treasures that make truly rich?

Although devoid of *beatus ille* echoes, the main themes of the complete retirement-lyric are all here: the invocation of solitude, the denunciation of earthly vanities and sins, the loving description of a grove which is somehow identified with Eden, and the mystic experience of the man who sees *'Invisibles'*.

This is even more true of two poems published in the *Thalia Rediviva* (1678). 'The Bee'[129] expresses ruthless condemnation of Cromwell's England. When corruption prevails 'Both in the Rulers and the Priest',

> To *Horeb* then *Elias* goes,
> And in the *Desart* grows the *Rose*.
>   Hail Christal Fountains and fresh shades,
>   Where no proud look invades,
> No busie worldling hunts away
> The sad Retirer all the day:

Haile happy harmless solitude,
Our sanctuary from the rude
And scornful world: the calm recess
Of faith and hope and holiness!
. . . . .
The truth, which once was plainly taught,
With *thorns* and *briars* now is fraught.
. . . . .
O lead me, where I may be free
In *truth* and *Spirit* to serve thee!
Where undisturb'd I may converse
With thy great self . . .

Although 'Retirement' [130] still dwells on the decay of the times, it displays a positive delight in retirement which marks it as of the period of Vaughan's finest verse:

All various Lusts in *Cities* still
Are found; they are the *Thrones* of Ill.
The dismal *Sinks*, where blood is spill'd,
Cages with much uncleanness fill'd.
But *rural shades* are the sweet fense
Of piety and innocence.
They are the *Meek*'s calm region, where
Angels descend, and rule the sphere:
Where heav'n lyes *Leiguer*, and the *Dove*
Duely as *Dew*, comes from above.
If *Eden* be on earth at all,
'Tis that, which we the *Country* call.

All Vaughan's religious verse is, in a way, concerned with retirement, in its rejection of the 'busy worldling' and its recommendation of solitary meditation inside a landscape in whose 'weaker glories' one may spy 'Some shadows of eternity'. Because

Vaughan focusses so completely on the religious vision itself, his connection with the *beatus ille* tradition is much less obvious than in Fane, Benlowes, or Marvell. He echoes neither Virgil nor Horace, and if it were not for his translations from Casimire, Claudian, and Guevara, one would have little evidence of his familiarity with this tradition. 'The World'[131] is without doubt the poem which presents the ecstatic vision most successfully; its denunciation of various types of folly places it within range of the tradition pursued in these pages. This denunciation, however, stems from a Hermetic source, rather than a classical one, or so it would seem if one compares Vaughan's lines with Casimire's Ode II, 5 ('E Rebus Humanis Excessus') and with his own epistle 'The importunate Fortune, written to doctor *Powell* of *Cantre*'.[132] Both Casimire's Ode II, 5 and lines 57-87 of Vaughan's epistle are poetic versions of the following Hermetic passage:

> And thereupon the man mounts upward through the structure of the heavens. And to the first zone of heaven he gives up the force which works increase and that which works decrease; to the second zone, the machinations of evil cunning; to the third zone, the lust whereby men are deceived; to the fourth zone, domineering arrogance; to the fifth zone, unholy daring and rash audacity; to the sixth zone, evil strivings after wealth; and to the seventh zone, the falsehood which lies in wait to work harm. And thereupon, having been stripped of all that was wrought upon him by the structure of the heavens, he ascends to the substance of the eighth sphere, being now possessed of his own proper power; and he sings, hymning the Father; and they that are there rejoice with him at his coming... And thereafter, each in his turn, they mount upward to the Father; they give themselves up to the Powers, and becoming Powers themselves, they enter into God.[133]

On the basis of this passage Casimire created a magnificent ode which in its turn became a source of literary inspiration from Abraham Cowley to John Norris and John Hughes.[134] G. Hills's translation is clumsy, but accurate:

Lift me up quickly on your wings,
Ye Clouds, and Winds; I leave all earthly things,
   How Devious Hills give way to mee!
And the vast ayre brings under, as I fly,
   Kingdomes and populous states! see how
The Glyst'ring Temples of the Gods doe bow;
   The glorious Tow'rs of Princes, and
Forsaken townes, shrunke into nothing, stand:
   And as I downward looke, I spy
Whole Nations every where all scattred lye . . .

The seven Hermetic spheres are recognised in the description
which follows of various types of human folly:

1. Sphere of the *Moon;* the force which works increase and decrease.

Oh the sad change that Fortune brings!
The rise and fall of transitory things!
   Here walled townes that threatned Heav'n,
Now old and ruin'd, with the earth lye even:
. . . . .

2. *Mercury;* machinations of evil cunning.

Here on safe Seas, as joyfull prize
Is strip'd away th' Ægyptian Merchandize,
   Whilst the full Havens thick beset,
Doe furiously with fierce contention fret.
. . . . .

3. *Venus;* the lust which deceives.

From the Adultresse smiling lookes
Pleasure doth fight, and unto Warre provokes,
   The doting world with *Helen* burnes.
. . . . .

4. *The Sun;* domineering arrogance.

This sordid man, oh base advantage! turnes
   Revenge of words to blowes;
Mischiefe begets it selfe, from mischiefe growes,
   Small sins by example higher dare.
. . . . .

207

5. *Mars;* unholy daring & rash audacity.	There th' Easterne Sea lyes coverd o're With warlike Fleets... Forbeare, cruell men to multiply With fire, Sword-wrack your single destiny.
6. *Jupiter;* evil strivings after wealth.	. . . . . Vast wealth I see swept downe with th' tyde Rich treasure in the Ocean floting glyde.
7. *Saturn;* false-hood that lies in wait to work harm.	The active world t' each others harmes Doth daily fight, and the pale Goddesse armes The bloudy scene with slaughters, warrs, With utter ruins, and with deadly jarrs.

The ode concludes with the ecstatic vision of the Deity:

> Oh the brim'd Ocean of the Deitie!
> Oh Glorious Island richly free
> From the cold Harbours of mortality!
> Yee boundlesse seas, with endless flouds of rest
> Girt round *Sarbinius* your panting Priest.

The Hermetic source has been treated with considerable freedom to permit a realisation of the lyric mood and form demanded by the ode. Casimire repeatedly infused a note of ecstasy into the more measured tone of the Horatian ode, an achievement which partly explains the great popularity of his poetry.

The nature of the epistolary form employed by Vaughan in 'The importunate Fortune' facilitates the enumeration of the various spheres, which is briefer and much more precise than in Casimire's lyric.

If one now turns to 'The World' ('I saw Eternity the other night') I believe it will become apparent that Vaughan again is concerned with portraying the influence of those seven spheres through which the soul must pass before it reaches Casimire's *refusum Numinis Oceanum.* If this is so, one must conclude that

the inspiration behind Vaughan's best known lyric is literary,
in other words that he derived much of his inspiration from the
Polish poet's presentation of the same ideas in his most widely
admired ode.

The first stanza presents a truly cosmic vision of Time and
Eternity:

> I saw Eternity the other night
> Like a great *Ring* of pure and endless light,
>   All calm, as it was bright,
> And round beneath it, Time in hours, days, years
>   Driv'n by the spheres
> Like a vast shadow mov'd, In which the world
>   And all her train were hurl'd;
> The doting Lover in his queintest strain
>   Did their Complain,
> Neer him, his Lute, his fancy, and his flights,
>   Wits sour delights,
> With gloves, and knots the silly snares of pleasure
>   Yet his dear Treasure
> All scatter'd lay, while he his eys did pour
>   Upon a flowr.

While Vaughan compares eternity to a ring 'of pure and endless
light', Casimire had referred to the 'brim'd Ocean of the Deitie'
which envelops the poet 'with endlesse flouds of rest'. Both are
no doubt traditional comparisons. Thus Benlowes speaks of
'wreaths of endless light' and of a 'ring of boundless justice'.[135]
The second image of time as a vast shadow driven by the spheres
suggests the Hermetic view of creation. If this is so, eternity itself
represents that sphere of the Divinity which lies beyond the eighth
sphere of the powers.

The rest of Vaughan's lyric, like Casimire's ode, describes, not
the seven spheres, but seven types of human conduct each of
which represents the influence of one Hermetic sphere. Since

some of these spheres are somewhat similar, it is not always possible to identify Vaughan's sinful types with complete assurance. The total number, however, is seven, and most of these are easily enough identified. Thus the fickle lover of stanza 1 is governed by the mutability of the Moon, while the 'darksome States-man' moving 'Like a thick midnight-fog' (stanza 2), obviously stands for the machinations of evil cunning or the second sphere of Mercury. The digging mole which works underground 'lest his ways be found' can represent nothing but the seventh sphere of Saturn with its concealed falsehood. Stanza 3 presents a number of personified evils. The 'fearfull miser on a heap of rust' has succumbed to the sixth sphere of Jupiter (evil strivings after wealth); the 'down-right Epicure' who has 'plac'd heav'n in sense' is the slave of the lust which deceives (the third sphere of Venus), while those who have 'slipt into a wide Excesse' most probably typify the unholy daring and rash audacity of the profligate (the fifth sphere of Mars). The men enslaved by 'triviall wares', may be relegated to the fourth sphere of the Sun, since their contempt for truth suggests the domineering arrogance of this sphere. The 'triviall wares' may consist in riches, honour, titles — the main attributes of the arrogant man. All seven spheres are therefore represented.

The fourth and last stanza contains the only suggestion of direct indebtedness to Casimire. Since Vaughan must have studied Casimire in Latin, we cannot expect verbal borrowing, but a more general similarity afforded by imitation. It seems to me that the following lines do reveal such a general resemblance:

Vaughan:
O fools (said I,) thus to prefer
dark night
Before true light,
To live in grots, and caves, and
hate the day

Casimire, tr. G. Hills:
Why stay I then, when goe I
may —
To'a house enlightned by the
Suns bright ray?
Shall I still dote on things

Because it shews the way,
The way which from this dead
    and dark abode
Leads up to God,
A way where you might tread
    the Sun, and be
More bright than he.

humane?
Lift up your longing Priest, yee
    Clouds, oh deigne
Lift m'up where th'aire a
    splendour yeilds
Lights the sun's chariot through
    the azure fields.

Both poets ask the same question: why remain on earth, under the dominion of the spheres (or Time), when it is possible to ascend to a height from which the sun may be trodden underfoot, and where the air yields a splendour which 'lights the sun's chariot'.

Under the impact of the physico-theological enthusiasm of the early eighteenth century, Casimire's vision of the ascent of the soul was frequently made the vehicle of Newtonian sentiments, and nowhere more so than in John Hughes's avowed paraphrase. At this time, too, the motif of the cosmic voyage was linked to the motif of the Happy Man. In transmuted form, therefore, the seventeenth-century motif of the religious ecstasy lived on into the age of rationalism, providing a cosmic background to the activities of the Newtonian *beatus vir*.

It is possible that I have overestimated the influence of Casimire's odes upon the poets of this chapter. One must nevertheless remember that he was viewed as the supreme neo-Latin religious poet of his age. It seems impossible to doubt that the poetry of Casimire formed one of the most important channels through which Vaughan became acquainted with motifs and descriptive techniques of great importance to himself. What Vaughan appropriated from the Polish poet was more important than verbal turns or phrases; he inherited from him a basic poetical technique. Vaughan's poetry in many ways represents a fusion of the tradition of George Herbert with that of Casimire. Herbert was no poet of nature. His concern was with the soul of man in its

211

relationship to God. In the lyrics of Casimire, however, spiritual truth was often conveyed through the description of the landscape. From no one else could Vaughan have learnt to use the landscape in this manner, and once he knew how to master the technique, he applied it independently.

4.

Abraham Cowley

The *Essays and Discourses* analysed in Chapter I have shown how completely Cowley's mind was preoccupied with the classical doctrine of the Happy Man. Cowley wrote these essays (published posthumously in 1668) as an explanation, and a defence, of his retirement from public life after the Restoration. In the words of Thomas Sprat, he intended them as a 'real Character of his own thoughts, upon the point of his Retirement'.[136] Although Cowley's first biographer admitted that the poet 'chose that state of Life, not out of any Poetical Rapture, but upon a steady and sober experience of Humane things',[137] he could not applaud his decision, since it deprived society of one of its most useful members. The high regard which Cowley enjoyed for several generations after his death was largely due to the high moral seriousness of his essays. Although his metaphysical poetry was unanimously deplored, his prose and his Pindaric odes received the stamp of approval and constituted a source of inspiration to poets and essayists like John Norris, Addison, and Steele.

Cowley's own epitaph neatly sums up the image of himself which he wished to perpetuate. This epitaph was 'supposed written on his House' while 'yet alive, but withdrawn from the busie World to a Country-Life':

> Here, Passenger, beneath this Shed
> Lies COWLEY, tho entomb'd, not dead;
> Yet freed from human Toil and Strife,

And all th' Impertinence of Life;
Who in his Poverty is neat,
And even in Retirement, Great ... [138]

Dr. Johnson satirically queried the truthfulness of this 'image'
when he wrote: 'By the lover of virtue and of wit it will be
solicitously asked, if he now was happy.' [139] By way of answer
Dr. Johnson inserts one of Cowley's letters, from which it is only
too apparent that the poet suffered acutely from illness and the
absence of congenial company. And Thomas Sprat neatly points
the paradoxical moral inherent in the story of the poet's life:

Who can here, Sir, forbear exclaiming on the weak hopes,
and frail condition of humane Nature? For as long as Mr. *Cowley* was pursuing the course of Ambition, in active life, which
he scarce esteem'd his true life; he never wanted a constant
health and strength of body: But as soon as ever he had found
an opportunity of beginning indeed to live, and to enjoy himself
in security, his contentment was first broken by sickness, and
at last his death was occasion'd by his very delight in the
Country and the Fields, which he had long fancied above all
other Pleasures. [140]

This dramatic irony on the part of Fate invests Cowley's praise
of country life with a peculiar air of pathos.

It was only to be expected that a poet who delighted in translating classical *beatus ille* passages, also would exploit similar
ideas in his original work.

Three poems should be placed together because of their
similarity: 'The Wish' (from *The Mistress)*, 'A Vote' *(Sylva)*
and the imitation of Martial's Epigram V, 21 *(Miscellanies)*.
Each offers a ready-made poetic prescription how best to achieve
happiness. Martial, as imitated by Cowley, stipulates *'Books*, and
wise *Discourse, Gardens*, and *Fields*, / And all the joys that
unmixt Nature yields', 'A few *Companions*, which our selves
should chuse, / A *Gentle Mistress*, and a *Gentler Muse'*. [141]

Horace's *modus agri non ita magnus* (Sat. II, 6, lines 1-2) hovers
over 'The Wish':

> Well then; I now do plainly see,
> This busie world and I shall ne're agree;
> The very *Honey* of all earthly joy
> > Does of all meats the soonest *cloy*,
> > And they (methinks) deserve my pity,
> Who for it can endure the stings,
> The *Crowd*, and *Buz*, and *Murmurings*
> > Of this great *Hive*, the *City*.
> > Ah, yet, e're I descend to th' Grave
> May I a *small House*, and *large Garden* have!
> And a *few Friends*, and *many Books*, both true,
> > Both wise, and both delightful too!
> > And since *Love* ne're will from me flee,
> A *Mistress* moderately fair ...
>
> Oh, *Fountains*, when in you shall I
> My self, eas'd of unpeaceful thoughts, espy?
> Oh *Fields!* Oh *Woods!* when, when shall I be made
> > The happy *Tenant* of your shade? ...[142]

Horace had similarly queried: *O rus, quando ego te aspiciam?*
(Sat II, 6). Or, as rendered by Philip Francis:

> ... 'Oh! when again
> 'Shall I behold the rural Plain?
> 'And when with Books of Sages deep,
> 'Sequester'd Ease, and gentle Sleep,
> 'In sweet Oblivion, blissful Balm!
> 'The busy Cares of Life becalm ...

'A Vote'[143] begins by rejecting various types of men — the Puritan,
the schoolmaster, the justice of the peace, the courtier, the lawyer
— instead asking for a Golden Mean in everything:

This only grant me: that my means may lie
Too low for envy, for contempt too high.
. . . . .
Books should, not business, entertain the light,
And sleep, as undisturb'd as death, the night.
    My house a Cottage more
Than Palace, and should fitting be
For all my use, no luxury:
    My Garden painted o'er,
With Natures hand, not arts, that pleasures yield,
Horace might envy in his *Sabine* field.

Cowley states that he wrote this poem at the age of thirteen and he quotes the last three stanzas in the essay 'Of My self' to prove that he had always been possessed by the desire to embrace retirement.

'The Wish' and 'A Vote' are early examples of a type of composition which later on was to become exceedingly popular, Pomfret's *The Choice* (1700) being the best known of them all.

The *Sylva* (1637) contains two further poems that are strongly indebted to classical *beatus ille* sentiments: 'Ode II. That a pleasant Poverty is to be preferred before discontented Riches'[144] and 'Ode IV. On the uncertainty of Fortune. A Translation'.[145] 'Ode II' stresses a motif dear to the heart of Cowley, to wit that unadorned Nature is much superior to art:

Give me a River which doth scorne to shew
    An added beauty, whose cleere brow
    May be my looking-glasse, to see
What my face is, and what my mind should be.
. . . . .
Here a fresh Arbor gives her amorous shade,
    Which *Nature*, the best *Gard'ner* made.
    Here I would set, and sing rude layes,
Such as the *Nimphs* and *me my selfe* should please.

Thus I would waste, thus end my carelesse dayes,
And *Robin-red-brests* whom men praise
For pious birds, should when I dye,
Make both my *Monument* and *Elegie*.

'Ode IV' is a fairly close translation of Casimire's Ode I, 2, 'That hee would not complaine too much of adverse fortune',[146] the moral being that one should remain *aequus mentis* whatever one's fortune may be. The story of the Emperor who returned 'To his old Country Farme of yesterday' illustrates the thesis.

Cowley's familiarity with Casimire is again apparent from 'The Extasie',[147] the first six stanzas of which are a free paraphrase of Casimire's Ode II, 5 ('E Rebus Humanis Excessus'). It is also possible that Cowley's 'Life' [148] may owe its inspiration to Casimire's Ode II, 8 ('Ad Asterium'). 'Life' touches on the Platonic theme of the deceptive surface appearance of things, and in his own comments Cowley refers to Plato and Hermes Trismegistus and their doctrine that nothing truly is, but God.

Cowley's finest retirement poems, the odes 'Upon Liberty' 'On Solitude' and 'The Garden' (attached to the essays on the same topics) present the Happy Man as a Hortulan Saint, who, like Moses, views 'Ev'n in a Bush the radiant Deitie'.

'Upon Liberty' places liberty in the obscure life, while it is totally absent from men governed by tyrants like wild ambition, avarice, and lust. Even though a great man might be free from these 'insulting Passions', he would nevertheless be fettered by 'Custom, Business, Crowds, and formal Decencie'. The true Happy Man is he who can 'With a few Friends, and a few Dishes Dine'.

The essay 'Of Solitude' states that only a certain type of person is fit for solitude:

> The truth of the matter is, that neither he who is a Fop in the world, is a fit man to be alone; nor he who has set his heart much upon the world, though he have never so much understanding; so that Solitude can be well fitted and set right,

216

but upon a very few persons. They must have enough knowledge of the World to see the vanity of it, and enough Virtue
to despise all Vanity; if the Mind be possest with any Lust or
Passions, a man had better be in a Fair, than in a Wood alone ...
In the second place, he must learn the Art, and get the Habit
of Thinking ... Cogitation is the thing which distinguishes the
Solitude of a God from a wilde Beast.

Learning and books are therefore necessary before solitude can
become profitable. If these are present, the 'first Minister of
State has not so much business in publick, as a wise man has
in private ... the one has but part of the affairs of one Nation,
the other all the works of God and Nature under his consideration'. The main business of the solitary man, then, is with 'all
the works of God and Nature', a point illustrated by the ode.

Virgil's praise of the happy life serves as a point of departure
for the ode: *O quis me gelidis sub montibus Æmi / Sistat, &
ingenti ramorum protegat umbra?* (*Georgics* II, 488-489: O for
one to set me in the cool glens of Haemus, and shield me under
the branches' mighty shade!). Like all the poets of this chapter,
Cowley praises the trees of the forest, its silver stream and soft
breezes, and, like Marvell, he rejects the presence of Eve and
focusses his mind on higher things. He denounces the 'Monster
London', proclaiming that Nature is the 'wisest Architect':

> Here Nature does a House for me erect;
> > Nature the wisest Architect
> > Who those fond Artists does despise
> That can the fair and living Trees neglect;
> > Yet the dead Timber prize.
>
> . . . . .
>
> A silver stream shall roul his waters near,
> > Guilt with Sun-beams here and there,
> > On whose enamel'd Bank I'll walk,
> And see how prettily they smile, and hear
> > How prettily they talk.

217

Ah wretched, and too Solitary He
    Who loves not his own Companie!
. . . . .

Oh Solitude, first state of Human-kind!
    Which blest remain'd till man did find
    Even his own helpers Companie.
As soon as two (Alas!) together joyn'd,
    The Serpent made up Three.
. . . . .

Thou the faint beams of Reason's scatter'd Light
    Dost like a Burning-glass unite,
    Dost Multiply the feeble Heat,
And fortifie the strength till thou dost bright
    And noble fires beget.

It is difficult to decide whether the process of focussing 'Reason's scatter'd Light' serves a religious, or a purely intellectual purpose. Upon the whole, Cowley appears more rationalistic than Vaughan, Benlowes, or Marvell. He seems more akin to Mildmay Fane, with whose ode to retirement he may possibly have been familiar. Cowley was best man at the wedding of the Duke of Buckingham to Fairfax's daughter Mary in 1658, which connects him with the Fairfax circle.

The eleven Pindaric stanzas of 'The Garden' come much closer to the ecstatic mood of the Hortulan Saint. Addressed to John Evelyn, it praises him for having chosen books and gardens rather than 'empty shows and senceless noys':

Happy art thou whom God does bless
With the full choice of thine own Happiness;
    And happier yet, because thou'rt blest
    With prudence how to choose the best:
. . . . .

Oh blessed shades! O gentle cool retreat

From all th' immoderate Heat,
In which the frantick World does burn and sweat!
. . . . .
    The Birds that dance from bough to bough,
    And sing above in every Tree,
    Are not from Fears and Cares more free,
    Than we who Lie, or Walk below,
. . . . .
These are the Spells that to kind Sleep invite,
And nothing does within resistance make,
    Which yet we moderately take;
    Who would not choose to be awake,
While he's incompass'd round with such delight,
To th' Ear, the Nose, the Touch, the Taste, and Sight?
. . . . .
    Who, that has Reason, and his Smell,
Would not among Roses and Jasmin dwell,
    Rather than all his Spirits choak
With exhalations of Dirt and Smoak?
    And all th' uncleanness which does drown
In pestilential Clouds a populous Town?
. . . . .
When *Epicurus* to the World had taught,
    That pleasure was the chiefest good,
(And was perhaps i'th' right, if rightly understood)
    His life he to his Doctrine brought,
And in a Gardens shade that Sovereign Pleasure sought.
Whoever a true Epicure would be,
May there find cheap and virtuous Luxurie.
. . . . .
Where does the Wisdom and the Power Divine
In a more bright and sweet Reflection shine?
Where do we finer strokes and colours see
Of the Creators real Poetrie,

219

> Than when we with attention look
> Upon the third days Volume of the Book?
> If we could open and intend our Eye,
> We all like *Moses* should espy
> Ev'n in a Bush the radiant Deity.

Cowley was perhaps the last poet to express belief in the actual presence of God in the Creation, and his statement, significantly enough, is given conditional form: '*If* we could open and intend our Eye . . .' The introduction of a carefully qualified statement in favour of Epicurus ('if rightly understood'), denotes a new departure. The Earthly Paradise mood of the garden theme has finally resulted in a tentative approach to the most important garden philosopher of Antiquity. From this time on the Hortulan Saint was destined to vanish out of sight like Elijah in Cowley's 'The Extasie', leaving in his wake the far more worldly figure of the Innocent Epicurean.

Cowley's literary production marks an important stage in the history of the Happy Man. His marshalling of classical sources, and his own comments on these in his *Essays and Discourses*, together with his original poetry along similar lines, constitute a striking presentation of the motif of the Happy Man, and a serious defence of the way of life recommended by Horace and Virgil, Claudian and Martial. Cowley's sincerity is apparent; this is indeed the 'language of his heart'. No wonder, therefore, that while the poetry of Fane and Benlowes, Marvell and Vaughan was consigned to the literary dustbin, Cowley's essays in prose and verse proved sturdy perennials in the garden of popular esteem. The serious poets of the Restoration derived much of their inspiration from Cowley. Thus Samuel Woodford, a minister best known for his paraphrase of *Canticles*, in 1679 published an ode to 'Solitude' which is nothing but a stanza-by-stanza paraphrase of Cowley's ode. Woodford's paraphrase was penned in 1668, which shows how Cowley's adaptation of the *beatus ille* formula commanded instant attention from the new generation.

5.

Thomas Traherne

Few of the poems of Thomas Traherne can be said to be in the tradition of Horace's second Epode, although in some respects they represent a logical development of *beatus ille* themes. The poetry of this Anglican minister[149] is the deeply personal record of a man who penetrated beyond mere argument concerning happiness to a fountain of spiritual bliss. Traherne's chief concern was with felicity as a spiritual achievement, and so in him we have the most extreme example of the type of *beatus vir* which is here referred to as the Hortulan Saint.

In Traherne's conception of felicity, Platonic ideas outweigh the Stoic. His picture of the *beatus vir* is almost entirely free of negative characteristics. His happiness is derived, not from an absence of ills or a rejection of vice, but from a positive enjoyment of life based on a Neoplatonic purification of sense experience. Speaking in terms of themes, this involves a focussing on the theme of the Earthly Paradise and the mystic vision, rather than on the Stoic theme of contentment with the *parva rura*.

Like Vaughan, and in strong contrast to Cowley, Traherne has a strong anti-intellectual bias; the deepest wisdom is found in the visionary powers of a child. 'Eden'[150] compares the innocent happiness of our parents before the Fall to those feelings which the poet recalled having had as a child:

> A learned and a Happy Ignorance
> Divided me, ...
> From all the Sloth Care Pain and Sorrow that advance,
> The Madness and the Miserie
> Of Men. No Error, no Distraction I
> Saw soil the Earth, or overcloud the Skie.
> . . . . .

221

Only what Adam in his first Estate,
Did I behold;
Hard Silver and Drie Gold
As yet lay under Ground; my Blessed Fate
Was more acquainted with the Old
And Innocent Delights, which he did see
In his Original Simplicitie.

Traherne seems a thoroughly original poet; echoes are not often found in his lines, and his allusion to Boethius Metre II, 5 (in the reference to 'Hard Silver and Drie Gold' being yet 'under Ground') was probably consciously intended to bring up the memory of the author of *De Consolatione Philosophiae*.

'Innocence' [151] describes childhood in terms usually applied to the Hortulan Saint. 'A Joyfull Sence and Puritie / Is all I can remember', and 'A Serious Meditation did employ / My Soul within'. In this meditation, mere outward show is avoided; the inner reality is everything. 'The Preparative' [152] discusses the same ideas, stressing the 'Naked Simple Pure *Intelligence*' of childhood. The last stanzas describe how the Platonic vision is achieved by the Stoic *beatus vir* in his contemplative retirement:

Tis not the Object, but the Light
That maketh Heaven; Tis a Purer Sight.
Felicitie
Appears to none but them that purely see.

A Disentangled and a Naked Sence
A Mind that's unpossest,
A Disengaged Brest,
An Empty and a Quick Intelligence
Acquainted with the Golden Mean,
An Even Spirit Pure and Serene,
Is that where Beauty, Excellence,

> And Pleasure keep their Court of Residence.
> My Soul retire,
> Get free, and so thou shalt even all Admire.

It is not often that Traherne praises the 'Disengaged Brest' of the Stoic; occasionally he would denounce it as an inadequate basis for human felicity:

> A quiet Mind is worse than Poverty!
> Unless it from Enjoyment spring!
> . . . . .
> Content alone's a dead and silent Stone:
> The real life of Bliss
> Is Glory reigning in a Throne![153]

Traherne conceived of meditation as an active force, charged with immense power. Thoughts, to him, were 'Engines of Felicitie', 'Springs / Of inward Pleasure', his 'Sweet Mysterious Shades / That do all Substances Excell.' [154]

Although Traherne in this manner looked upon happiness as a psychological or spiritual state, there is a strong love for the country in his poetry.[155] Nature, to Traherne, partook of the magic glory inherent in life if man would but see it. However, unlike Vaughan and Marvell, Traherne did not often convey spiritual truth by means of descriptions of the landscape of retirement. For this reason, his was the more disembodied voice.

6.

The Hortulan Saint enjoyed a remarkably flourishing existence in the lean years of the Commonwealth, but this was only to be expected from a figure which emerged as the result of a fusion between two of the strongest philosophic trends of the mid-century. When Stoicism wedded Neoplatonism, the theme of the Happy

Man entered its most distinctive religious phase. The *beatus ille* themes were infinitely enriched by becoming associated with a spiritual interpretation of Nature, and the somewhat austere attitude of the Serene Contemplator was considerably softened by the infusion of the new belief in a transcendent reality (or Earthly Paradise) which may be grasped once the senses have been purified. After the sixteen-forties rural retirement no longer was a mere defence mechanism against a corrupt world; it became an open gateway to Paradise before the Fall.

Since Paradise before the Fall was such a pleasant place, there entered into the ascetic life of the saint a sensuous element of pure delight in the beauty of the garden. To the eye which sees that Apollo is as much part of the Laurel tree as Daphne, the vegetable world assumes a secret life of its own in God. More, Benlowes, Marvell, and Vaughan for this reason drew a sharp line of distinction between the true delights of the garden, and the fallacious pleasures of depraved sense.

No one has ever accused Benlowes or Casimire Sarbiewski of sensuality, since even their most sensuous lines carry the stamp of being imitations of *Canticles* or the *Psalms*. Marvell disguised this connection more cleverly, and hence his garden mood has been suspected of betraying an abandonment to that life of the senses which the Hortulan Saint condemned so strongly. Nothing could be more erroneous. It is only to the modern ear that the sensuous passages in Marvell's retirement poetry fails to provoke an association with *Canticles*, and with the poetic tradition which stems from it. Marvell's 'amorous green' was no libertine concept, but an abstraction which can be perceived only by means of the nobler light of the intellect, and as such it carried religious implications. To a generation thoroughly familiar with this great commonplace of Neoplatonic or Hermetic thought, it was enough to hint at pre-lapsarian delights, and the point, we can be sure, was immediately taken.

Despite the prevalence of religious or occult ideas, we have seen that there is a clear connection with classical *beatus ille* sources in most cases. The Horatian influence was particularly strong in this period, whether it came directly from the poet of the Sabine farm, or indirectly through interpreters such as Casimire Sarbiewski. During the Civil War and the Commonwealth the Horatian ode and verse epistle were the chief vehicles for the expression of the philosophy of rural retirement. No other form exhibits a similar vitality. Henry More who preferred an Elizabethan diffuseness to the Horatian clarity and brevity, did not succeed very well, and it is chiefly in his few briefer lyrics that he achieves a manner and a style which come close to the tradition which we are pursuing.

The finest expressions of the philosophy of the Hortulan Saint are found among the odes and epistles of Fane, Marvell, Vaughan, and Cowley. From the time of Cowley, however, the Pindaric form was destined to supersede the more measured and regular type of ode associated with Horace. At the same time, as we shall soon see, the Hortulan Saint was changed into the Lucretian Detached Spectator of the Restoration period.

This chapter has endeavoured to show how the figure of the classical *beatus vir*, re-interpreted in terms which suited the religious sensibility of the age, was definitely established during the Civil War as a Royalist counterpart to the Puritan pilgrim. In the years from Habington's *Castara* (1634-1640) to Cowley's essays (1668) no other poetic theme was more truly expressive of the spirit which prevailed in humanist circles in England. In the Restoration period the political character of the *beatus vir* was to become more pronounced, at the same time that the intellectual preferences of the new generation were to shift the emphasis away from Stoic or Platonic thought to a prevailingly Epicurean bias. This new phase in the career of the Happy Man forms the topic of the next chapter.

CHAPTER V

THE INNOCENT EPICUREAN, OR THE DETACHED SPECTATOR

The reaction of the English nation in 1660 was largely caused by the feeling that a period of fear and insecurity was at an end. With the re-establishment of the old regime something of the order long vanished again returned to the English scene. As John Evelyn phrased it in his *Panegyric to Charles the Second* (1661): '... no sooner were we possess'd of your sacred Majestie, but you suddainly gave form to our confused Chaos.'

At the same time that order was introduced into Church and State, the work of the scientists performed a similar office for the universe. Joseph Glanvill's *Vanity of Dogmatizing* (1661) has been called a 'paean of triumph in celebration of the new philosophy.' [1] In this work the airy speculations of the schoolmen received the same condemnation which had been extended to the religious enthusiasts. To the men of the Royal Society, greater truth value was felt to inhere in the Cartesian principles of motion and extension than in dogmatic assertions concerning the 'idea' of a thing. Nature, no longer a divine hieroglyph, was advanced (or reduced) to the status of a mathematical formula.

The influence of this turning of the tides was necessarily profound. With the general relaxation of tension came a fondness for leisured ease, and the dimpled god of the bacchanalian love feast entered into the landscape of retirement. Instead of Seneca and Boethius, the poets of the Restoration began to echo Anacreon, Lucretius, Ovid, and the more wanton of the Horatian odes. In the realm of philosophy, the doctrines of Epicurus received serious consideration. In the first half of the century the name of Epicurus had been synonymous with everything that was self-indulgent, sensual, and reprehensible, and the true nature of his teaching was not made clear until Walter Charleton and Thomas Stanley took it upon them to give an unbiassed exposition of the Epicurean philosophy. [2] The gradual waning of Stoic moroseness in favour of more urbane philosophical views was fittingly commented upon in the commendatory poem prefixed to John Evelyn's translation of Lucretius' *De Rerum Natura*, Book I (1656):

> How spruce (thus trimm'd) Philosophy looks now,
> Which was *morose* before in beard and brow?
> What we abhorred then, we now embrace;
> A Nymph is seated in a Satyrs place.

Philosophy, it would seem, has suddenly developed sex appeal.

To the hedonistically inclined court of Charles II, Epicurean ideas were far from repugnant, and the materialism inherent in the new science predisposed many serious men to accept the doctrine that nothing exists after death: *post mortem nihil est*. One can observe a transition from a prevailingly introvert to a more extrovert position even in the quarters where the tenets of the Church were honoured. What took place (in the words of Basil Willey) was nothing less than 'a general transference of interest from metaphysics to physics, from the contemplation of Being to the observation of Becoming.' [3]

The Restoration interpretation of the philosophy of retirement reflects this fundamental change in outlook very clearly. What used to be a defence of an introspective, half religious way of life was transformed, some time after the turn of the half-century, into an apology for the enjoyment of a secular way of life, pursued, it is true, in the country-side and often in solitary state, but under the auspices of Epicurus or Catullus rather than Seneca or Plato. The Hortulan Saint who fights on bended knees was ousted by an urbane gentleman who chose retirement because he abhorred business, preferring instead a life marked by pleasant ease and privacy. Rural scenes became the accepted setting for elegant and licentious courtship to such an extent that a poet like Mrs. Behn was led to embrace the theme of retirement because she automatically associated rural solitude with free love.

Even in the more serious Restoration poets one can observe a definite loss of the consciousness that God is part of His creation. The double vision of the mid-century, the ability to live in two distinct and separate worlds at one and the same time, was lost. The contemplating gentleman, learning to put increasing emphasis on clear and precise ideas of a reality conceived in terms of mechanics rather than secret correspondences, no longer dwelt in his garden as in a place made holy by the Divine presence. To the new generation, the only real properties of matter were those capable of mathematical demonstration. The old feeling of awe and wonder gradually faded in the grey dawn of a Cartesian universe. Instead of ultimate truth, the Restoration contemplator was left to seek intellectual satisfaction in considering the immutable laws of nature and their moral implications for man, or again he could find satisfaction in an abandonment to physical beauty. The consequences of late seventeenth-century Cartesianism, Deism, and Epicureanism were far-reaching. The one changed the concept of Nature, the second the concept of God, and the third the concept of man. The Restoration idea of a gentleman reflects this great change in outlook. The idealistic definitions of Castiglione, Spenser, and Milton had to yield to Locke's more worldly idea of men characterised by good breeding and fitted for elegant conversation. The heroic tone of the Renaissance was lost in a society which favoured the scepticism of the new science, the rationalism of the new theology, and the psychological empiricism of Locke. In the process, intrinsic virtues were traded against external accomplishments, and the *beatus vir* became a pursuer of elegant pastimes rather than absolute truth.

Nevertheless, the Innocent Epicurean of the Restoration was by no means a contemptible figure. His purpose was not primarily sensual abandonment, but the achievement of indolence of body

and tranquillity of mind. Like the great master himself, he valued
the pleasures of rest above those of motion:

> For it is not perpetuall feasting, and drinking; not the con-
> versation of beautifull women; not rarities of fish, nor any
> other dainties of a profuse table, that make a happy life; but
> reason, with sobriety, and a serene mind ... [4] Happy indeed,
> who knowes The chief good and a blessed life, consists not in
> Soveraignty or power, not in numerous wealth and plenty, but
> in indolence, composure of affections, and such a disposition
> of mind, as, circumscribing all things by the boundaries of
> nature, makes him, in being content with little, obtain that
> which they, who rule over many, and possesse great treasures,
> despair ever to arrive at.[5]

Public employment was therefore carefully avoided by the new
beatus vir, and the thesis that '*solitude*, Contemplation, or a
Country-life, have more of pleasure in them than publick Employment' was seriously defended by Sir George Mackenzie in *A Moral
Essay, Preferring Solitude to Publick Employment* (1666).

Mackenzie makes a number of interesting points. Thus he
argues in Epicurean fashion that pleasure is an act of the fancy
(that is, the mind), and hence the things which affect the fancy
should be preferred to those which affect the senses only. For
this reason one ought to court retirement because it affords more
complete freedom to the fancy than an active life. Like Owen
Feltham, Sir George Mackenzie praises the pleasures of contemplation, but in terms which would have shocked the Stoic
moralist: 'Contemplation does often drive our souls into extasies,
and is so charming, that it may be rather said to ravish then
please ...'[6] The terms used ('charming', 'ravish' 'please') are
characteristic of the Restoration attitude. Contemplation, no
longer a duty but a pleasure, is praised in terms usually applied
to a mistress. The nymph has indeed been seated in the satyr's
place.

Mackenzie's defence of retirement leads him to paraphrase
Lucretius' lines on the detached spectator:

The world is a Comedy... I know no securer box, from which to behold it, then a safe *Solitude*, and it is easier to feel then to express the pleasure which may be taken in standing aloof, and in contemplating the reelings of the multitude, the excentrick motions of great men, and how fate recreats it self in their ruine...[7]

This Lucretian picture of the man who enjoys the spectacle of the world as a passive observer, was destined to become the leading feature in the portrayal of the Restoration Happy Man. The *alterius spectare laborem* was the most important pastime of the Innocent Epicurean; it assured him of his own superiority and provided ample material for serious moral reflection.

The philosophy of Epicurus was admirably suited to offset a serious limitation in the Restoration milieu. To Sir William Temple's generation the 'reelings of the multitude' and the 'excentrick motions of great men' were only too plainly visible. Surely one of the chief reasons why the philosophy of Epicurus became so popular was the fact that it provided such a potent antidote, not only to the enthusiastic notions of the sectarians, but also to the ambitious schemes of politicians and court favourites. For those who scorned both the reeling multitude and the scheming politicians the garden of Epicurus, or the Lucretian pinnacle, became the logical refuge.

Although a love of ease and tranquillity was the basic Restoration motive for seeking country retirement, certain more austere ideas persisted as part of the philosophy of happiness. The complete abandonment of some Restoration writers to the inner life can scarcely be adequately explained solely in terms of Epicurean influence. The Duchess of Newcastle is an extreme example of the tendency to reject the external world in favour of the regions of the mind. Although no doubt a pathological case, the Duchess may, for all we know, have been trying to realise the ideal outlined by a French writer in a work translated by Walter Mountague, the Neoplatonist, in 1656. The treatise dealt with *The Accomplish'd*

233

Woman and was dedicated by Mountague to the Duchess of Buckingham. The chapter 'Of Cheerfulnesse and Melancholy' praises the contemplative life, not only for the *repose* which it affords to the mind, but also (and more importantly) because the inner life only is seen to have any reality:

> We are to be found truly no where but in our selves, every where else we meet but with our fantasme or our shadow. And therefore many have reason to say, That Meditation is harder then Extasie, as its easier to go out of our selves, then to re-enter into them, without the use of this noble Thoughtfulnesse, to which the temper of Melancholy is disposed.[8]

This Platonic doctrine is not incompatible with a refined and serious Epicureanism, and the two are in fact often encountered in conjunction. The Platonic impulse persisted even in the works of scientists, who tended to describe the ordered beauty of the universe in a manner indebted to Plato. Like Benlowes and Marvell, Mackenzie insisted on a contemplation of God and His works, the prime reward of which would consist in 'that tranquillity of spirit which is peculiar to Philosophy, and is the guest of *solitude*'.[9] And in the poetry of Mrs. Philips, John Norris, and the Countess of Winchilsea a pensive retirement appears as the *summum bonum*, the only perfect pleasure, the only activity which is truly self-contained and productive of tranquillity of mind and indolence of body. Despite their Epicurean leanings, these poets retained some of the spiritual fervour of the Hortulan Saint.

It may seem strange that the man who took it upon himself to publish a refutation of Mackenzie's essay, was no less a person than John Evelyn, himself a lover of gardens and rural retirement. Perhaps Evelyn's reply was more a *tour de force* than a record of honest opinion; this seems indicated by his confession to Abraham Cowley that his defence of public life was undertaken in a jesting spirit, and that he apologised for forsaking a cause which both of them held dear.[10] However, Evelyn was undoubtedly serious enough in some of his arguments, and particularly when he stressed the importance of polite conversation. Evelyn picked no quarrel with Mackenzie's defence of the meditative life; what he attacked was the Scottish lawyer's assumption that wisdom could be achieved in *solitude*: ' . . . not to read men, and converse with living libraries, is to deprive ourselves of the most useful and profitable of studies... The wisest men are not made in chambers and closets, crowded with shelves, but by habitude and active conversations.' [11] Mackenzie's essay was a little behind the times in its advocacy of complete solitude; Evelyn's rejection of solitude in favour of a more polite version of rural retirement was to be echoed by increasing numbers. The Neoclassical *beatus vir* could by no means be allowed to suffer from pedantic moroseness induced by too much book learning; if he were to conform with the times he had, instead, to be an exponent of polite manners and a fine conversationalist.

After their exchange of words, Evelyn and Mackenzie were easily reconciled and no further controversy followed.

A second essay by Mackenzie presented *A Moral Paradox: Maintaining That it is much easier to be VIRTUOUS than VITIOUS* (1669). Mackenzie's main thesis is that 'all Creatures design ease', and that 'happiness consists in ease'.[12] Ease is no less than 'That happiest of States, and root of all Perfections'.[13] The author reconciles this position with that of the moralist by maintaining that virtue is inherent in the nature of man, and that therefore the pursuit of virtue is conducive to ease, while conversely the pursuit of vice implies effort because against man's natural bent and bias. The argument that most men nevertheless are not virtuous, would seem irrefutable, but Mackenzie counters this objection with the reply that mankind is mad. This seventeenth-century Scottish advocate in other words actually formulated a moral philosophy along the lines which later made the philosophy of the third Earl of Shaftesbury so popular. A belief in the perfection of natural man can be traced through a number of Restoration poems on the happy country life, and notably those of Aphra

Behn. It is difficult to assess the extent to which the tradition outlined in this study conduced to a belief in the superior virtue of natural, or primitive, man, but it cannot be doubted that it played a part in the process. Nevertheless, the stronger trend was in the direction of a retirement marked by a love of books, select company, and leisured ease — in other words, a highly civilised existence.

In the biographical annals of the Restoration, the life of Sir William Temple is a vivid expression of that fondness for leisured ease which marks the age. Temple professed that he 'was made for a farmer & not a courtier, & understood being a shepheard & a gardener better then an Ambassadour'.[14] Temple's statement reveals that pastoral and rural elements combined in his concept of retirement; gardening and agriculture have been placed on the same level. The same confusion can be found in professional treatises of agriculture, like John Worlidge's *Systema Agriculturae* (1669), which makes no difference between the labour of the farmer and the pleasant pursuit of gardening as a gentlemanly pastime. The virtues inherent in the former are generously attributed also to the latter. In this manner the austerity of the *beatus ille* philosophy was considerably softened. To Temple and Worlidge, the gentleman supervising his estate was actually living the happy life of the humble husbandman. For this reason Worlidge recommended agriculture for its restfulness and tranquillity. His bias in favour of gentlemanly pursuits is further shown in the fact that his encomium of agriculture includes a long passage in the spirit of the Royal Society on the intellectual satisfaction arising out of a study of the scenes of nature:

> This Country-life improves and exercises the most Noble and Excellent parts of our Intellects, and affords the best opportunities to the insatiable humane spirit to contemplate and meditate on; and to penetrate into, and discover the obscure and hitherto occult Mysteries and Secrets of Nature,... and to attain the highest perfections in Science and Art.

236

Worlidge supports his defence of country life by first paraphrasing and then quoting a passage from Ogilby's translation of Virgil's *Georgics*:

> Here they enjoy all things necessary for the sustentation of Life, and are freed from the perturbations, cares, and Troubles, that in other places disturb the mind; and live content with their Lot, in tranquility and moderation of Spirit. Here they enjoy
>
>> Rest secure, an innocent Life in Peace,
>> Variously Rich, in their large Farms at ease.
>> *Tempe's* cool shades, dark Caves, and purling Streams,
>> Lowings of Cattel, under Trees soft Dreams.[15]

When Dryden, in his dedication of his translation of Virgil's *Georgics* to the Earl of Chesterfield,[16] praised the latter for preferring a private life, he placed him in a *garden* and not on a farm. The argument is worth following. 'You, my Lord', so Dryden writes, 'have ... forsaken the common track of business, which is not always clean: you have chosen for yourself a private greatness, and will not be polluted with ambition.' Next Dryden ironically points out that he has observed how all public figures were desirous of retiring to a private life; 'greatness, they said, was nauseous, and a crowd was troublesome; a quiet privacy was their ambition.' Most of these nevertheless still lingered at court, 'because they thought they had not yet enough to make them happy: they would have more, and laid in, to make their solitude luxurious — a wretched philosophy, which Epicurus never taught them in his garden.' The argument is clearly conducted with the Epicurean philosophy in mind; the ideal state is found, not on a Sabine farm, but in the garden of Epicurus. Dryden also introduces the Lucretian picture of the detached spectator who views the tempests of the sea from a safe distance:

> You, my Lord, enjoy your quiet in a garden, where you have not only the leisure of thinking, but the pleasure to think of nothing which can discompose your mind. A good conscience

is a port which is landlock'd on every side; and where no winds can possibly invade, no tempests can arise. There a man may stand upon the shore, and not only see his own image, but that of his Maker, clearly reflected from the undisturb'd and silent waters.

And, like Cowley, Dryden insists on intellectual pursuits, referring to Virgil by way of proof:

> Virgil seems to think that the blessings of a country life are not complete without an improvement of knowledge by contemplation and reading:
>> *O fortunatos nimium, bona si sua norint,*
>> *Agricolas!*
>
> 'Tis but half possession not to understand that happiness which we possess ... Such only can enjoy the country, who are capable of thinking when they are there, and have left their passions behind them in the town. Then they are prepar'd for solitude; and in that solitude is prepar'd for them:
>> *Et secura quies, et nescia fallere vita.*

Dryden associated the retired life with the Epicurean philosophy to such an extent that he proclaimed Horace an Epicurean: 'let his Dutch commentators say what they will, his philosophy was Epicurean.' [17] While the translators and commentators of the first half of the century had stressed Horace's Stoic ideas, the Restoration exaggerated his Epicureanism to the almost complete exclusion of all Stoic elements.

1.

Translations

Dryden's chief contribution to the *beatus ille* tradition lies in the realm of translations. One would have thought that the market for translations would have been saturated by 1685, when Dryden published his version of parts of Lucretius and Theocritus, and four of Horace's odes, among them two rural lyrics: Ode III, 29 and the second Epode. Yet this was not so; translations were as popular as ever. The poets and the reading public seemed equally enthusiastic. Dryden jokingly refers to having suffered from 'the disease of translation' for 'this last half-year', that is, the last half year before publishing his second miscellany, *Sylvae* (1685). In the act of translation Dryden discovered 'something that was more pleasing' than his 'ordinary production', and the basis of selection was his own personal response to a passage.[18] The popularity of Dryden's miscellanies is shown by the frequency with which they were published. Dryden's technical craftsmanship far exceeded that of his predecessors, and his literary sensitivity made him alive to the peculiar characteristics distinguishing the poetry of a particular author. He endeavoured to feel his way into a text, rendering its spirit rather than the letter, and boldly departed from the 'learned Dutch commentators' for whom he felt nothing but contempt, seeing that they were mere pedants, 'heavy gross-witted fellows, fit only to gloss on their own dull poets'.[19] Dryden sometimes contracted a text, sometimes enlarged it, and he defended the latter practice by alleging that the additions either 'are secretly in the poet, or may be fairly deduc'd from him; or at least if both those considerations should fail, that my own is of a piece with his, and that if he were living, and an Englishman, they are such as he would probably have written.'[20]

One of the passages in Lucretius to which Dryden responded, is the one at the beginning of the second book which presents the Happy Man as a detached spectator of mankind. Dryden's translation is vigorous and thoroughly congenial with the spirit of the original:

> 'Tis pleasant, safely to behold from shore
> The rolling ship, and hear the tempest roar:
> . . . . .
> 'Tis pleasant also to behold from far

239

The moving legions mingled in the war;
But much more sweet thy lab'ring steps to guide
To virtue's heights, with wisdom well supplied,
And all the magazines of learning fortified:
From thence to look below on humankind,
Bewilder'd in the maze of life, and blind:
To see vain fools ambitiously contend
For wit and pow'r...
  O wretched man! in what a mist of life,
Inclos'd with dangers and with noisy strife,
He spends his little span, and overfeeds
His cramm'd desires with more than nature needs!
For nature wisely stints our appetite,
And craves no more than undisturb'd delight:
Which minds, unmix'd with cares and fears, obtain;
A soul serene, a body void of pain.
. . . . .
If golden sconces hang not on the walls,
To light the costly suppers and the balls;
If the proud palace shines not with the state
Of burnish'd bowls, and of reflected plate;
. . . . .
Yet on the grass, beneath a poplar shade,
By the cool stream our careless limbs are laid;
With cheaper pleasures innocently blest,
When the warm spring with gaudy flow'rs is dress'd.[21]

One realises the basic kinship between this passage and Virgil's praise of the *agricola* in the second *Georgic*, but one also notices a striking difference. Lucretius is not interested in the hardy toil of the farmer; the motif of the *parva rura* is totally absent, since the *beatus vir* must be presented in a state of complete rest in contrast to the frantic activity of the wretched man.

Horace's peculiar characteristics, according to Dryden, are 'his

briskness, his jollity, and his good humor; and those I have chiefly
endeavor'd to copy. His other excellencies, I confess, are above
my imitation'. Dryden adds that one particular ode pleased him
infinitely in the reading, and that he took some pains 'to make
it my masterpiece in English'. This is Ode III, 29, paraphrased
in Pindaric verse, and dedicated to the Earl of Rochester. Its
leit motif is the advice to enjoy the present hour; its form is that
of a letter from Horace to Maecenas, requesting the latter to
leave the town and join him on his country estate. The text is
much expanded (from 64 to 104 lines), as is seen if one compares
the translation with the original. I quote from Horace in the
translation of John Marshall:

Horace: Quit for a time the luxury that cloys,
    And thy high towers which touch the dizzy clouds;
      Admire not so Rome's smoke and crowds,
        And all her prosperous noise.[22]
                (stanza 3)

Dryden: Leave for a while thy costly country seat;
    And, to be great indeed, forget
  The nauseous pleasures of the great:
    Make haste and come;
  Come, and forsake the cloying store;
    Thy turret that surveys, from high,
  The smoke, and wealth, and noise of Rome;
    And all the busy pageantry
  That wise men scorn, and fools adore:
Come, give thy soul a loose, and taste the pleasures
              of the poor.[23]

The Horatian terseness has been exchanged for an impassioned
eloquence, but one must grant the point that the additions 'are
secretly in the poet, or may be fairly deduc'd from him'. The

difference is largely one of style, but the style of a poem cannot be kept entirely distinct from its content. For this reason the overall impression of Dryden's version is more lush, more luxurious; his abandonment to the joys of the moment is much more intense. Thus Horace had written in stanzas 9 and 10:

> Learn calm to face what's pressing. For the rest,
> Life's like a river's flow, which now shall glide
> > Straight on to meet the Tuscan tide:
> > > Now on its storm-tost breast
>
> Sweeps cattle, trees uprooted, loosened stones,
> Ev'n houses, all in one...

Dryden's version transforms Horace's *memento componere aequus* into the advice to enjoy the present moment:

> Enjoy the present smiling hour,
> And put it out of Fortune's pow'r;
> The tide of bus'ness, like the running stream,
> > Is sometimes high, and sometimes low,
> A quiet ebb, or a tempestuous flow,
> > And always in extreme.

The same exaggeration is felt in Dryden's rendering of lines 41-43: *Ille potens sui / Laetusque deget, cui licet in diem / Dixisse 'Vixi'*. ('Self-centred he, / And blest, who can make boast each coming night / "This day I've lived".')

> Happy the man, and happy he alone,
> > He, who can call to-day his own;
> > He who, secure within, can say:
> 'To-morrow do thy worst, for I have liv'd to-day.
> > Be fair, or foul, or rain, or shine,
> The joys I have possess'd, in spite of fate, are mine...'

Dryden's version of the second Epode[24] seems closer to the spirit of the original, despite the fact that he expanded Horace's 70 lines into 102. This is largely due to the compactness of the form; Dryden employed tetrameters varied with occasional trimeters and rhyming abab, aa bb, or abba. The superiority of Dryden's translation is apparent, if we compare it with earlier versions. The four first lines will serve as a basis of comparison.

Ben Jonson:
> Happie is he, that from all Businesse cleere,
>> As the old race of Mankind were,
> With his own Oxen tills his Sires left lands,
>> And is not in the Usurers bands:

Thomas Randolph:
> Happy the man which farre from city care;
>> (Such as ancient Mortals were)
> With his own oxen plows his fathers land,
>> Free from Usurers griping hand.

Abraham Cowley:
> Happy the Man whom bounteous Gods allow
> With his own Hands Paternal Grounds to plough!
> Like the first golden Mortals Happy he
> From Business and the cares of Money free!

Common to all these versions are a fairly awkward rhythm and an unnatural syntax. Cowley's syntax is the best, but it will be seen to fall short of the ease displayed by Dryden's version. Dryden's syntax is unforced; his rhythm both vigorous and smooth, his phrasing more pregnant. The paradox of the second line is particularly felicitous:

Dryden: How happy in his low degree,
>> How rich in humble poverty, is he,

243

Who leads a quiet country life;
Discharg'd of business, void of strife,
And from the griping scrivener free!
(Thus, ere the seeds of vice were sown,
    Liv'd men in better ages born,
Who plow'd with oxen of their own
    Their small paternal field of corn.)

In the preceding year (1684) John Harington and Thomas Creech had published translations of Horace, and that of Creech apparently provided Dryden with a few useful hints. Thus Creech employed tetrameter couplets with an occasional pentameter, and his phrasing, too, bears a certain similarity to that of Dryden. Harington's translation is too inferior to deserve quotation. As Dryden remarked, one must be a thorough poet before one can be a thorough translator.

Dryden's version of the second Epode, when compared with the original, tends to stress the 'harmless easy joys' of the husbandman. The Horatian question, 'Who amid sports like these forgets not quite / Love's ill desires and pestering plight?' is expanded into a quatrain:

    Amidst his harmless easy joys
      No anxious care invades his health,
    Nor love his peace of mind destroys,
      Nor wicked avarice of wealth.

If one similarly compares various versions of Virgil's praise of the *agricola* with that of Dryden, the impression of Dryden's superiority is greatly strengthened, and further instances are discovered of a deliberate heightening of those passages which describe the 'substantial Blessedness' of the husbandman. The translations by Thomas May (1628) and John Ogilby (1654) are without distinction; neither of these was a poet in his own right, unlike Cowley and Dryden. Dryden's translation is again marked by that easy grace which is so peculiarly his own, and by the addition of sensuous details suggesting a life of pleasant ease rather than strenuous toil and sparse living:

639   O happy, if he knew his happy state,
    The swain, who, free from business and debate,
    Receives his easy food from Nature's hand,
    And just returns of cultivated land!
    No palace, with a lofty gate, he wants,
    T'admit the tides of early visitants,
645   With eager eyes devouring, as they pass,
    The breathing figures of Corinthian brass.
    . . . . .
651   He boasts no wool whose native white is dyed
    With purple poison of Assyrian pride;
    No costly drugs of Araby defile,
    With foreign scents, the sweetness of his oil;
655   But easy quiet, a secure retreat,
    A harmless life that knows not how to cheat,
    With home-bred plenty the rich owner bless,
    And rural pleasures crown his happiness.
    Unvex'd with quarrels, undisturb'd with noise,
660   The country king his peaceful realm enjoys:

To the last six lines correspond two lines in the original: '*at secura quies et nescia fallere vita, / dives opum variarum, at latis otia fundis . . . non absunt.*' The Loeb classical edition translates: 'Yet theirs is repose without care, and a life that knows no fraud, but is rich in treasures manifold. Yea, the ease of broad domains . . . are theirs.' The *secura quies* has been expanded into 'easy quiet, a secure retreat', the *dives opum variarum* has become a 'home-bred plenty' which blesses the 'rich owner' whose happiness is crowned by untold 'rural pleasures'. The more non-committal phrase *latis otia fundi* has been transformed into a 'peaceful

realm' enjoyed by a 'country king'. In all these phrases there is
a subtle exaggeration emphasising the pleasures of rest, the ease
of mind and indolence of body typical of the Epicurean *beatus vir*.

The same is true of the following passage:

688   My next desire is, void of care and strife,
        To lead a soft, secure, inglorious life —
690   A country cottage near a crystal flood,
        A winding valley, and a lofty wood.
        Some god conduct me to the sacred shades
        Where Bacchanals are sung by Spartan maids,
        Or lift me high to Hæmus' hilly crown,
695   Or in the plains of Tempe lay me down,
        Or lead me to some solitary place,
        And cover my retreat from human race!
         Happy the man, who, studying nature's laws,
        Thro' known effects can trace the secret cause;
700   His mind possessing in a quiet state,
        Fearless of fortune, and resign'd to fate!
        And happy too is he who decks the bow'rs
        Of Sylvans, and adores the rural pow'rs;
        Whose mind, unmov'd, the bribes of courts can see,
705   Their glitt'ring baits, and purple slavery;

To the first four lines correspond less than two in the original:
*Rura mihi et rigui placeant in vallibus amnes, / flumina amem
silvasque inglorius* ('let my delight be the country, and the
running streams amid the dells — may I love the waters and the
woods, though fame be lost'). The addition of the epithets *soft*
and *secure* to *inglorious*, and of the phrase *void of care and strife*,
tends to stress the Epicurean implications of the text, and so do
lines 696-697, which are Dryden's own elaboration.

The main impression of Dryden's translation is one of clarity,
ease, and power. Although slightly expanded, it has retained much
of the terseness of the original, which is partly due to the clear

and emphatic rhymes, the simple syntax, and the frequent use of alliteration and other devices of sound.

Dryden's translation of Juvenal's satires, published in 1692, provide two further examples of classical *beatus ille* sentiments. Satires 3 and 10 describe the contrast between town and country in terms of the contrast between misery and happiness, sin and virtue. Both expose the stupidity of those who exchange 'solid quiet, to obtain / The windy satisfaction of the brain' (Tenth Satire, 11. 218-219). Man is betrayed by his ignorance of his own good:

1   Look round the habitable world: how few
         Know their own good; or knowing it, pursue,
3   How void of reason are our hopes and fears!
                    (Tenth Satire)

As Dryden explains in his prose argument, the poet's design 'is to represent the various wishes and desires of mankind, and to set out the folly of 'em.' The satirical mode suited Dryden's genius; the parallels between the age of Juvenal and that of his own are obvious. Thus the following lines from the Tenth Satire could easily be applied to an English minister of state:

144   Now, tell me truly, wouldst thou change thy fate
         To be, like him, first minister of state?
         To have thy levees crowded with resort,
         Of a depending, gaping, servile court;
         Dispose all honors of the sword and gown,
         Grace with a nod, and ruin with a frown;
150   To hold thy prince in pupilage, and sway
         That monarch whom the master'd world obey?
         While he, intent on secret lusts alone,
153   Lives to himself, abandoning the throne.

The concluding lines depict the true Happy Man as one who can 'stand confin'd / To health of body, and content of Mind'.

17

550   A soul, that can securely death defy,
       And count it nature's privilege to die;
       Serene and manly, harden'd to sustain
       The load of life, and exercis'd in pain;
       Guiltless of hate, and proof against desire;
555   That all things weighs, and nothing can admire;
       That dares prefer the toils of Hercules
       To dalliance, banquets, and ignoble ease.
            The path to peace is virtue: what I show,
       Thyself may freely on thyself bestow:
       Fortune was never worship'd by the wise;
561   But, set aloft by fools, usurps the skies.

Juvenal's *beatus vir* seems purely Stoic in his austerity and in his insistence that the path to peace is virtue.

Among the great bulk of Dryden's translations, those discussed here cannot be said to loom large quantitatively. They reveal one bias among many. Once this has been granted, one may, I think, contend that Dryden's selection of *beatus ille* passages from Lucretius, Horace, and Juvenal was a conscious choice, and that his superior poetic powers resulted in translations of such high quality that they must be considered as much a work of art as the originals. Never before had the classical versions of the happy life been presented with greater poetic intensity.

The Restoration miscellanies are fertile hunting-grounds for translations of *beatus ille* poetry. The sixteen-eighties in particular saw the publication of a number of miscellanies crammed with translations of briefer classical poems or selections from longer works.

In Dryden's first miscellany (*Miscellany Poems*, 1684) Thomas Otway's translation of Horace's Ode II, 16 shifts the emphasis away from the Horatian *parva rura* to the happiness of 'soft content'. In the same volume is found Rochester's translation of Horace's Ode I, 4[25] — if one can call it a translation. It is much

248

more of a free paraphrase. Horace's ode describes the advent of spring in impersonal terms, and concludes with the grave moral that the brevity of life should teach us to moderate our wishes. Rochester's version is frankly erotic; while Horace had described the stately dance of nymphs and graces, Rochester permits his Shepherdesses and their Swains to 'steal in private to their covert Groves, / There finish their well heighten'd Loves.' Rochester finally adds a story of the 'City Dame' who leaves town for the country solely in order to 'bribe, then grasp some Country Clown'. And the moral of it all is summed up as follows: 'Since all the World's thus gay and free, / Why should not we? / Let's thus accept our Mother Nature's Treat, / And please our selves with all that's sweet.' I suppose Rochester felt that the many erotic Horatian odes warranted his introducing the same note into poems where it is not present. The bias of the age was in favour of erotic poetry, and Horace's love poems therefore came in for a great deal of attention. Thus the sixteen Horatian odes translated by Flatman for Dryden's second miscellany are pervaded by a mood fittingly summed up in these lines from Ode IV, 11:

> Come *Phillis*, gentle *Phillis!* prithee come,
> I have a Glass of rich old Wine at home,
> And in my Garden curious Flowers do grow,
>   That languish to adorn thy brow.[26]

Even the grave Sir George Mackenzie praised country life only when it was graced by love:

> O happy country life, pure like its air,
> Free from the rage of pride, the pangs of care!
> Yet all these country pleasures, without love
> Would but a dull and tedious prison prove.[27]

In his preface to *Sylvae* (1685) Dryden admits that he translated the passage on love from the fourth book of Lucretius, because 'the obscenity of the subject' pleased him: ' ... without the least formality of an excuse, I own it pleas'd me: and let my enemies make the worst they can of this confession.'

The anonymous translation of Horace's Epistle I, 18 in the 1684 miscellany offers a further instance of the deliberate softening of the Horatian ideal. The epistle discusses the problem of human virtue or happiness, placing it in the golden mean: *virtus est medium vitiorum et utrimque reductum* ('Virtue is a mean between vices, remote from both extremes'). Horace's advice is to read and question the wise men of this earth, so that one can learn to pass one's days in tranquillity, and he concludes with a pious wish for a settled mind and a competence. The translator expands the last six lines into fourteen:

> What thoughts d'ye think those easie Joy's inspire?
> What do you think I covet and desire?
> 'Tis, that I may but undisturb'd possess,
> The littl' I have, and if Heaven pleases, less;
> That I to Nature and my self may give,
> The little time that I have left to live;
> Some Book's in which I some new thoughts may find,
> To entertain, and to refresh my mind;
> Some Horses, which may help me to partake
> The lawful pleasures which the seasons make;
> An easie plenty, which at least may spare
> The frugal pains of a Domestick care;
> A Friend, if that a faithful Friend there be,
> Who can love such an idle life, and me;
> Then Heav'n, give me but life and health, I'le find
> A grateful Soul, and a contented Mind.[28]

The Horatian emphasis on simplicity, frugality, and mental serenity has been exchanged for one on idleness and easy joys. The translator, however, was probably in good faith, and would surely have protested most vigorously if faced with the charge of having distorted the text. To him, Horace was an Epicurean whose wish for obscurity was tantamount to a desire for ease; when Horace recommends country life and simple fare, he really means a pleasant and carefree existence marked by an 'easy plenty'.

Two further examples of the same tendency are found in Dryden's third miscellany (1693). Rochester's friend, Wolsley, translated Catullus's 35th poem under the title 'Invitation into the Country'.[29] Wolsley seized upon the town-country aspect, and expanded the description of the rural joys into an Anacreontic passage. The anonymous translator of Horace's Ode II, 3[30] commits a similar indiscretion by transforming this grave Horatian ode on the necessity of preserving an even mind, into an apology for 'sweet ease and rest':

> Be thy Lot good, or be it ill,
> Life ebbs out at the same rate still:
> Whether with busy Cares opprest,
> You wear the sullen time away;
> Or whether to sweet Ease and Rest,
>   You sometimes give a day:
>   Carelessly laid,
>   Underneath a friendly Shade
> By Pines, and Poplars, mixt embraces made;
>   Near a River's sliding Stream,
> Fetter'd in Sleep, bless'd with a Golden Dream.
>
> Here, here, in this much envied state,
> Let every Blessing on thee wait...

It was said of Archbishop Tillotson that he conveyed such a 'charming Idea' of God that 'it is alone sufficient, without any further Argument, to make the *Atheist* wish there were a Deity'.[31] Similarly Lord Halifax stated that 'A wise Epicure would be religious for the sake of Pleasure'.[32] It is therefore logical enough that the *beatus ille* philosophy was similarly treated, so that the motivation for seeking solitude or country life was given an Epicurean slant. As the century wore on, the *res rusticae* were gradually covered by a veneer of fine polish which made them as attractive as any of the scenes of ambition so ostentatiously spurned. Obscurity became synonymous with ease, and a frugal simplicity with true pleasure. In the light of this development, it is easier to understand how a man like Sir William Temple could seriously protest that he was made for a farmer, and not a courtier. Like the probing psychoanalyst, the Restoration translators stripped all Stoic camouflage off the core of the classical philosophy of the happy life, courageously displaying it in complete Epicurean nakedness. Never before had a nymph been so nude; the philosophic strip-tease could go no further, and the acclaim of the public was correspondingly enthusiastic.

2.

From Orinda to Wycherley

In the poetry of Mrs. Philips retirement is a major motif, but hers is a retirement *à deux* rather than the uncompromising solitude of the religious devotee. It is typical of the period that even the latter came to cultivate the noble art of friendship. The Platonic friendship between John Evelyn and the saintly Mrs. Godolphin springs to mind, and even that archetypal rake, the Earl of Rochester, confessed that 'if there bee a reall good upon Earth 'tis in the name of friend, without wch all others are meerly fantasticall'.[33] The Restoration cult of friendship is a further development of the Platonic *précieuse* cult of the first half of the century, the chief difference being the addition of Epicurean arguments. Thus Anthony Collins's *Discourse of Free-Thinking* (1713) praises Epicurus for having placed the virtue of friendship so high in his scale of values:

... *Epicurus* declares it to be his Opinion, That of all things which Wisdom can procure towards a happy Life, Friendship

is the noblest, most extensive, and delicious Pleasure ... what
a numerous, what an harmonious Company of Friends, did
Epicurus croud into his own little Habitation! And the *Epi-
cureans* follow his example at this day.

Collins did not hesitate to draw the conclusion that Christians
would do well to listen to Epicurus: '... we Christians ought
still to have a higher Veneration of *Epicurus* for this Virtue of
Friendship than *Cicero*: Because even our *Holy Religion it self*
does not any where *particularly* require of us that Virtue.' [34]

Mrs. Philips's pronounced preference for retirement has a
biographical background. Although possessed of strong Royalist
sympathies, she married a Puritan from South Wales. Placed in
an inimical environment, what more natural than that she should
try to establish a charmed circle of happiness over which the
'boisterous world' would have no control? Whether she was as
successful in real life as she pretends to be in her poetry, is doubtful. Against her poems on the blessings of true friendship should
be put those where she exclaims bitterly at the faithlessness of
her chosen intimate. It is also doubtful that Mrs. Philips ever
presided over a literary salon or circle; if it existed, it did so
chiefly on paper.

The poetry of the 'matchless Orinda' is marked by the fusion
of Neoplatonic with Epicurean ideas. It has been pointed out
that her views on the nature of true friendship were strongly
influenced by Francis Finch's *Discourse on Friendship*, written
in 1653 and circulated in manuscript among the friends of the
author.[35] However, decidedly Epicurean ideas can also be traced,
and her emphasis on the joys of friendship often seems more
Epicurean than Platonic. She was moved much more strongly by
the desire to create a circle of perfect happiness for herself and a
friend, than by the wish to penetrate to the source of all being;
nor did she discover traces of the actual presence of God in the
landscape of retirement. She loved retirement for the sake of
pleasure, just as Halifax loved God for the sake of pleasure. Arch-

bishop Tillotson tried to convert the atheist and the sceptic by painting a picture of a God, intent on procuring the greatest happiness for the greatest number.[36] Similarly, Mrs. Philips tried to gain converts to the creed of retirement through her spirited poetic descriptions of the supreme happiness of retirement *à deux*. In so doing she leaned heavily on the Lucretian description of the happiness of the gods in the first book of the *De Rerum Natura*:

> The *Gods*, by right of Nature, must possess
> An everlasting Age of perfect Peace:
> Far off remov'd from us and our Affairs;
> Neither approach'd by *Dangers*, or by *Cares*:
> Rich in themselves, to whom we cannot add:
> Not pleas'd by *Good* Deeds; nor provok'd by *Bad*.[37]

This is the archetypal pattern of happiness which men must try to copy.

The key concepts in Mrs. Philips's portrayal of happiness are *innocence, friendship, retreat* from 'all bold noise', *privacy*, and *happy quiet*. 'Content,[38] and 'A retir'd Friendship. To Ardelia'[39] denounce courts, mere physical beauty, riches, and ambition in the traditional style. However, instead of placing content in that 'serious evenness that calms the breast'[40] or in the ecstatic garden experience, she prefers to define it as the state of mind enjoyed by two loving friends in their complete retirement from the world:

> These far remov'd from all bold noise,
> And (what is worse) all hollow joys,
> Who never had a mean design,
> Whose flame is serious and divine,
> And calm, and even, must contented be,
> For they've both Union and Society.
> Then, my Lucasia, we who have
> Whatever Love can give or crave;
> Who can with pitying scorn survey

> The trifles which the most betray;
> With innocence and perfect friendship fir'd,
> By Virtue join'd, and by our choice retir'd
>
> Whose mirrors are the crystal brooks,
> Or else each other's hearts and looks;
> Who cannot wish for other things
> Than privacy and friendship brings:
> Whose thoughts and persons chang'd and mixt are one,
> Enjoy Content, or else the World hath none.
>   (Stanzas 10-12 of 'Content')

'A retir'd Friendship' makes the same points:

> Come, my Ardelia, to this Bower,
>   Where kindly mingling souls awhile,
> Let's innocently spend an hour,
>   And at all serious follies smile.
>
> Here is no quarrelling for crowns,
>   Nor fear of changes in our fate;
> No trembling at the Great One's frowns,
>   Nor any slavery of state.
> . . . . .
> Here let us sit and bless our stars,
>   Who did such happy quiet give,
> As that remov'd from noise of wars,
>   In one another's hearts we live.

Like the Lucretian gods, Orinda's retired friends enjoy complete detachment from every-day affairs; they are not even faintly stirred by a wish to engage in any action outside their own circle. The centre of existence is no longer outside man, in God; it is in man himself, in his 'soul self-mov'd'.[41] The *beatus vir* is neither saint nor contemplator, but one who

23   ... in the beauty of his ordered mind
     Doth still a new, rich satisfaction find.
     Innocent epicure! whose single breast
     Can furnish him with a continual feast.
     . . . . .
33   Others do court applause and fame, but he
     Thinks all that giddy noise but Vanity.
     . . . . .
37   He's still himself, when company are gone,
     Too well employ'd ever to be alone.
     For studying God in all his volumes, he
     Begins the business of Eternity;
     And unconcern'd without, retains a power
42   To suck (like bees) a sweet from ev'ry flower.[42]
                                ('Happiness')

If *innocent* is one of Mrs. Philips's favourite epithets, *unconcerned* is another. Her ode 'Upon Mr. Abraham Cowley's Retirement' [43] states directly that in order to be happy one must have no concern for the rest of the world: 'Who will be happy, must be unconcern'd, / Must all their comfort in their bosom wear, / And seek their treasure and their power there.' The ode is a sustained defence of a Lucretian retreat from the world:

18   In my remote and humble seat
      Now I'm again possest
     Of that late fugitive, my breast,
    From all thy tumults and from all thy heat
22   I'll find a quiet and a cool retreat;
     . . . . .
33   For thy inconstant sea, no more
     I'll leave that safe and solid shore:
     . . . . .
47   No other wealth will I aspire,
     But that of Nature to admire;

Nor envy on a laurel will bestow,
50   Whilst I have any in my garden grow.
            And when I would be great,
            'Tis but ascending to a seat
        Which Nature in a lofty rock hath built;
        A throne as free from trouble as from guilt.
55   Where when my soul her wings does raise
            Above what worldlings fear or praise,
        With innocence and quiet pride I'll sit,
        And see the humble waves pay tribute to my feet.
        O life divine, when free from joys diseas'd,
60   Not always merry, but 'tis always pleas'd!

Those only can boast of possessing the world, who enjoy it least;
Cowley was such a man:

73   For lo, the man whom all mankind admir'd,
            (By ev'ry Grace adorn'd, and ev'ry Muse inspir'd)
            Is now triumphantly retir'd.
            The mighty Cowley this hath done,
        And over thee [i. e. the world] a Parthian conquest won:
78   Which future ages shall adore...

Although Orinda, like Marvell, spurns the laurel, her soul soaring
above the sordid world like a bird, one feels nevertheless that
hers is a much more superficial existence. Her attention is directed
at herself rather than at God or the divine principle in life.

Mrs. Philips's Epicurean definition of happiness appears
plainly from her panegyric on a deceased friend, whom she praises
for having been an 'unconcern'd spectator' of the world:

17   Thy even mind, which made thee good and great,
            Was to thee both a shelter and retreat.
        Of all the tumults which this World do fill,
20   Thou wert an unconcern'd spectator still...[44]

257

Whenever Mrs. Philips describes country life, one can observe a perceptible softening of the Stoic elements in the classical tradition. 'A Country-life'[45] begins with the traditional denunciation of the world and praise of solitude:

1   How sacred and how innocent
            A country-life appears,
        How free from tumult, discontent,
            From flattery and fears!
5   This was the first and happiest life,
            When man enjoy'd himself;
            . . . . .
25   What blessings doth this World afford
            To tempt or bribe desire?
        Her courtship is all fire and sword,
            Who would not then retire?
        Then welcome, dearest Solitude,
30   My great felicity;
        Though some are pleas'd to call thee rude,
            Thou art not so, but we.

In the succeeding lines a thoroughly Restoration love of rest and of unconcerned aloofness modifies the Stoic mood:

33   Them that do covet only rest,
            A cottage will suffice:
            . . . . .
41   When all the stormy World doth roar
            How unconcern'd am I!
        I cannot fear to tumble lower
            Who never could be high.
45   Secure in these unenvied walls
            I think not on the State,
            . . . . .
69   Let others (nobler) seek to gain
            In knowledge happy fate,

258

> And others busy them in vain
>   To study ways of State.
> But I, resolved from within,
>   Confirmed from without,
> 75 In privacy intend to spin
>   My future minutes out.
> And from this hermitage of mine
>   I banish all wild toys,
> And nothing that is not Divine
> 80   Shall dare to tempt my joys.

The 'Invitation to the Country' in the same manner places the *summum bonum* in rural retirement graced by the company of one true friend. Friendship has usurped the throne erected by the Hortulan Saint for his solitary ecstasy:

> 39 Kings may be slaves by their own passions hurl'd,
>   But who commands himself commands the World.
>   A country-life assists this study best,
>   Where no distractions do the soul arrest:
>   There Heav'n and Earth lie open to our view,
>   There we search Nature and its Author too;
> 45 Possess'd with freedom and a real state
>   Look down on Vice, and Vanity, and Fate.
>   There (my Rosania) will we, mingling souls,
>   Pity the folly which the World controls;
>   And all those grandeurs which the World do prize
> 50 We either can enjoy, or will despise.

'A Reverie'[46] gives a fair summary of Orinda's attitude towards retirement and also reveals both her strength and her weakness as a lyric poet:

> 1 A chosen privacy, a cheap content,
>   And all the peace a friendship ever lent,
>   A rock which civil Nature made a seat,

A willow that repulses all the heat,
5   The beauteous quiet of a summer's day,
A brook which sobb'd aloud and ran away,
Invited my repose, and then conspir'd
To entertain my Fancy thus retir'd.
As Lucian's ferry-man aloft did view
10   The angry World, and then laugh'd at it too:
So all its sullen follies seem to me
12   But as a too-well acted tragedy.

The philosophic lyric could be effectively handled by Mrs. Philips, but not always did she manage to express her reflections with sufficient lyric grace. The brook which 'sobb'd aloud and ran away' is a glorious example of the worst effects of the pathetic fallacy. However, many of her poems have a positive charm of their own, and they are interesting for the light which they shed on the process whereby the Hortulan Saint was metamorphosed into an Innocent Epicurean. Mrs. Philips clearly seized upon the theme of retirement as she found it in the works of Cowley, Vaughan, and St. Amant (whose ode to solitude she translated), and then proceeded to give it her own interpretation or bias. The clear spirituality of the earlier group did not survive this process. To Mrs. Philips the landscape of retirement served largely to entertain her fancy or to provide a soft background against which could be sketched the outlines of two loving friends. In her terminology retirement became synonymous with the repose enjoyed by an unconcerned, innocent Lucretian spectator; the ecstatic, transcendent element was lost, and the enjoyment of oneself and a friend furnished the chief motivation for seeking rural retirement.

The Matchless Orinda to-day may be known only to the specialist, but in her own day and age she was greatly admired and widely read. Editions of her poems were issued in 1664, 1667, 1669, 1678, and 1710, and we know that they passed from hand to hand in manuscript long before they were published. Much of this popularity must have been due to the simplicity of her style. Tired with metaphysical obscurity, the reader of the 1660's turned with pleasure to the uncomplicated, yet pleasantly philosophical lyrics of the Matchless Orinda. In her work they could find a sort of reader's digest of the more difficult themes of the better poets, and there was also enough original material in it to provide a stimulus not afforded by anybody else. What Vaughan and Marvell had written about retirement may have been far superior in poetic merit, but neither of these succeeded in reaching the public to the same degree.

If it is felt that it shows poor judgment in readers and critics alike to favour Mrs. Philips above more competent masters, it must not be forgotten that the vogue for metaphysical poetry declined sharply after 1660. The development, during the Restoration, of a new poetical style and of new poetical genres, was inevitable since it was the result of the changing intellectual preferences of the century. It has also been convincingly argued by Mr. Bateson that it was connected with the growth of the English language.[47] The new era frowned upon obscurity and ambiguity; it disliked individual eccentricities and took no interest in problems of mere personal relevance. What was wanted was a 'clear, unerring, universal Sense' which 'Cheers like the Sun with gen'ral Influence'.[48]

To a lover of Marvell, the greatest deficiency of Mrs. Philips's verse probably is found in the utterly superficial treatment of the landscape of retirement. However, in this respect Mrs. Philips reflects the tendency of the age. Most Restoration poets viewed Nature, like Mrs. Philips, as an elegant setting suitable to the detached spectator of the folly of the world. This is true of the Earl of Roscommon, Charles Cotton, Thomas Flatman, Nahum Tate, John Norris, and the Countess of Winchilsea. It will be recognised that these exponents of the theme of retirement are the minor poets of the period. The major stars were busy in

261

other hemispheres, penning satires and mock epics, or erotic lyrics without much depth or sincerity of passion. Lyrics were still being written, but the most significant poems of this era were satirical and argumentative rather than lyrical. It may be tempting to present our minor poets as an opposition party which voiced the sentiments of the non-classicist part of the English Parnassus, and to describe them as a slighted minority group whose rights received no vindication until the dawn of the Romantic period. This has also been done. The nature lyrics of Anne, Countess of Winchilsea, have often enough been classified as pre-Romantic, particularly since Wordsworth explicitly recommended her 'Nocturnal Reverie' for its lovely descriptions of natural scenes. Coleridge did the same for Charles Cotton. However, a belated benediction from Wordsworth or Coleridge can scarcely be said to make any one a pre-Romantic. This minority group was actually firmly linked with the growing interest in classical motifs, and their wistful poems on the happiness of country life were as much a product of English Neoclassicism as Pope's *Rape of the Lock*. The nature poetry even of Charles Cotton and the Countess of Winchilsea, so far from being isolated examples of a unique character (as Myra Reynolds suggests[49]), fits into the general pattern formed by the fortunes and misfortunes of the predominantly classical tradition of the *beatus vir*.

If one were to choose a single poem that could serve as a typical example of the Restoration interpretation of this classical tradition, no better choice can be made than the Earl of Roscommon's popular 'Ode Upon Solitude'.[50]

The theme of Roscommon's ode is the traditional one of the vanity of the world and the wisdom of remaining aloof from all ambitious pursuits. The voice and manner, however, are those of the new age. Despite its lyric form, which is that of the Pindaric, the poem is plainly didactic. Roscommon was more concerned with imparting a general lesson than with recording his own experience of the happiness of solitude:

> Hail, Sacred *Solitude!* from this calm Bay,
> I view the World's Tempestuous Sea,
>   And with wise Pride despise
>   All those senseless Vanities:
> With Pity mov'd for others, cast away
> On Rocks of hopes, and Fears, I see 'em toss'd,
> On Rocks of Folly, and of Vice I see 'em lost:
> Some the prevailing Malice of the Great,
>   Unhappy Men, or Adverse Fate,
> Sunk deep into the Gulphs of an afflicted State.
> But more, far more, a numberless prodigious Train,
> Whilst Virtue courts 'em, but alas in vain,
>   Fly from her kind embracing Arms,
> Deaf to her fondest Call, blind to her greatest Charms,
> And sunk in Pleasures, and in brutish Ease,
> They in their Shipwreck'd State themselves obdurate please.

This opening stanza derives its most effective imagery from Lucretius' description of the Detached Spectator. The *beatus vir* has been removed from his Sabine farm and instead placed on the cliff by the edge of the treacherous sea of the world. The stanza impresses by its passionate sincerity, and may be characterised as the Restoration counterpart to the vision of the Hortulan Saint.

The second stanza blends the manner of Cowley with that of the Matchless Orinda, perhaps in a conscious effort to emulate them both:

> Hail, Sacred *Solitude*, Soul of my Soul,
>   It is by thee I truly live,
> Thou dost a better Life and nobler Vigour give;
> Dost each unruly Appetite controul:

Thy constant Quiet fills my peaceful Breast,
With unmix'd Joy, uninterrupted Rest.
    Presuming Love does ne'er invade
    This private Solitary Shade;
And, with fantastick Wounds by Beauty made,
The Joy has no Allay of Jealousy, Hope, and Fear,
The Solid Comforts of this happy Sphere;
    Yet I exalted Love admire,
    Friendship, abhorring sordid Gain,
And purify'd from Lust's dishonest Stain:
Nor is it for my Solitude unfit,
For I am with my Friend alone,
    As if we were but one;
'Tis the polluted Love that multiplies,
But Friendship does two Souls in one comprise.

Roscommon's ode provides a perfect example of the refined intellectual Epicureanism of the Restoration. Unstirred by mere sensual delights, his *beatus vir* knows the true peace and serenity of the Lucretian gods. Characteristically enough, his solitude has ample room for a friend, and in the third stanza the pronoun changes from 'I' to 'we'. In this stanza, too, the emphasis is thrown emphatically on the pleasures of rest, which by definition are those of intellectual pursuits and true friendship:

Here in a full and constant Tide doth flow
    All Blessings Man can hope to know;
Here in a deep Recess of Thought we find
Pleasures which entertain, and which exalt the Mind;
Pleasures which do from Friendship and from Knowledge rise,
Which make us happy, as they make us wise:
Here may I always on this downy Grass,
Unknown, unseen, my easy Minutes pass:
'Till with a gentle Force Victorious Death

My *Solitude* invade,
And, stopping for a-while my Breath,
With Ease convey me to a better Shade.

The tone of this ode is admirable in its sustained serenity; the mood and the style are perfectly co-ordinated. This may not be very profound poetry, but as far as it goes it is extremely successful as an expression of the Restoration attitude to life. This attitude is almost completely Epicurean; the largely Stoic *beatus ille* formula has been abandoned in favour of the Lucretian description of the happiness of the Detached Spectator. There is not even a glancing allusion to the husbandman and his rural pursuits; the *beatus vir* is a Restoration gentleman, devoted to 'constant Quiet' and 'uninterrupted Rest' in quest of pleasures which both entertain and exalt the mind.

The poetry of Charles Cotton, published posthumously in 1689, is somewhat less typical of the age than the Earl of Roscommon's. His philosophy of life was more influenced by Stoic thought than was the general rule after 1660, as is evidenced by his translations of Montaigne's essays and Guillaume du Vair's *Morall Philosophy of the Stoicks* (1664). Cotton's *Planter's Manual* (1675) and, above all, his continuation of Walton's *Compleat Angler* (1676), demonstrate his fondness for the sports and occupations of the countryside. Cotton was a thorough country squire (and a pure-bred Tory Anglican) who confessed himself never really happy except at Beresford Hall, as well as a student of philosophy, a translator, and a minor poet.

This background of a necessity predisposed Cotton to accept the philosophy of retirement, which he so interpreted as to strike a golden mean between Horace and Lucretius. This compromise is no where better expressed than in 'The Retirement,' [51] some irregular stanzas addressed to Walton and printed in the expanded 1676 edition of the *Compleat Angler*.

The key-note of 'The Retirement' is delight in solitude. Solitude provides the only true happiness, which consists in leisured ease and innocence. I quote stanzas 2-5:

Good God! how sweet are all things here!
How beautiful the fields appear!
How cleanly do we feed and lie!
Lord! what good hours do we keep!
    How quietly we sleep!
What peace! what unanimity!
How innocent from the lewd fashion
Is all our bus'ness, all our conversation!

Oh how happy here's our leisure!
Oh how innocent our pleasure!
Oh ye valleys, oh ye mountains,
Oh ye groves and crystal fountains,
    How I love at liberty
By turn to come and visit ye!

O Solitude, the soul's best friend,
That man acquainted with himself dost make,
And all his Maker's wonders to intend;
    With thee I here converse at will,
    And would be glad to do so still;
For it is thou alone that keep'st the soul awake.

How calm and quiet a delight
        It is alone
To read, and meditate, and write,
By none offended, nor offending none;
    To walk, ride, sit, or sleep at one's own ease,
And pleasing a man's self, none other to displease!

Cotton's lyric reflects the influence of Cowley in form and content. Its mood favours both Stoic serenity and Epicurean ease, and in

the lines on the cleanness of the country we sense the reaction of
the north countryman to the London 'Clowds of Smoake and
Sulphur, so full of Stink and Darknesse.'[52] The third stanza quoted harks back to the more spiritual interpretation of the function
of solitude, but there is no trace of the mystic vision of the
Hortulan Saint.

Political allusions are sometimes encountered in Cotton's praise
of country life. In the politically unstable years of the Stuart
regime, the classical philosophy of happiness could obviously be
used by the Tories to pour ridicule upon their Whig opponents.
'Contentation'[53] displays a pleasing formal simplicity reminiscent
of the ballad, but its content makes it a philosophic ode. Cotton
characterises 'Titles and Wealth' as 'Fortune's Toyls / Wherewith
the Vain themselves ensnare',

> Nor is he happier than these,
>   Who in a moderate estate,
> Where he might safely live at ease,
>   Has Lusts that are immoderate.
>
> . . . . .
>
> A very little satisfies
>   An honest, and a grateful heart,
> And who would more than will suffice,
>   Does covet more than is his part.
>
> That man is happy in his share,
>   Who is warm clad, and cleanly fed,
> Whose Necessaries bound his Care,
>   And honest Labour makes his Bed.
>
> Who free from Debt, and clear from Crimes,
>   Honours those Laws that others fear,
> Who ill of Princes in worst Times
>   Will neither speak himself, nor hear.

. . . . .

Who, with his Angle, and his Books,
  Can think the longest day well spent,
And praises God when back he looks,
  And finds that all was innocent.

That man is happier far than he
  Whom publick Business oft betrays,
Through Labyrinths of policy,
  To crooked and forbidden ways.

The classical message is parodied very entertainingly in 'Saphick
Ode':

How easie is his Life, and free,
  Who, urg'd by no necessity,
Eats chearfull Bread, and over night does pay
    For's next day's *Crapula.*

No suitor such a mean estate
  Invites to be importunate,
No supple flatt'rer, robbing Villain, or
    Obstreperous Creditor.

This man does need no Bolts nor Locks,
  Nor needs he start when any knocks,
But may on careless Pillow lie and snoar,
    With a wide open door.[54]

Cotton had every reason to speak feelingly on the topic of importunate creditors; his straitened circumstances prompted a
deeply-felt ode on poverty,[55] where he exclaims against his 'bloody
Persecutors', asking, 'For Heav'ns sake, let me but be quiet'.

The carefree and happy angler re-appears in 'The Angler's
Ballad',[56] a singularly pleasant poem:

The Angler is free
From the cares that degree
   Finds it self with so often tormented;
And although we should slay
Each a hundred to-day,
   'Tis a slaughter needs ne'er be repented.

And though we display
All our Arts to betray
   What were made for man's Pleasure and Diet;
Yet both Princes and States
May, for all our quaint Baits,
   Rule themselves and their People in quiet.

. . . . .

Whilst quiet we sit
We conclude all things fit,
   Acquiescing with hearty submission;
For, though simple, we know
That soft murmurs will grow
   At the last unto down-right Sedition.

And the ballad ends with a pious wish for 'long life to our King *James* the Second'.

   'To my Freind Mr. John Anderson'[57] compares city life with rural retirement. The tone is again humorous:

     First, wee have here no bawling Dunnes,
     Nor those feirce things ycleped Bummes,

     . . . . .

     And then, wee've no unwholsome Dames,
     To broil us in their bawdy flames,
    Nor need inquire after Physitians names,
       That may befriend us.

The same tone marks the 'Epistle to John Bradshaw Esq.' the purpose of which is to describe the poet's relief at returning home from his travels:

> And now I'm here set down again in peace,
> After my troubles, business, Voyages,
> The same dull Northern clod I was before,
> Gravely enquiring how Ewes are a Score,
> How the Hay-Harvest, and the Corn was got,
> And if or no there's like to be a Rot;
> Just the same Sot I was e'er I remov'd,
> Nor by my travel, nor the Court improv'd;
> . . . . .
> My River still through the same Chanel glides,
> Clear from the Tumult, Salt and dirt of Tides,
> And my poor Fishing-house, my Seat's best grace,
> Stands firm and faithfull in the self-same place
> I left it four months since ...
> So that (my Friend) I nothing want but thee
> To make me happy as I'd wish to be;
> And sure a day will come I shall be bless'd
> In his enjoyment whom my heart loves best;
> Which when it comes will raise me above men
> Greater than crowned Monarchs are, and then
> I'll not exchange my Cottage for *White-hall*,
> *Windsor*, the *Louvre*, or th' *Escurial*.[58]

Cotton's fondness for country life was no mere philosophic pose; his appreciation of the pursuits of the country, and his delight in rural scenes appear in everything he wrote. The idea of a convivial retirement was particularly congenial to his frame of mind. 'Then let the chill Sirocco blow', he observes in his lines on 'Winter',

> Whilst we together jovial sit
> Careless, and Crown'd with Mirth and Wit;

Where though bleak Winds confine us home,
Our Fancy round the World shall roam.[59]

John Norris (1657-1711) was poet, priest, and philosopher.
Henry More was his avowed spiritual father, and many of his
poems are pervaded by Neoplatonic thought. However, his treatment of *beatus ille* motifs reveals such a profound indebtedness
to Epicurean ideas that it is impossible to place him among the
Hortulan Saints. Although little known to-day, Geoffrey Walton
has recently entered a plea for recognition of his poetic talent,[60]
and I think that one must agree that Norris has undoubted poetic
charm.

Like Cowley and Mackenzie, Norris wrote an essay on solitude,
proving that 'the *Satisfactions* and *Advantages* of Solitude (to a
person that knows how to improve it) are very great, and far
transcending those of a *Secular* and *Popular* Life'.[61] When describing the supreme pleasures inherent in a solitary life, Norris
had recourse to Lucretian terms and phrases:

... the Solitary and Contemplative man sits as safe in his
Retirement as one of *Homer's Heroes* in a Cloud, and has this
only trouble from the follies and extravagancies of men, that
he *pitties* them ... he lives to himself and God, full of serenity
and Content.

Norris's 'Divine Hymn on the Creation'[62] similarly defines God
in Epicurean terms as 'one unmov'd self-center'd point of rest'.
If this is true, the question naturally arises why God troubled
to create a world at all, 'why not indulge his self-sufficient state,
/ Live to Himself at large, calm and secure, / A wise eternal
epicure?' The answer is that God was moved to create 'Beings
that might participate / Of their Creator's happy state'. The
desire of the individual for self-centred bliss is thus sanctioned
by God himself as an expression of His divine purpose. The Innocent Epicurean in this manner becomes a deeply religious figure.

271

In accordance with this view Norris, in his ode 'To Dr. More',[63] addresses the Cambridge Platonist as an 'intellectual epicure':

> Whilst to be great the most aspire,
> Or with low souls to raise their fortunes higher.
> Knowledge ...
> Was made thy choice; for this thou hast declin'd
> A life of noise, impertinence, and state,
> . . . . .
> How calm thy life, how easie, how secure,
>   Thou intellectual epicure.

Norris's translation of Seneca's well-known choral ode reveals the same Epicurean bias. While Seneca had merely expressed a wish for the sweet quiet of an obscure position, Norris requests permission of the gods to lie at ease, enjoying the 'soft minutes':

> Let me in some sweet shade *serenely lye*,
> Happy in *leisure* and *obscurity*:
>   Whilst others place their joys
>   In *popularity* and *noise*.
> Let my soft minutes glide *obscurely on*
> Like *subterranean* streams, *unheard, unknown*.[64]

Stanzas 3-4 of 'The Retirement',[65] a poem inspired by Cowley's 'The Wish', depict the *beatus vir* inside a solitary grove, where he enjoys a state of self-contained happiness. Norris's rejection of political responsibility is absolute; the ideal state is that of Adam before Eve was created:

> Here in this shady lonely grove,
> I sweetly think my hours away,
> Neither with business vex'd, nor love,
> Which in the world bear such tyrranick sway:
> No tumults can my close apartment find,
> Calm as those seats above, which know no storm or wind

Let plots and news embroil the State,
Pray what's that to my books and me?
Whatever be the kingdom's fate,
Here I am sure t' enjoy a monarchy.
Lord of myself, accountable to none,
Like the first man in Paradise, alone.

Stanza 5 removes the Happy Man out of his grove, transforming
him to a Lucretian detached spectator of the follies of the world:

While the ambitious vainly sue,
And of the partial stars complain,
I stand upon the shore and view
The mighty labours of the distant main,
I'm flush'd with silent joy, and smile to see
The shafts of Fortune still drop short of me.

'Sitting in an Arbour'[66] opens in a Stoic vein, and its first
stanza may owe something to Horace's Ode III, 16:

Thus ye good powers, thus let me ever be
Secure, retir'd, from love and business free;
The rest of your great world I here resign
  To the contentions of the great;
  I only ask that this retreat,
  This little tenement be mine.
All my ambition's to this point confin'd;
Others inlarge their fortunes, I my mind.

In the rest of the poem, however, the pious Anglican minister
proves as self-centred as the Earl of Rochester:

How calm, how happy, how serene am I!
How satisfy'd with my own company!
. . . . .

273

Thus I affect an independent state,
And — as a creature can — in self I terminate.
. . . . .

That bliss which others seek with toil and sweat
    For which they prodigally wast
      Their treasures, and yet miss at last,
    Here I have at an easie rate.
So those that costly physick use in vain,
Sometimes by cheap receipts their health obtain.

These lines should be compared to Rochester's statements: 'Born to myself, I like myself alone',[67] and

    In my Dear Self I center every Thing,
    My Servants, Friends, my Mistress, and my King,
    Nay Heaven and Earth to that one Point I bring.[68]

In their complete self-sufficiency, the Restoration divine and the Restoration rake are made to share the same Lucretian mantle.

Of all Norris's poems on retirement, 'My Estate'[69] reveals the strongest feeling for Nature, and for this reason comes closest to the mood of the mid-century:

    Throughout the works divine I cast my eye,
    Admire their beauty, and their harmony,
      I view the glorious host above,
      And Him that made them, praise and love,
      The flowery meads and fields beneath,
      Delight me with their odorous breath.
. . . . .
Nay — what you'd think less likely to be true —
I can enjoy what's yours much more than you.
      Your meadow's beauty I survey,
      Which you prize only for its hay.
      There can I sit beneath a tree,
      And write an ode or elegy.

What to you care, does to me pleasure bring.
You own the cage, I in it sit and sing.

Although Norris depicts his *beatus vir* as a solitary contemplator of rural scenes, his interpretation of the landscape of retirement differs radically from that of the Hortulan Saint. Despite his discipleship to Plato, Norris reveals no preoccupation with mystic beliefs concerning the penetration of the material universe by the world of the spirit. What Norris discovers, is evidence of the absolute prevalence of a visible order and harmony so often mourned for lost by the previous generation. As we read on in the poetry of the final years of this century, we shall discover that praise of the ordered universe tends to assume increasing importance. Its connection with the new world view associated with the names of Descartes and Newton will also become apparent, as will the fact that the insistence on the beauty of the universe represents a continuation of the Neoplatonic impulse.

Few Restoration poets wrote as persistently about retirement, or as significantly, as John Norris. In his poetry echoes of the past mingle with visions of the future. By virtue of his Neoplatonism Norris was the direct descendant of the Hortulan Saints, while his pronounced Epicureanism aligns him with the generation of John Dryden and the Earl of Rochester. Finally, through his exploitation of the new motif of the ordered universe Norris anticipated one of the most typical strains of the age of Pope.

John Rawlet (1642-1686) is another Anglican clergyman-poet whose attitude towards retirement was based upon the Epicurean principle of self-enjoyment. Rawlet's paraphrase 'On *Psalm* 39. 6, 7'[70] printed in his *Poetick Miscellanies* (1687) expresses a clear preference for the Lucretian pinnacle:

> In a retired Hermitage I dwell,
> Where no disturbance can approach my Cell;
> Where scarce with any noise my ears are struck,

But th' gentle murmurs of a purling Brook,
Or the soft whispers of the Winds that move
The trembling Leaves of an adjoyning Grove;
Or the sweet musick of the winged Quire,
Unto whose mirth and freedom I aspire.
Here with a calm and easie mind I sit,
From throngs, from bus'ness, and from passions quit:
And hence, as from an higher Region, I
The ways of mortals on this Earth descry...

Rawlet's ode 'On Solitude' [71] bears witness to the pervasive influence of Cowley's retirement poetry. Through its seventeen stanzas sound all the well-known arguments in favour of solitude. Solitude improves the mind and provides the only real pleasure, which is to love oneself properly by retiring into oneself:

1

Welcome sweet Solitude, who loves not thee,
    Loves not himself: for only he
    Who from the busie throng is quit,
He to retire into himself is free,
    He with himself may sit.

2

Than our Dear self is any thing more Dear?
    Shall we then seem to hate or fear
    What most we love? yet so do they
Who rather had been rambling here, and there,
    Than with themselves to stay.

8

Then welcome, Solitude, abhor'd by none,
    But Fools and vicious Men alone;
    Whilst courted by the Wise and Good,
Who by Fruition have its blessings known,
    Its pleasure's understood.

276

9

Whilst they hither, from the World remove,
  In all that's Good they do improve,
  And here where nothing can annoy,
Rendring themselves worthy of their own love,
  Themselves they do enjoy.

17

Thus on the Banks of *Thames* great *Cowley* chose
  His private *Chertsey* for repose;
  Cowley whose Verse like those rich streams,
So deep, as clear, in various numbers flows,
  And long shall last as *Thames*.

Among the court wits of the Restoration William Wycherley
(1640-1716) has an honourable place. Few other Restoration poets
damned middle-class industry and morality with more masculine
vigour, or were more persistently preoccupied with the analysis
and defence of *ease*.

Wycherley's '*Song, in praise of Solitude*'[72] is more thoroughly
Epicurean than even Roscommon's ode on solitude. Despite its
title, the poem is argumentative rather than lyrical, and it exhibits
the same fondness for the moral paradox which marks the essays
of Sir George Mackenzie. The key concepts of Wycherley's song
are *innocence, wise selfishness,* and *self-sufficiency*:

Most Happy, he himself may boast,
  Whose Happiness depends on none;
Who, for his knowing this World most,
  Lives in it, to it, most unknown;
Who scorning to Proud Knaves, or Fools, to creep,
For Want of Pride, does Distance with 'em keep;
Who, but the more for his Self-Love,

For others has more Charity;
His Innocence, but more to prove,
　Does hide his Head most Hon'rably;
Who but the more, for his Wise Selfishness,
Of Avarice, or Vanity, has less;

Who but much more the wiser grows,
　As of the World more ignorant;
More Self-sufficiency he shows,
　Shows less his Pride, his Fear, or Want,
Is to himself a God on Earth alone,
In Want of no Good, since in Care for none;

So Solitude, just Selfishness,
　Does the World's Selfishness prevent;
Makes Man's Peace more, as his Fear less,
　Him more safe, as more innocent;
To gain more Honour, Ease, for want of Pelf,
By Content, all-sufficient to himself.

This defence of wise selfishness comes close to seeming cynically insincere, a *tour de force* or a mere display of the art of the paradox. The style is greatly influenced by the terseness of the fashionable maximes of which Wycherley wrote a great number.

The Lucretian spectator of the world also appears in the argumentative poem 'For *Solitude* and *Retirement* against the *Publick, Active Life*':

Alone, remov'd from Grandeur and from Strife,
And ev'ry Curse that loads a publick Life,
In Safety, Innocence, and full Repose,
Man the true Worth of his Creation knows.
. . . . .
To him, the Rural Cottage does afford
What he prefers to the *Patrician* Board:
. . . . .

But all is quiet, jocund, and serene,
A Type of Paradise, the Rural Scene!
Here may he sit, and on the Rocky Shore
See distant Storms, and hear the Billows roar,
And count the Wrecks on the tost Ocean spread,
Safe from each Surge that curls its ridgy Head.
Here he may laugh, in Privacy and Ease,
At guilty Grandeur, and its Fopperies;
. . . . .
For all true Happiness, we must confess,
Is more, as it depends on Others less.
His Happiness we then must greatest own,
When it depends upon Himself alone.
. . . . :
More Ease, Peace, Safety to our selves we gain,
As we from Publick Commerce more abstain.[73]

A private life is best, because the private man is least in the
power of fickle fortune. The more a man comes to know the
world, the fonder will he grow of solitude. Soldiers, lawyers,
merchants, and ministers of state sacrifice present ease for a toil
which postpones the enjoyment of life till a future and very
uncertain date. Towns are dangerous, because full of infections,
and passions sway one more easily when one is in company. Only
in solitude can one attain to anything like serenity of mind. The
happiest men, therefore, are those 'who themselves of publick
Life deprive, / Interr'd in peaceful Solitude alive.'

The feeling that Wycherley argues for the sake of the clever
phrasing of the argument, is confirmed on reading his lines 'For
the publick Active Life, against Solitude'.[74] The fact that this
poem is only one fourth the length of the defence of solitude
may suggest a certain bias, but may also simply be due to the
fact that the former topic lent itself more readily to paradoxical
statements.

19

Although Wycherley scarcely can be called an exponent of the philosophy of retirement, his belief in the superior happiness induced by ease and privacy cannot be doubted. Other of his poems can be quoted in this context, such as his lines on *'Ease, the Wish and Endeavour of all Men, lost by their too eager Pursuit of it'*, *'In Praise of Laziness'*, and *'Upon the Idleness of Business. A Satyr'*.

Wycherley's poems, controversial as their tone often is, and wilfully abusive, constitute a strong attack by a man of wit on the men of sense. His frequent attacks on business, zeal, ambition, and avarice are strong and vigorous, a circumstance partly due to the character of his verse. So far from padding his lines, Wycherley pressed so much paradoxical meaning into them that they often are difficult to understand.

3.

The Amorous Grove

In an age of erotic poetry it was inevitable that the *beatus ille* themes should be incorporated into the popular love songs of the day. Patterns for this sort of writing could be found in French poetry as translated by Thomas Stanley, the Earl of Roscommon, Philip Ayres, and Mrs. Aphra Behn. Thomas Stanley's translation of St. Amant's 'La Jouyssance'[75] may serve as an example:

> Far from the court's ambitious noise
> Retir'd, to those more harmless joys
> Which the sweet country, pleasant fields,
> And my own court, a cottage, yields;
> I liv'd from all disturbance free,
> Though prisoner (Sylvia) unto thee;
> . . . . .
> Now, in some place where Nature shews
> Her naked beauty, we repose;
> . . . . .

Now with delight transported, I
My wreathed arms about her tie;
The flattering Ivy never holds
Her husband Elm in stricter folds:
To cool my fervent thirst, I sip
Delicious nectar from her lip.

The *beatus ille* themes sounded initially have been completely subordinated to the erotic scene, which is the real topic, and even Nature herself is turned into an innocent voluptuary who delights in showing her naked beauties.

Similar use is made of the landscape of retirement in the Earl of Roscommon's 'The Grove,' a translation of part of the fifth scene of the second act of Guarini's *Pastor Fido*. Few other poems were reprinted more frequently in the poetic miscellanies of this period. Other examples are found in the *Lyric Poems* (1687) by Philip Ayres. Love is the main motif of 'His Retirement,' 'Being retired, complains against the Court,' and 'Invites his Nymph to his Cottage,' all of which are translations from Girolamo Preti.[76] 'In Praise of a Country Life' [77] pretends to be 'An Imitation of Horace's Ode, Beatus ille,' but, as Mr. Praz has shown, is in reality a rendering of Garcilaso de la Vega's imitation of Horace's second Epode. In this imitation, as rendered by Ayres, country life has become a 'divine retirement' with prevailingly idyllic features:

The bliss which souls enjoy above,
He seems on Earth to share,
Who does divine retirement love,
And frees himself from care,
Nor thought admits which may his peace control,
But in a quiet state contents his bounded soul.

The Happy Man hates all faction, servility, and dishonesty and instead enjoys a pastoral serenity:

281

In pleasant shades enjoys his ease,
  No project spoils his sleep,
With rural pipe himself can please,
  And charm his wand'ring sheep,
Till to his cottage in some quiet grove,
By dusky night's approach he's summon'd to remove.

The open fields of the Sabine farm have been exchanged for the closed confines of the grove with its idyllic cottage, the husband-man for a shepherd.

Thomas Otway provides an English version of the erotic *beatus ille* poem in the 'Epistle from Mr. Otway to Mr. Duke.' [78] The desire for liberty is primarily a desire for free love:

How happy are we in this sweet Retreat?
Thus humbly blest, who'd labour to be great?
· · · · ·
No Cares or Business here disturb our Hours,
While underneath these shady, peaceful Bow'rs,
In cool Delight and Innocence we stray,
And midst a thousand Pleasures waste the Day.

Horace's erotic verse is highly praised: 'With Thoughts of Love, and Wine, by him we're fir'd, / Two Things in sweet Retirement much desir'd.' At night, 'Each takes th' obedient Treasure of his Heart, / And leads her willing to his silent Bed,' where 'ev'ry Sense with perfect Pleasure's fed,' until 'in full Joy dissolv'd, each falls asleep / With twining Limbs, that still Love's Posture keep.'

It was no doubt this type of poem which provoked Thomas Shadwell to pen the following lines in 'The Tory-poets: A Satyr' (1682):

Happy are they in Amorous Fields, that Rove
And Sing no other Songs then those of love;
Whose Verses treat of nought but careless ease,
And in their Sonnets only strive to please.[79]

One Tory poet who deservedly would have felt the point of Shadwell's satire, was Mrs. Aphra Behn. Thus T. C., in a commendatory poem, praised the poetess for her ability to stimulate erotic passion: 'In the same Trance with the young pair we lie, / And in their amorous Ecstasies we die.' [80]

Mrs. Behn stressed two different points in her treatment of the theme of rural retirement: (1) the Epicurean innocence and happiness of rural life and of earlier ages, and (2) the erotic freedom enjoyed by men before society grew corrupt. Like Sir George Mackenzie, Aphra Behn believed that it is easy to be virtuous; it consists in nothing but a reversion to a state of nature. Strip away all corrupt ambition and perverted desires, and you will achieve physical health, mental serenity, and moral superiority.

This kind of reasoning, so far from denoting a relapse from the growing rationalism of the century, was a direct outcome of the belief in reason as the noblest part of man and the magic cure-all of all afflictions. If reason is inherent in all men and the equal inheritance of all, a reversion to a state of nature becomes tantamount to a revival of the reign of reason, and the Golden Age (or state of innocence) becomes the age in which blind and destructive passions as yet had not upset the original mental and emotional balance of man. Mrs. Behn interpreted this reign of reason as a state in which the noble passion of love was unhampered by false conceptions of honour, dignity, or worth, and so to the classical denunciation of ambition she added her own of false honour and modesty. Apart from this additional qualification, she did not change the current definition of a happy life. In all other respects, her *beatus vir* is the same innocent Epicurean who occupies the stage in the poetry of Mrs. Philips, the Earl of Roscommon, John Norris, and Thomas Otway.

Mrs. Behn was the first to popularise the concept of the Noble Savage. As we shall soon see, there is little difference between Mrs. Behn's Noble Savage and the Restoration *beatus vir*. The similarity is such that one suspects a genetic connection between the two.

Mrs. Behn's familiarity with the philosophy of retirement is easily established. Most of her literary friends were interested in the idea of retirement (Dryden, Otway, Nahum Tate, Cotton), and one of her early plays — *The Amorous Prince* (1671) — contrasts the innocence of rural life with the corruption of court and city. Moreover, in a letter to Mrs. Price we find her defending her prolonged stay in the country-side with the usual *beatus ille* formula:

> My Dear,
> In your last, you admir'd how I cou'd pass my Time so long in the Country: I am sorry your Taste is so deprav'd as not to relish a Country-Life. Now I think there's no Satisfaction to be found amidst an Urban Throng (as Mr. *Bayes* calls it).
> The peaceful Place where gladly I resort,
> Is freed from noisy Factions of the Court:
> There joy'd with viewing o'er the rural Scene,
> Pleas'd with the Meadows ever green,
> The Woods and Groves with tuneful Anger move,
> And Nought is heard but gentle Sighs of Love.[81]

Mrs. Behn's most important poem on rural retirement, 'The Golden Age,' [82] is a paraphrase of a translation of a French poem. In addition to the traditional features of the Golden Age — a serene climate, peace, rich crops from untilled soil, and contentedness derived from a total absence of all ambition — supreme importance is attached to the freedom to love. Then, no scorned shepherds were tortured by love, jealously, or fear, 'Then it was glory to pursue delight.' The greatest enemy of this *beatus vir* is not so much business or avarice or ambition — although these are bad enough — as a wrong sense of honour. Honour, it seems, belongs only among the vicious and those fired by ambition: be gone, therefore, 'and make thy Fam'd resort / To Princes Pallaces,' 'Be gone and interrupt the short Retreat, / Of the Illustrious and the Great.' Mrs. Behn's praise of the Golden Age exploits traditional *beatus ille* arguments:

Then no rough sound of Wars Alarms,
Had taught the World the needless use of Arms:
Monarchs were uncreated then,
Those Arbitrary Rulers over men:
. . . . .
Till then Ambition was not known,
That Poyson to Content, Bane to Repose;
Each Swain was Lord o'er his own will alone,
His Innocence, Religion was, and Laws.
. . . . .
Right and Property were words since made,
When Power taught Mankind to invade:
When Pride and Avarice became a Trade;
Carri'd on by discord, noise, and wars . . .

In the total absence of greed, ambition or wild desires, no form
for external government would be needed. Reason does all the
work, in co-operation with the benevolent scheme of Nature. As
soon as the passions rebel, the light of reason is obscured, wars
follow, and governments assume tyrannical sway. There is no
reason to suspect that Mrs. Behn's general assault upon tyrannic
monarchies had special application to the Stuart regime.[83] Her
lines on honour ('Go break the Politician's sleep, / Disturb the
Gay Ambitious Fool, / That longs for Scepters, Crowns, and Rule')
can easily be interpreted as a reference to the Whig intrigues. The
moral of the poem as a whole is definitely Tory in its recommendation of peaceful acquiescence and its denunciation of the miseries imposed upon men by the pride and avarice of merchants. Her
ideal of free love would, of course, be acclaimed only by the aristocratic wits clustering around the court.

Ever since its first popularity in the years before the Civil War,
the semi-primitivistic philosophy of rural retirement had flourished almost exclusively in Royalist, conservative circles. From the
days of William Habington and Mildmay Fane to Charles Cotton

and the Countess of Winchilsea, the chief exponents of the *beatus ille* creed were strongly anti-Puritan and anti-Republican. It is scarcely possible to decide whether Mrs. Behn scorned commerce, industry, and capitalist enterprise simply because she was a Tory, or whether she was led to adopt this attitude because she had accepted the half Stoic, half Epicurean formula for happiness. Both reasons may have played their part. A third possible reason is her attitude towards love. Scenes of rural retirement logically enough form the best environment for a pair of passionate lovers.

Mrs. Behn's well-known prose story *Oroonoko* presents an appealing picture of the Noble Native. His chief characteristic is his tranquillity. He is *sibi imperiosus* to a much higher degree than the civilised Europeans, because taught to be so by Nature. There is little actual primitivism in such an interpretation, nor was Mrs. Behn persistently partial to natives as such, since Oroonoko's father, the king, is as much a slave to passion as the white slave-owners and the governor of Surinam. Mrs. Behn's scale of values depended, not upon the degree of civilisation, but upon psychological factors. Whoever embodied the virtues characteristic of the Golden Age, was a hero and a shining example to others. Oroonoko obviously represents the ideal man; he was the true lover of Mrs. Behn's erotic dreams as well as the detached spectator of the vices and follies of men. He was also the complete gentleman, well versed in history and languages.[84]

A more traditional picture of rural retirement is found in 'A *Farewel to* Celladon, *On his Going into* Ireland.' The poem opens with a violent diatribe against 'business' in the best Restoration style:

> Bus'ness Debauches all his hours of Love;
> Bus'ness, whose hurry, noise, and news
> Even Natures self subdues;
> Changes her best and first simplicity,
> Her soft, her easie quietude
> Into mean Arts of cunning Policy.[85]

Celladon's soul, however, was framed for 'Glorious and Luxurious Ease,' and he should not let ambition destroy the intention of Heaven and Nature. Ireland is described as a veritable earthly paradise, where true happiness may be achieved:

> Divert him all ye pretty Solitudes,
> And give his Life some softning Interludes:
>> That when his weari'd mind would be,
>> From Noise and Rigid Bus'ness free;
> He may upon your Mossy Beds lye down,
>> Where all is Gloomy, all is Shade,
>> With some dear Shee, whom Nature made,
>> To be possest by him alone ...

The motif of amorous retirement can be traced through a number of Mrs. Behn's lyrics, so suffice it here to single out perhaps the best specimen, 'A Voyage to the Isle of Love.' [86] Although a paraphrase of a French poem, it is one of Mrs. Behn's best poetic efforts. A short extract will suffice to convey an idea of Mrs. Behn's ideal world:

> A thousand gloomy Walks the Bower contains,
>> Sacred all to mighty *Love*;
> A thousand winding turns where Pleasure reigns;
> Obscur'd from day by twining Boughs above,
>> Where Love invents a thousand Plays,
>> Where Lovers act ten thousand Joys:
> . . . . .
> Recesses Dark, and Grotto's all conspire,
>> To favour *Love* and soft desire;
>> Shades, Springs, and Fountains flowry Beds,
>> To Joys invites, to Pleasure leads,
> To Pleasure which all Humane thought exceeds.

Before the century was out, the partly Hedonistic, partly Epicurean impulse of the Restoration was definitely on the wane, and a more serious and reflective tendency again makes itself felt. The change from aristocratic immorality to a more serious code of behaviour was gradual. Attempts to reform the manners and morals of the age were made as early as the sixteen-eighties, but not till the days of Addison and Steele did it become possible seriously to recommend the sober ideal of a Christian gentleman and to apply it to the upper classes. This transition to a more serious moral note will now be traced through the work of certain minor poets from the last few years of the century.

4.

End of the Century

Nahum Tate (1652-1715), who in 1692 succeeded Thomas Shadwell as Poet Laureate, may easily have been awarded this distinction because of the professed moral bias of his verse. Tate's first volume of poetry (1677) contains moralising reflections 'On the Present Corrupted State of Poetry,' [87] and fourteen years later he declared in the preface to *Characters of Vertue and Vice* that the true task of poetry is the 'Representing of *Vertue* and *Vice* in their respective *Beauties* and *Deformities*.' Poetry should provide useful 'Prescriptions of Politic and Private Life,' and the *Miscellanea Sacra* published in 1693 and 1698 were obviously designed to provide such prescriptions.

Tate's attitude, however, was not always consistent, just as his personal behaviour was far from blameless; he was given to drink and was constantly harassed by creditors. Moreover, his early connection with Dryden and with the court of the Stuarts marks him as a Tory and a man of wit rather than a man of sense. Tate's poems on retirement reflect the same dual tendency. Some of these profess an aristocratic distaste for 'business' and for any kind of public responsibility, while others advocate a positively bourgeois morality.

'Stephen's Complaint on quitting his Retirement' [88] is a vigorous diatribe against business, in the vein of Cowley, John Norris, and Aphra Behn. A more serious note is heard in 'The Gratefull Shepheard' [89] — a poem which describes the innocence of country life and the corruption of town and court. The value of a contented mind and the prudence of lying low form the topic of 'The Gold-hater,' 'The Ingrates,' and 'Disappointed.' [90] 'The Prospect' [91] pursues the same ideas and, in so doing, employs the Lucretian image of the detached spectator who views the tempest-tossed seas, wisely deciding that it is much safer to be a looker-on.

'The Choise' [92] is an excellent example of the middle-of-the-road wish which was to become so popular after the publication of John Pomfret's poem by the same name in 1700. In its attempt to establish a rational compromise between extremes it is prophetic of the spirit of moderation which was to prevail before the century was out. Tate's lines, it is true, are indebted to the Horatian wish for the *parva rura* (see particularly Satire II, 6) and to the Senecan wish for obscurity in the choral ode from *Thyestes*; however, his prudent compromise between a religious life and a life of pleasure is a completely original departure:

> Grant me, indulgent Heav'n, a rural Seat,
>   Rather contemptible than great;
> Where though I taste Life's Sweets, still I may be
>   Athirst for Immortality.
> I wou'd have Business, but exempt from Strife;
>   A private, but an active Life.
> A Conscience bold, and punctual to his Charge;
>   My Stock of Health, or Patience large.
> Some Books I'd have, and some Acquaintance too;
>   But very good, and very few.
> Then (if one Mortal two such Grants may crave)
> From silent Life I'd steal into my Grave.

One is tempted to paraphrase: 'I would like to have my cake, and eat it, too!' Cowley's 'The Wish' had revealed no such desire to make the best of two worlds, and Rowland Watkyns, too, aimed at a true classical mediocrity when he wrote a poem by the same name for his collection *Flamma Sine Fumo* (1662):

> A little house, a quiet wife,
> Sufficient food to nourish life,
> Most perfect health, and free from harm,
> Convenient cloths to keep me warm.
> The liberty of foot, and mind,
> And grace the ways of God to find.
> This is the summe of my desire,
> Until I come unto heavens quire.[93]

Tate, in contrast to Cowley and Watkyns, is not intent on limiting his desires; he seems, instead, to be outlining a type of existence which might be his, only if 'indulgent Heav'n' would give it to him. His series of compromises is prompted by prudent considerations; he would like to enjoy himself, but without incurring censure for being worldly. Tate is obviously the middle-class poet, whose uncertain income makes him yearn for the security of a rural seat, and one suspects him of glancing hopefully at some prospective patron capable of supplying that which is needed. In the first half of the eighteenth century this sort of poem was to become increasingly common, and many of them were nothing but a hopeful bid for patronage on the part of would-be poets. While pretending to scorn ambition, these poets actually describe an existence far beyond their own means, and an existence based on a number of external requirements. Tate's poem is the first hint of a development in this direction.

In the dissenting Whig pamphleteer, John Tutchin (1661?-1707), we have the first exception to the rule that only Tories

and Anglicans would write about the happiness of rural retirement. Tutchin adopted the classical philosophy in an effort to
clean out the Augean stables of Restoration literature, Cowley's
moral essays providing the inspiration. Tutchin himself refers
to Cowley in the preface to his *Poems* (1685), where he complains
that 'the Abuse of *Poetry* has been very great in these latter Ages;
and since Mr. *Cowley,* there has been none that has endeavoured
to Rectifie it.'[94] Cowley, therefore, was the poet whom Tutchin
wished to imitate, and in so doing he fastened almost exclusively
on that part of Cowley's authorship in which the philosophy of
happiness is expounded. Tutchin's essay, 'A Discourse of Life',[95]
is nothing but a summary of the contents of Cowley's essays, and
it is also written in the same style. Like Cowley, Tutchin decided
that the life of a country gentleman was the happiest:

> Were Envy a Vertue, I should exercise it in nothing more
> than in coveting a Country-Man's Life, who has... enough to
> make him an ordinary Gentleman, and not enough to advance
> him to the place of a Justice of the Peace; enough to secure
> him from Contempt, and not enough to make him Honourable,
> or Miserable, which you please: For Honour is a perplexing
> Plague, the damn'd Fatigue of Life, the Devil that bewitches
> Mortals, the *Ignis fatuus*, that leads Men into Ruine...

Rural solitude is an imitation of the state of innocence:

> What greater Pleasure can there be than to live retir'd?...
> To live Retired, is to imitate our pristine state of Innocence,
> e're Rapine and Cruelty had invaded our World. But, Alas!
> herein is our Misery, we never can attain to the Happy State
> of our Fore-Father: He lived in a Garden, so may we; but it
> cannot be an *Eden:* He was retir'd in a glorious obscurity, we
> may be so too; but here is the fatal consequence, our Passions,
> our Lusts, our Inordinate Desires still accompany us: But yet
> for all this, Solitude is a thing the nearest Happiness of any;
> for though we have our Passions always with us... yet in
> Solitude they are better tamed... Indeed Solitude is an Anti-
> dote against all the raging Plagues of the Tumultuous World.[96]

Still following Cowley, Tutchin breaks out into Pindaric praise
of solitude. I quote stanzas 2 and 3:

> First State, and Best of Men!
> Free from all Cares!
> *Ancorite Adam* happy still had been,
> Free from Lust, and free from Fears
> Had not Company and Vice come rowling in;
> And with it all that Mortals vex:
> Envy pale, and Discontent
> Hand in hand together went;
>
> . . . . .
>
> The greatest *Scipio* Thee admir'd,
> After his Conquests to a Grove retir'd.
> 'Tis Solitude that gives us Rest;
> 'Tis Solitude inspires each noble Breast.
> In vain's the giddy Noise of worthless Schools,
> Or Taverns cramm'd with loads of Knaves and Fools;
> Let them boast on of Wit in Company,
> While all the Wise grow Great in good Obscurity.[97]

The attack on taverns and the knaves and fools who boast of
wit, sufficiently reveals Tutchin's concern with a reformation of
manners, and the antagonism felt by a man of sense for the men
of wit. Tutchin concludes his essay with a passage in the tradition
of Cowley's 'The Wish':

> Grant me, good *God!* a Melancholy Seat,
> Free from the Noise and Tumults of the Great:
> Like some Blest Man, who his Retinue sees
> A Tall and sprightly Grove of servile Trees,
>
> . . . . .
>
> A Place where *Lust* and *Passion* die away,
> And some good Friends make long the tedious Day.
> Fraught full of Mirth, the Hours more Joy would bring,
> Than the black Days attend a Regent King.[98]

292

Despite his close imitation of Cowley's tone and manner, Tutchin has failed to re-capture that magic which turns words into poetry. The chief interest of his work therefore lies in the fact that a moral reformer realised the usefulness of Cowley's *Essays and Discourses* (and of the poetry imbedded in them) and hence imitated them in an effort to invest literature with moral dignity. The philosophy of rural retirement, so far the exclusive possession of Tory poets, with Tutchin entered the parlour of the middle-class Whig and moral reformer. However, not till the publication of John Pomfret's *The Choice* (1700) can it be said to gain the general acclaim of this part of the English nation.

A moralised Epicureanism marks Thomas Heyrick's *Miscellany Poems* of 1691. 'A Pindarique *Ode in Praise of* Angling'[99] echoes sentiments popularised by Charles Cotton:

> May I (far from desire of being Great)
>   Enjoy a little Quiet Seat,
>   That overlooks a *Chrystal* Stream:
>   With Mind as Calm, as is her Brow,
> Pure as the Fountain, whence her Waters flow;
> Those Pleasures tast a *Cynick* could not blame.

'On Sleep'[100] praises the innocent pleasures which dwell in 'Humble Cotes and silent Cells', deploring the *'Noise* of Business' which robs the soul of ease. Heyrick's panegyric 'On the Right Honourable *John* Earl of *Rutland*'[101] depicts the Earl as a Lucretian spectator:

> A scheme of Life, like Yours, *Lucretius* laid,
> (Whose Boundless Wit all Nature's works survey'd)
> And fitted to th' Immortal Gods, he made:
> He gave them what would most Divinely please;
> And lull'd them up in bless'd *Content* and *Ease.*

In imitation of Lucretius Heyrick wrote 'The Submarine Voyage. A Pindarique Ode',[102] which covers sixty-seven pages, and whose purpose is to describe life under and by the sea in all the oceans of the world. The opening stanzas depict the poet as standing on a Lucretian promontory by the sea; then comes the inevitable storm which wrecks a ship, and the poet moralises in accepted fashion on the instability of earthly glory and the dimness of man's intellectual vision. In the course of his imaginary journey through the seven seas, Heyrick arrives at undiscovered South Sea islands, where noble natives live in perfect happiness amid scenes of uncorrupted Nature:

> Here fixt *Content* doth place her Seat,
> Beyond ev'n Philosophick Notions Great.
> Happy in Ignorance, they know no more,
> Than Nature's humble Store;
> Pleas'd with their state, they Strangers are to Care,
> They nothing hope for, and they nothing fear.
> [Book IV, stanza 6]

Heyrick did not confuse these noble natives with real savages, whose 'bloody Teeth on Men's Entrails lay'. Like Thomson (and Mrs. Behn) he distinguished between savagery and an ideal state of Nature.

'The Retirement' [103] by William Walsh, one of Dryden's friends, gives conventional praise to a highly stereotyped grove. Equally conventional are the lines 'On the Happyness of a Retir'd Life' [104] written by Dryden's son, Charles, and sent to his father from Italy. Of greater interest is *The Innocent Epicure: Or, The Art of Angling* (1697), written by J. S. and published by Nahum Tate. In its interpretation of the happy life, this poem combines new and old features. Tate's preface refers to the landscape of retirement drawn by the poet as a good 'Copy of that Original Landskip of Retirement, which was long since so admirably drawn by *Horace*.' The introductory poem ('From J. S. to C. S.') paraphrases Horace's Epistle I, 10, and does so in a manner influenced by Abraham Cowley. The halieutic is completely pervaded by the refined Epicureanism of this generation. Angling represents, not only content, simplicity, and innocence, but also 'the Pleasures of the Wise' and 'unrepented Ease'. After a passage in praise of life on one's own paternal acres, the poet deplores his own lack of such an estate. His wealthier friend, however, has everything a man could wish for:

> Oh Friend! oh Friend! what Fortune's so Divine,
> What Fate's so safe or sweet as that of thine?
> . . . . .
> Thou chear'st the Minutes, for to thee they bear
> Scarce the minutest part of human Care:
> Thus by the Streams, and there supinely laid,
> With Thoughts for which Mankind was chiefly made:
> No Care, no Mischief in thy worst Intent,
> All, like thy Recreation's innocent.
> Through Nature's Opticks thou dost wisely look,
> And readst thy Maker in the fairest Book.[105]

J. S. seems to have borrowed the tone of voice of his patron, Nahum Tate, in this passage, which in fact is a disguised request for financial aid. The conclusion points a similar moral:

> Blest might I live an honest Country Swain,
> And with content in little compass Reign:
> No spacious Fabricks would I care to boast,
> Convenient Neatness would delight me most;
> Where from my Shades I could with joy survey
> Expanding Meads...
> If falling Waters reach'd from far my Ear,
> 'Twould raise the Landskip and depress my care:
> Far off some good old Tow'r shou'd strike my view,
> And teach the certain state of things below.
> There neighb'ring grandeur might unenvi'd reign,
> While I'm allow'd by all the Happy Man.

All this is nothing but a series of accepted clichés, and the poem would have been entirely unremarkable, if it had not been for the introduction of the motif of the 'beauteous order' of the world, an order which can be established by rational inquiry. This motif was to predominate in the next century. Although closely connected with contemporary science, this motif has retained something of the Neoplatonic fervour so typical of the seventeenth century:

> Come here ye Fools, though in Opinion Wise.
> Come here and see with natural Reason's Eyes.
> Reason, your Boast, though an imperfect Guide,
> The weighty Controversy shall decide.
> In beauteous order see the Waters move,
> And show like Motion in the Spheres above.
> . . . . .
> Though Gay the Sun his Course each Morn renews,
> Chance cannot hold the Reins could she the Work produce.
> No! here consistent Beauty Rules the whole,
> Mov'd by an Ardent and Continual Soul.[106]

After the turn of the century, this appeal to natural reason came to outweigh any other, and the landscape of retirement was praised primarily because it offered visible proof of the existence of God by virtue of the ordered beauty everywhere visible.

The Happy Man portrayed by J. S. is quite a composite character. He combines the features of the Innocent Epicurean with those of an 'honest country Swain', seasoning the mixture with the intellectual spice provided by the rational contemplation of the ordered universe. His landscape is similarly composite: partly rural fields, partly country estate, and partly the whole cosmic frame.

The poetry of George Granville (Lord Lansdowne), the Countess of Winchilsea, and Lady Mary Chudleigh remained unpublished until the next century, but is included here because it was largely written in the last two decades of the seventeenth. Their prevailing Lucretian interpretation of the *beatus vir* also marks their poetry as of the preceding age.

George Granville, Lord Lansdowne (1666-1735) has been described as 'politically honest in an age when political honesty was a plant of rare growth'.[107] As a result of the Glorious Revolution of 1688, Granville was forced into retirement on his Yorkshire estate, where he proceeded, like so many before him, to apply a Horatian therapy to his mental wounds.

Granville's version of the second Chorus in the second act of Seneca's *Thyestes*[108] uses the text as a pretext for imparting a political lesson:

> When will the gods, propitious to our prayers,
> Compose our factions and conclude our wars?
> . . . . .
> Place me, ye Pow'rs! in some obscure retreat;
> O keep me innocent, make others great!
> In quiet shades, content with rural sports,
> Give me a life remote from guilty courts,
> Where, free from hopes or fears, in humble ease,
> Unheard of, I may live and die in peace.

The verse epistle 'To Mrs. Higgons Occasioned by some verses written by that lady, and sent to the Author in his retirement, 1690'[109] presents Granville's refusal to leave his peaceful obscurity. When penning this refusal, Granville had recourse to the Lucretian figure of the Detached Spectator, rather than the Horatian husbandman. The larger part of the poem expresses contempt for the England of William of Orange, 'an impious world, contriv'd for knaves and fools'. In such circumstances, who can blame the poet for wishing to imitate the aloofness of the Lucretian gods?

When the winds blow, and loud the tempests roar,
What fool would trust the waves and quit the shore?
. . . . .

Happy the man, of mortals happiest he,
Whose quiet mind from vain desires is free;
Whom neither hopes deceive nor fears torment,
But lives at peace, within himself content;
In thought or act accountable to none,
But to himself and to the gods alone.
. . . . .

From hence, as from a hill, I view below
The crowded world, a mighty wood in show!
Where sev'ral wand'rers travel day and night
By diff'rent paths, and none are in the right.

The retirement of Anne Finch, Countess of Winchilsea (1666-1720), was also politically motivated. Unable to reconcile themselves to the Revolution settlement, Anne Finch and her husband (then Colonel Finch) retired into the country-side to glean whatever comfort they could find from the peaceful obscurity of rural scenes.

'The Petition for an Absolute Retreat' [110] is one of her best known poems. It adheres to the pattern already established by Cowley, Tate, and others, but Lady Winchilsea's version is poetically superior and patently sincere:

> Give me O indulgent Fate!
> Give me yet, before I dye,
> A sweet, but absolute Retreat,
> 'Mongst Paths so lost, and Trees so high,
> That the World may ne'er invade,
> Through such Windings and such Shade,
> My unshaken Liberty.

This absolute retreat should be free from false alarms and malicious gossip, and, although solitary, should include the presence of a devoted husband and equally devoted friends. Like Horace, she would serve no extravagant delicacies at her table ('spread without my Care'), only the seasonal produce of the soil, and her costume should be modest and expressive of 'Unaffected Care-lessnesse'. Lady Winchilsea's ideal life is marked, above all, by a sincere piety and great moral earnestness, and her final desire for 'Contemplations of the Mind' is ripe with the yearnings of the soul to whom the world has nothing to offer.

'A Poem, Occasion'd by the Sight of the 4th Epistle Lib. Epist: 1 of Horace'[111] praises the quiet retreat of a friend, while 'Love, Death, and Reputation'[112] associates love with rural plains and soft repose. 'An Invitation to Dafnis'[113] strikes a humorous note only too infrequently encountered:

> The Cristall springs, shall murmure as we passe,
> But not like Courtiers, sinking to disgrace;
> Nor, shall the louder Rivers, in their fall,
> Like unpaid Saylers, or hoarse Pleaders brawle;
> But all shall form a concert to delight,
> And all to peace, and all to love envite.

Lady Winchilsea's claim to fame is based almost entirely on 'A Nocturnal Reverie',[114] the poem which Wordsworth applauded for its detailed observation of natural scenes. The 'Reverie' gives fine lyrical expression to the desire for that 'serious evenness' which calms the breast; it is also thoroughly original and seems to owe little to literary inspiration:

> In such a *Night*, when every louder Wind
> Is to its distant Cavern safe confin'd;
> And only gentle *Zephyr* fans his Wings,
> And lonely *Philomel*, still waking, sings;
>   . . . . .
> When in some River, overhung with Green
> The waving Moon and trembling Leaves are seen;
>   . . . . .

299

When a sedate Content the Spirit feels,
And no fierce Light disturb whilst it reveals;
But silent Musings urge the Mind to seek
Something, too high for Syllables to speak;
Till the free Soul to a compos'dness charm'd,
Finding the Elements of Rage disarm'd,
O'er all below a solemn Quiet grown,
Joys in th' inferiour World, and thinks it like her Own:
In such a *Night*, let Me abroad remain,
Till Morning breaks, and All's confus'd again;
Our Cares, our Toils, our Clamours are renew'd,
Or Pleasures, seldom reach'd, again pursu'd.

'A Nocturnal Reverie' occupies the half-way mark between Milton's *Il Penseroso* and Gray's *Elegy Written in a Country Churchyard*. Like Milton, the Countess stressed the sweetness of midnight walks and silent musings, and, like Gray, she leant towards the pathetic or slightly sentimental. There is nothing overtly 'Romantic' about Lady Winchilsea's wish for retirement. What she desires is complete tranquillity of mind and body based on a withdrawal from the world and strengthened by the reflective mood of the midnight scenes.

Lady Mary Chudleigh (1656-1710) has been characterised as a seventeenth-century gentlewoman, neglected by her husband, who tried to find solace in retirement and reading, and whose interest in friendship was not as Platonic as it is presented in her verse.[115] Her moral seriousness, however, cannot be denied, and her interest in the new vision of the ordered universe points forward to the age of Pope. Historically she is a very useful figure, since her poetry clearly shows how the new motif of the ordered universe was closely connected with the Lucretian version of the *beatus ille* philosophy. There is also a clear line from John Norris, the avowed Platonist, to Lady Chudleigh; in her praise of retirement she followed both Norris and Mrs. Philips.

Lady Chudleigh's *Essays Upon Several Subjects in Prose and Verse* (1710) follow in the footsteps of Cowley, Mackenzie, and Norris in their comprehensive defence of retirement as the only happy way of life. 'Of Knowledge'[116] and 'Of Solitude' touch most directly on the issues with which we are concerned. The influence of the new science (including the psychology of Locke) is discernible in the exhortation to attend to *things* rather than *words*, and in the programme outlined for the education of women, the contemplation of Nature plays an important part because it is seen to provide knowledge of God. There is an unmistakable Platonic fervour in the passage which describes how the soul, by contemplating the effects, may rise to a contemplation of the First Cause and the 'Foundation of all Perfections'. However, a certain amount of logic, geometry, and physics is required in order to derive the most benefits from such a contemplation. History, characteristically enough, is reduced to a moral spectacle; in its pages the reader can observe the turbulent sea of the world and notice the striking difference between the frantic activity of fools and the wise passivity of the detached spectator. Since the chief activity of the retired person consists in studies and contemplation of Nature, not everybody is qualified to profit from it:

> To render a private Life truly easie, there must be Piety, as well as humane Knowledge, uncorrupted Morals, as well as an Insight into Nature, a Regardlessness of Wealth, at least no eager Solicitude for it, a being wean'd from the World, from its Vanity, its Applause, its Censure, its Pomp ...[117]

The preface to *Poems On Several Occasions* (1703) defines happiness in terms which underline the necessity of remaining completely aloof from the world. The only way to be truly easy, to be always serene, is to 'retire into our selves, to live upon our own Stock'.

'On the Death of his Highness the Duke of *Glocester*'[118] opens with a confession of the personal faith of the poetess:

301

I'le take my Leave of Business, Noise and Care,
And trust this stormy Sea no more:
Condemn'd to Toil, and fed with Air,
I've often sighing look'd towards the Shore:
And when the boistrous Winds did cease,
And all was still, and all was Peace,
Afraid of Calms, and flatt'ring Skies,
On the deceitful Waves I fixt my Eyes,
And on a sudden saw the threatning Billows rise:
Then trembling beg'd the Pow'rs Divine,
Some little safe Retreat might be for ever mine:
O give, I cry'd, where e'er you please,
Those Gifts which Mortals prize,
Grown fond of Privacy and Ease,
I now the gaudy Pomp of Life despise.

Although she desires to live 'in my Books, and thoughts entirely',
— a highly intellectual existence — she nevertheless blithely compares her life to the Golden Age. There is apparently no difference
between the cultured retirement of an educated person and the
state of innocence enjoyed by the first men. As long as the state
of Nature was felt to be identical with the rule of reason, the
retired life remained prevailingly intellectual, and so did the
concept of primitive man.

Lady Chudleigh, like Lord Lansdowne and the Countess of
Winchilsea, scorned contemporary society:

Those few who dare be good, must live alone
To all Mankind, except themselves, unknown:
From a mad World, to some obscure Recess,
They must retire, to purchase Happiness.[119]

Similar sentiments are found in 'The Resolution',[120] a poem
reminiscent of John Norris's 'The Retirement'. 'The Resolve',[121]
clearly inspired by Norris's 'The Refusal', attributes a Platonic

view of the world to the *beatus vir*, while 'The Happy Man'[122] paints a definitely Epicurean picture of happiness:

> He is the happy Man whose constant Mind
> Is to th' Enjoyment of himself confin'd:
> . . . . .
> Who all his Passions absolutely sways,
> And to his Reason cheerful Homage pays,
> Who's with a *Halcyon* Calmness ever blest,
> With inward Joy, untroubl'd Peace, and Rest:
> . . . . .
> To whom a Grove, a Garden, or a Field,
> Much greater, much sublimer Pleasures yield,
> Than they can find in all the Charms of Pow'r . . .

Like so many others, Lady Chudleigh wrote a Pindaric ode on solitude in the manner of Cowley, and, like him, attributes the ability to enjoy solitude only to the intellectual type:

> Happy are they who when alone
>   Can with themselves converse;
> Who to their Thoughts are so familiar grown,
> That with Delight in some obscure Recess,
> They cou'd with silent Joy think all their Hours away.
>
> But few, ah! few are for Retirement fit;
> But few the Joys of Solitude can taste;
>   The most with Horror fly from it,
> And rather chuse in Crouds their Time to waste;
> In busie Crouds, which a Resemblance bear
>   To th' unshap'd Embryo of the World.[123]

Lady Chudleigh's attitude towards the landscape of retirement was conditioned partly by Platonic thought (scaling the ladder of the Creation to the source of all being), partly by a Lucretian desire to explore the 'boundless Realms of Chance'. However, her religious orthodoxy made her refute the basic assumption of Lucretius, that the gods do not interfere with the world after it has been created. On the other hand, she gave enthusiastic assent to the doctrine that virtue is happiness, and that the soul has nothing to fear after death:

> *Lucretius* with his Philosophick Strains,
> My Mind at once delights, and entertains:
> Thro' Paths untrod, I see him fearless go:
> His Steps I tread, with eager hast to know:
> With him explore the boundless Realms of Chance,
> And see the little busie Atoms dance:
> See, how without Direction they combine,
> And form a Universe without Design,
> While careless Deities supremely blest,
> Enjoy the Pleasures of eternal Rest,
> Resolv'd that nothing here their Quiet shall molest.
> Strange that a Man of such a Strength of Thought,
> Could think a World was to Perfection brought
> Without Assistance from the Pow'rs above,
> From the blest Source of Wisdom, and of Love!
> All frightful Thoughts he from my Soul does chase,
> And in their room glad, bright Ideas place:
> Tells me that Happiness in Virtue lies,
> And bids me Death, that dreaded Ill, despise.[124]

Lady Chudleigh was much more preoccupied with surveys of 'the Works of Nature' than with the more limited rural scene. And in her treatment of this theme, she stressed the cosmic aspects, preferring to describe imaginary voyages through the universe, rather than the traditional landscape. Her poetry, therefore, provides an interesting record of the influence of the new science on the poetic imagination. The motif of the voyage through space was nevertheless still linked with the Neoplatonic motif of the mystic ecstasy, as is shown by her paraphrase of Norris's 'The Elevation' in a poem by the same name.[125] Norris's poem, in its turn, was an imitation of Casimire Sarbiewski's most famous mystic ode, 'E Rebus Humanis Excessus' (II, 5). It will be remembered that Casimire's ode had inspired Abraham Cowley's Pindaric ode, 'The Extasie', and in the near future Isaac Watts and John Hughes were to follow suit. The reason for the popularity of Casimire's ode is obvious: it provided a literary vehicle for the description of voyages through space. While Cowley and Norris had retained much of the mystic fervour of the Polish Jesuit, Lady Chudleigh (like Hughes and Watts later on) invested the theme with scientific, rather than mystic, overtones. She also introduced Lucretian ideas by describing the soaring soul as a detached spectator of the folly of men:

> How ambitious is my Soul,
>   How high she now aspires!
> There's nothing can on Earth controul,
>   Or limit her Desires.
> Upon the Wings of Thought she flies
>   Above the reach of Sight,
> And finds a way thro' pathless Skies
>   To everlasting Light.

The third stanza transforms the ecstatic visionary into an amused Lucretian spectator:

> From whence with blameless Scorn she views
>   The Follies of Mankind;
> And smiles to see how each pursues
>   Joys fleeting as the Wind.

The vision of the receding earth is found also in the opening stanzas of *The Song of the Three Children Paraphras'd*,[126] a long poem inspired by the *De Rerum Natura*. Like Heyrick, Lady

Chudleigh takes the reader on a tour of the world, and, like him, prefers the medium of the Pindaric. The visionary nature of the voyage through space evidently demanded the noble enthusiasm of the Pindaric form:

> Ascend my Soul, and in a speedy Flight
> Haste to the Regions of eternal Light;
> Look all around, each dazling Wonder view,
> And thy Acquaintance with past Joys renew.
> Thro' all th' Æthereal Plain extend thy Sight,
> On ev'ry pleasing Object gaze;
> On rolling Worlds below,
> On Orbs which Light and Heat bestow:
> And thence to their first Cause thy Admiration raise
> In sprightly Airs, and sweet harmonious Lays.
> . . . . .
> Oh the vast Prospect! O the charming Sight!
> How full of Wonder, and Delight!
> How mean, how little, does our Globe appear!
> This Object of our Envy, Toil, and Care,
> Is hardly seen amidst the Croud above;
> There, like some shining Point, do's scarce
> distinguish'd move.

The poem refers to God in Epicurean fashion as being 'of all Felicity possest, / And in himself supremely blest'. Not content to follow Epicurus only, Lady Chudleigh then combines the Platonic concept of the purified vision with the new psychology of Locke: the soul after death comes face to face with true reality, and forms new ideas on the basis of the bright images transmitted by its unclogged senses. Then, man's reason will be

> Bless'd with a free, distinct, unclouded Sight
> Of all those Glories which adorn the happy Realms of Light.

Our Faculties will all awake,
And each will sprightly grow,
Exert its Pow'r, and its whole Force will show.

The simplicity and happiness of earlier ages is praised in a manner
which recalls Boethius:

How happy shou'd we be, if we agen
To the first Rules of Living cou'd return,
By Nature, the best Tut'ress taught,
Her just and easie Laws obey,
Like those she on th' early Stage of Action brought?
Who to few Things their Wishes could confine,
On Herbs and Fruits contentedly cou'd dine;
. . . . .
They sought no Pomp, no Delicacies knew
Nor Wealth admir'd,
That greatest Plague of Life;
Nor glorious Palaces desir'd;
But underneath some pleasant Shade,
Strangers to toil, to Care and Strife,
Did sweetly sleep, or calmly think.

The various echoes from Sarbiewski, Boethius, and Lucretius may
seem to form a curious mixture, together with the psychology of
Locke and the new Cartesian world view, yet these were the impulses from which Lady Chudleigh fetched the inspiration for
her poem. A diluted Neoplatonism goes rather well with the
psychology of Locke, just as the Lucretian Detached Spectator
could easily be transformed into a scientific observer of the universe. The inherent materialism of Lady Chudleigh's thought
stands revealed in the fact that she lets the departed soul gather
its ideas, like a scientist, from the close study of material objects.
Her imagined soul encounters no spiritual realm on its ascent,
but very concrete 'rolling Worlds' and 'Orbs which Light and

Heat bestow'. Under Lady Chudleigh's hands, therefore, the mystic
ecstasy of the Hortulan Saint turns into a scientific excursion
among the stars. Despite the semi-mystical terminology there is
here no attempt to describe a mystic vision, only a scientific
desire to think 'more accurately' on the basis of clear sense im-
pressions. Lady Chudleigh's poetry for this reason provides an
admirable demonstration of the way in which the mystic vision
of the seventeenth century was being superseded by the thoroughly
rationalistic outlook of Locke's generation. In her poetry it is
possible to observe the point at which the tradition of the late
seventeenth century begins to be influenced by the trends of the
new era. It is still possible to trace the patterns established by
Abraham Cowley, Mrs. Philips, the Earl of Roscommon and
John Norris, but they are in the process of becoming significantly
modified by that nexus of ideas which cluster round the names
of Descartes and John Locke. This nexus was eventually destined
to cause a radical re-arrangement of the old patterns, as will be
shown in the second volume of this study.

5.

The poetry reviewed in this chapter has been remarkably ample
and remarkably consistent in its interpretation of the *beatus vir*.
From the *précieuse* poetry of Mrs. Philips and the erotic verse
of Mrs. Behn, to the Neoplatonism of John Norris and the Whig
morality of John Tutchin, the emphasis throughout was on the
ability of the individual to 'live to himself at large, calm and
secure, A wise eternal Epicure' (Norris). The self-centredness of
the Restoration Happy Man is his most outstanding characteristic.
A Norris and a Rochester both were equally convinced that they
were born to themselves alone and accountable to none. Self-love
and self-sufficiency provided the only true basis for the happiness
of court wits as of Anglican ministers: 'Than our Dear self is any
thing more Dear?' (Rawlet) and 'all true Happiness, we must

confess, Is more, as it depends on Others less' (Wycherley). The Epicurean bias of this generation manifested itself in a blithe negation of all responsibility for the state of the nation: 'Let plots and news embroil the State, pray what's that to my books and me?' (Norris). Of all our poets, not a single one was entirely uninfluenced by the Epicurean definition of happiness, while the great majority was completely dominated by it. Whether the personal bias of a poet was Stoic or Platonic, Hedonistic or plain moralistic, tranquillity of mind and indolence of body was the commonly accepted aim: 'Here may I always on this downy Grass, Unknown, unseen, my easy Minutes pass ...' (Roscommon).

Thomas Franklin Mayo has maintained that the spirit of Epicurus was 'essentially alien to the English temperament, [and] found a welcome on English soil only during that moment when the exasperated aristocrat was likely to include all piety and idealism in his hatred of the pious and idealistic bourgeoisie.'[127] It is not my intention to deny that the aristocratic bias of the Restoration Royalists was one of the reasons why Epicurean ideas gained such wide acceptance in this period. However, there was more at the root of the Restoration love of leisured retirement than a mere aversion for the religious and moral code of the Puritans. The positive elements in the Epicurean philosophy must not be overlooked; basically noble characters like John Norris were strongly influenced by these elements. The Lucretian ideal of happiness could not possibly have inspired so many and so varied poetic utterances, unless it had stirred more potent emotions than those of a mere aversion for bourgeois piety and morality.

Much of the despair which marked the poetry of the first half of the century vanished with the Restoration. The search for happiness no longer focussed on a reality which was felt to lie just beyond the world of sense. The materialism inherent in the doctrines of Epicurus and in the new science combined with the classical exhortation to seek happiness here and now, to pro-

duce a new type of *beatus vir* whose most important features
were borrowed from the self-contained Lucretian gods. At the
same time the landscape of retirement lost its Sabine flavour and
its mystical connotations, while it gained the Lucretian pinnacle
of the Detached Spectator and the elegant garden of the Innocent
Epicurean. The Restoration poets also made the solitary life more
convivial without, apparently, any feeling of logical inconsistency.
Solitude, it was felt, could include friends and books and conversation.

The Neoplatonic theme of Nature as a divine hieroglyph lost
ground tremendously in the last four decades of the century.
Except for Lady Winchilsea, this period offers few examples of
a belief in the spiritual effect of the solitary contemplation of
rural scenes. The double vision of the Hortulan Saint did not
survive in the sceptical atmosphere of the Restoration. Although
we have traced a definite line of influence from the religious
odes of Casimire Sarbiewski in the age of Dryden too, we have
seen how his Neoplatonic themes were modified in an Epicurean
direction, or in the direction of the new science. In this manner
the theme of the ordered universe (often presented in the form
of an imaginary voyage through space) came to replace that of
Nature as a divine hieroglyph. This means that the chief object
of the contemplation of the *beatus vir* was not God himself so
much as His creation.

CHAPTER VI

SUMMING UP

The first, very obvious conclusion is concerned with quantity rather than quality. It must be conceded that the mere bulk of the material presented in the preceding pages is impressive. Indeed, the very richness of the evidence has been a constant hazard since it has invited a procedure whereby quotation is heaped on quotation until the context is in danger of a total eclipse through the massed array of single specimens. On the other hand, some sort of statistical effort seemed required in order to establish beyond all doubt the actual existence of a poetic tradition which so far has received but scant attention. While much relevant material has been omitted, enough has been left to suggest that the number of poems concerned with the philosophic ideal of the Happy Man is indeed overwhelming. From the days of Ben Jonson, John Milton, and William Habington, this ideal enjoyed a popularity which only increased with the passing of time.

The second conclusion must be that the classical tradition was seldom rendered accurately, since in most cases it came to be coloured by the prevailing mood of each succeeding generation. As we read on in the poetry of this century, it becomes increasingly clear that practically all original versions of the *beatus ille* themes reveal an admixture of contemporary thought. We have also seen that this tendency can be traced even in the work of the translators.

The first conscious departure from the classical norm was in a religious direction, and occurred in the first half of the century under the impact of the strong neo-Stoicism of the period. Milton and Habington in particular — the Puritan and the Roman Catholic — were the creators of poetry which transformed the classical

313

Happy Husbandman into a neo-Stoic Serene Contemplator of the world. Milton's assimilation of this part of the classical tradition is proof of his deeply humanistic world view, just as his treatment of the character of the pensive man aligns him with contemporary neo-Stoic prose writers like Joseph Hall and Wye Saltonstall.

The second metamorphosis occurred in the fifth and sixth decades of the seventeenth century, at a time when civil dissent forced a large part of the nation to court retirement out of sheer necessity. This fact, together with the pronounced influence of Neoplatonic and of mystic or semi-mystic thought at exactly this point, must be considered responsible for the transformation of the neo-Stoic Serene Contemplator into an ecstatic Hortulan Saint. While the neo-Stoic poets had added the motif of solitary contemplation to the classical *beatus ille* motifs, the Neoplatonic poets of the mid-century added two further themes: the Biblical theme of the Earthly Paradise (or the classical motif of the Golden Age), and the partly Hermetic, partly Neoplatonic theme of Nature as a divine hieroglyph which, when properly studied, bespeaks a secret, spiritual connection with the Deity. Andrew Marvell invested these themes with perfect poetic form, and by so doing bequeathed to posterity one of the most intriguing lyrics to come to us from an age renowned for its gift of poetic utterance.

With the more sceptical intellectual climate of the Restoration, the *beatus vir* entered the third distinctive phase of his career. Under the influence of the current Epicurean interpretation of happiness as a state of pure tranquillity and ease, he turned into a man who, though blind to the divine character of the Creation, was extremely conscious of the divine character of the pleasures of rest and their superiority over the pleasures of motion. At this time, therefore, the Lucretian portrayal of the Detached Spectator nearly ousted the Horatian picture of the Happy Husbandman as the ideal type of *beatus vir*. As a consequence, the *hortus conclusus* of the Hortulan Saint was exchanged for a more extensive scene which could provide an adequate epitome of the world.

The garden setting, however, was not abandoned; it was re-interpreted in an Epicurean direction. The Restoration Happy Man viewed his garden as an elegant setting for a life, dignified through its refusal to share in the noise and tumult of the political scene. This interpretation of the *beatus vir* as a gentleman-gardener was to become the generally accepted view of the next century, and it is therefore important to underline its connection with Epicurean thought. The germ of much eighteenth-century retirement poetry must be sought in the interpretation given by poets like Abraham Cowley, Mrs. Philips, and the Earl of Roscommon to the *beatus ille* tradition.

This tradition was also exploited by a number of Restoration poets, who made it serve as an impeccable philosophic front for their Hedonistic indulgence in erotic pursuits. In the licentious poetry of Mrs. Aphra Behn in particular, the *beatus vir* endured a process whereby his disinterested aloofness from the world was strongly modified by a keen interest in the weaker sex.

The question of literary indebtedness may seem to have loomed rather large in the preceding pages. None, I think, will dispute the conclusion that a number of the lesser poets were imitators and occasionally downright plagiarists. The situation is somewhat different when we approach the acknowledged masters. Major poets seldom borrow as crudely as lesser minds, and a belief in poetic independence is almost always tacitly assumed in cases of supreme poetic excellence. However, it must not be forgotten that the poets of this century were capable of being inspired by literary experience to a degree seldom suspected to-day. Nevertheless, the absence of direct verbal borrowing is an effective restriction. No specific indebtedness can be assumed on the basis of mere general similarity in themes or imagery. What can be assumed, is the presence of a vital poetic tradition connecting a number of poems so far viewed as independent productions.

The larger part of this tradition was derived from classical sources. Direct or indirect indebtedness to such sources has

315

been evident throughout this study. However, once such passages had become the familiar property of the age, the poets often preferred to follow contemporary interpretations of the *beatus ille* message. Thus at the mid-century the neo-Latin Horatian odes of Casimire Sarbiewski exerted considerable influence, particularly on Edward Benlowes and Henry Vaughan. Andrew Marvell, too, may have derived from him his habit of combining Neoplatonic or Hermetic ideas with *beatus ille* motifs. While some indebtedness to the 'divine Casimire' can be traced in a few of Abraham Cowley's odes, the latter's translations and imitations of *beatus ille* passages represent an independent handling of the classical tradition. The importance of Cowley's work in this field cannot be overestimated; the pattern created by his *Essays and Discourses* was imitated again and again. Thus John Norris and Lady Chudleigh as well as John Tutchin wrote essays in prose and verse, closely copying Cowley's ideas as well as his style. Interestingly enough, some of the Neoplatonic terminology of the mid-century survived in those poems which echo Cowley's or Casimire's treatment of the divine ecstasy experienced by the *beatus vir*. But, as we have seen, this mystic vision was transformed into a Cartesian rapture arising from the magnificent spectacle of the ordered universe. This transformation or change of focus should be connected with the Restoration interest in the *De Rerum Natura* by Lucretius (translated by Thomas Creech in 1684), which logically enough led to a close association between the philosophy of retirement and the pursuit of scientific studies. Virgil's *Georgics* also furnished a precedent for this particular combination of ideas. The growing interest in science, particularly physics and astronomy, caused the mystic voyage through the Hermetic spheres to be transformed into a scientific excursion among the stars. In the poetry of the early eighteenth century this new motif of the ordered universe was to loom so large that it often obscured the other themes clustering around the nucleus of the *beatus ille* tradition.

A second final tendency of the seventeenth century was the movement towards greater moral seriousness. As a rule, the poets who wrote about the Happy Man were conservative in their political and religious affiliation. We have seen how the figure of the Happy Man was created, more or less consciously, as a Royalist or humanist counterpart to the grim figure of the Puritan pilgrim. After the Restoration the theme of the Happy Man continued as the typical expression of that part of the nation which was most strongly opposed to Puritan views in morals as well as religion. Lady Chudleigh, the Countess of Winchilsea, and Lord Lansdowne were all Tory die-hards who never were reconciled to the new regime of William of Orange. The hedonistic implications so often encountered in Restoration poems on happiness naturally would repel all serious-minded Englishmen. The aristocratic and Epicurean version of the *beatus vir* was consciously opposed to middle-class morality in the poetry of William Wycherley. The total disregard for the moral values found in an active life devoted to good works was nowhere given more pointed expression than in the works of this eminent court wit. Nevertheless, towards the end of the century this aristocratic monopoly of an important poetic tradition shows signs of breaking down. In the poetry of John Tutchin the tradition was actually enlisted in the service of a Whig moralist desiring to bring about a reformation of manners. This was a definite novelty, and it was only to be expected that Tutchin turned to Abraham Cowley's *Essays and Discourses* for inspiration; he wanted no truck with the intervening court poets. In the eighteenth century the *beatus ille* motifs finally penetrated into the ranks of pious non-conformist poets like Isaac Watts, as the second volume of this study will show.

Finally some remarks on the connection between poetic motifs and poetic techniques. We have encountered *beatus ille* motifs in separate poems after the manner of Horace, or embedded in longer poems as distinct passages after the manner of Virgil's praise of the husbandman in the second *Georgic*. Since Horace

317

wrote more copiously about the Happy Man than any other classical poet, the *beatus ille* motifs tended to become associated with the form of the Horatian ode (or epode) and the Horatian epistle. Characteristically enough, when William Habington turned from Elizabethan love lyrics to the motif of the Happy Man, he also abandoned the sonnet sequence in favour of the philosophic lyric and the epistle.

One basic characteristic of the Horatian ode is the tightness of its structure. The Horatian ode is an extremely well-plotted lyric; its ideas are presented with precision and clarity, so that the over-all impression is one of lyric grace combined with vigorous thought. Of the English poets, Andrew Marvell achieved this difficult combination with the greatest degree of success.

The epistolary form was skilfully handled particularly by William Habington, who deserves more attention on this score than he has so far achieved. There is more of the true Horatian manner in Habington's epistles than in any other seventeenth-century poet — Cowley not excepted. Cowley, as Coleridge has pointed out, lacked the fine precision of Horace's pen. He was too discursive to achieve quite the same effect of a well-planned totality. However, to the Restoration poets it was Abraham Cowley who was the great exponent of *beatus ille* themes, in prose, in translations, and in original compositions. The structure of the Pindaric ode favoured by Cowley was extremely loose, and its enthusiastic manner perceptibly changed the whole character of the praise of country life. Instead of proceeding by means of rational argument, the Pindaric ode emphasised the complete *rapture* of the Happy Man in a way tending to obscure his Stoic aspects. Roscommon's ode on solitude is a fine example of the new enthusiastic manner induced by the choice of the Pindaric form.

However, despite the great popularity of Cowley's Pindarics, the various lyric forms associated with the Horatian ode did not completely vanish. Through the last four decades of the century runs a fairly steady trickle of *beatus ille* lyrics that might be said to be Horatian in form. Of these, the poem in tetrameters was most popular, as evidenced by the poetry of Mrs. Philips and Lady Winchilsea. Tetrameters had been extensively used by English poets in their translations of Horatian odes, and therefore had come to be closely associated with this type of poem.

Since the poetry included in this study has been analysed from the point of view of content rather than form, it would be inadvisable to attempt conclusions concerning the extent of the formal influence of the Horatian ode upon seventeenth-century lyric poetry. One point, however, should have emerged with sufficient clarity, namely the fact that the philosophic nature lyric ought to be more firmly linked with the Horatian ode than it hitherto has been. The classical landscape of retirement in a number of cases was the direct inspiration of poets who delighted in painting rural scenes in a style patently indebted to the poet of the Sabine farm. We have also seen that this landscape was strongly modified in the course of the years through the addition of motifs which induced a different attitude to it. As a result of the introduction of the religious theme of Nature as a divine hieroglyph or mystic ladder leading to God, the landscape of retirement came to be described in terms suggesting a subtle animation of the scene. This new descriptive technique was traced in the popular neo-Latin Horatian odes of Casimire Sarbiewski, and subsequently in Denham's *Cooper's Hill* and Marvell's garden poems. Whatever the extent of Casimire's direct influence on English poetry, one thing remains clear, namely that the landscapes of Vaughan's and Marvell's nature lyrics represent a further development, in a mystic direction, of the classical landscape of retirement. The moment which saw the birth, in Poland as in England, of a new kind of nature lyric, was the moment when Hermetic or Neoplatonic motifs combined with the neo-Stoic version of the *beatus ille* tradition.

This moment was not sustained for any length of time.

319

With the restoration of the Stuarts, Stoicism and Platonism both had to yield the palm of pre-eminence to Epicurus and Lucretius. Hence the language of natural description, as we encounter it in the poetry of rural happiness, was again changed. The 'Sabine farm' of Restoration poetry was described in terms which belonged more properly to the garden of Epicurus, and one also observes a perceptible standardisation of the language. It is in the Restoration period that we first encounter those purling streams, those painted meads and winged choirs which became the curse of Neoclassical lyrics. By 1670, after the publication of Cowley's *Essays and Discourses* and Mrs. Philips's poems, the happiness of rural retirement had become an accepted poetic motif, and the gradual standardisation of the landscape of retirement was surely one of the consequences of its popularity. It was, of course, the result also of that poetic diction which evolved towards the end of the century. It is not here the place to discuss the probable reasons for the emergence of this diction, although one might underline the circumstance that the idyllification of the landscape of retirement during the Restoration period reflects the same increasing respect for the proper, the decorous, and the elegant, which was so largely instrumental in creating the poetic diction of the next century. Suffice it here to state that the language of natural description which had flourished so magnificently in the poetry of the mid-century, endured an increasing standardisation as the century wore on, one or two poems by Charles Cotton and the Countess of Winchilsea offering the only remarkable exceptions. One reason for this may be connected with the fact that the attention of the Restoration poets was focused, not on the landscape itself (or on the reality behind the landscape), but on the pleasant ease and tranquillity enjoyed by the *beatus vir*. Perhaps an additional clue may be found in the circumstance that the mystic vision was transformed into a Cartesian rapture. If the eyes of the meditating poet are fixed either on himself or on the grand scheme of the universe, can one really expect him to notice more than the very general features of the landscape which surrounds him?

In view of this close connection between poetic techniques and poetic motifs one is surely justified in concluding that seventeenth-century English poetry developed a number of its most distinctive forms and descriptive techniques as a result of the popularity of certain motifs. Milton's companion poems, Habington's epistles, Denham's *Cooper's Hill*, Marvell's garden lyrics, Cowley's translations and imitations, Roscommon's ode on solitude, and Lady Winchilsea's pensive nature lyrics — all these owe their creation to the pervasive influence of the classical *beatus ille* tradition.

A clear understanding of the way in which succeeding generations received this tradition — and, in receiving, transformed it — should therefore provide a sound basis for new insights into the poetic trends of this century.

NOTES

PREFACE

1. Josephine Miles, *Eras & Modes in English Poetry* (University of California Press, 1957).
2. Edward Niles Hooker, 'Humour in the Age of Pope', *The Huntington Library Quarterly*, XI (1948), p. 385.

CHAPTER I

1. Carol Maddison, *Apollo and the Nine. A History of the Ode* (London, 1960).
2. Perhaps the most convenient edition is the one edited by A. R. Waller: Abraham Cowley, *Essays, Plays and Sundry Verses* (Cambridge, 1906). No page references will be offered for quotations from Cowley's essays and translations since these are easily located.
3. The Loeb Classical Library translates as follows: 'Who then is free? The wise man, who is lord over himself, whom neither poverty nor death nor bonds affright, who bravely defies his passions, and scorns ambition, who in himself is a whole . . .'
4. From Horace's Epistle I, 18.
5. Dudley North, *A Forest Of Varieties* (1645), p. 68.
6. Timothy Nourse, 'Essay upon the Fuel of London,' in *Campania Faelix* (1700).

CHAPTER II

1. A. H. Bullen, ed., *England's Helicon* (London, 1887), p. 174 f.
2. *The Muses Sacrifice* (1612), pp. 121r-122v.
3. *Reliquiae Wottonianae* (1651), p. 522 f.
4. Gordon Goodwin, ed., *The Poems of William Browne of Tavistock* (The Muses' Library, no date), II, 299.
5. William Drummond, *Flowres of Sion* (1623), p. 22.
6. C. H. Herford Percy and Evelyn Simpson, ed., *Ben Jonson* (Oxford, 1947), VIII, 289-291.
7. *Ibid.*, VIII, 295.
8. *Ibid.*, VIII, 96-100.
9. *Ibid.*, VIII, 93-96.
10. *Ibid.*, VIII, 116-120.
11. Frederick S. Boas, ed., *The Poetical Works of Giles and Phineas Fletcher* (Cambridge, 1906), II, 337.

325

THE HAPPY MAN

12. Compare Canto I, stanza 26 with Sylvester's *Du Bartas His Deuine Weekes and Workes Translated* (London, 1611), pp. 86-89. See also Canto I, stanzas 28-30 and XII, 3-5.
13. Fletcher, *op. cit.*, II, 228 f.
14. *Ibid.*, II, 233-235.

CHAPTER III

1. Owen Feltham, *Resolves* (1840), p. 176.
2. Kenneth Allot, ed., *The Poems of William Habington* (London, 1948), p. 96.
3. Little is known about his life, beyond the fact that he acquired fame as a poet during his stay in Rome, and that later he became the favourite of the Polish king. The following sources will be found useful: *The Catholic Encyclopedia*, XIII, 471 f.; *Biographie Universelle Ancienne et Moderne*, XXXVIII, 12 f.; *Lexicon für Theologie und Kirche* (1937), IX, 182; Alexander Baumgartner, *Geschichte der Weltlitteratur* (Freiburg im Breisgau, 1900), IV, 642-45; C. L. Langbein, *Commentatio de Matth. Casimir Sarbievii vita, studiis et scriptis* (Dresden, 1754); 'On the Life and Writings of Casimir', *The Classical Journal*, XXV (1822), 103-110; H. E. Wideck, 'Casimir, the Polish Horace', *Philological Quarterly*, XVI (1937), 307-316, and Antonius Bacci, 'De Mathia Casimiro Sarbiewski Polonorum Horatio', *Latinitas* (1954), II, 94-101.
   Sarbiewski was born in 1595; he became a member of the Society of Jesus at the age of 17, and was ordained priest in Rome in 1623. Cardinal Barberini sponsored him during his stay in Rome 1622-1624, and so did the Pope. When S. left for Poland in 1624, Urban VIII presented him with a gold medallion of great value, and some also relate a story of how S. was actually crowned 'poet laureate' on this occasion. This episode, however, seems apocryphal.
   At least seven editions of S.'s poetry appeared before 1650. See Carlos Sommervogel, *Bibliothèque de la Compagnie de Jésus* (Brussels and Paris, 1896), VII, 627-646. The first Latin edition printed in England appeared in 1684.
4. *The Odes of Casimire (1646)*, Augustan Reprint Society Publication No. 44 (Los Angeles, 1953). Except when otherwise stated, all quotations from Casimire are taken from this volume. Since the poems are numbered, I have omitted all page references.
5. See below, pp. 164-165.
6. Vaughan paraphrased the same sections in his epistle 'The importunate Fortune, written to doctor *Powell of Cantre*'. This particular ode was imitated more frequently than any other in the Restoration period and in the early years of the 18th century. Abraham Cowley paraphrased it, and so did John Hughes.
7. Herman Hugo, *Pia Desideria Emblematis* (Antverpiae, 1628), p. 210 f.
8. Walter Mountague, *Miscellanea Spiritualia* (1648), p. 65.
9. Joseph Hall, *Characters of Virtues and Vices*, ed. Rudolf Kirk (Rutgers Studies in English No. 6), p. 166.
10. Wye Saltonstall, *Picturae Loquentes*. Luttrell Reprints No. 1 (Oxford, 1946), p. 74.

11. L. C. Martin, ed., *The Works of Henry Vaughan* (Oxford, 1914), I, 86 f.
12. John Earle, *Microcosmographie (1628)*, The Temple Classics (London, 1899), p. 49.
13. Owen Feltham, *Resolves* (1840), p. 296 f. First ed. 1623, second 1628.
14. Robert Sanderson, *Works* (Oxford University Press, 1854), I, 420. Here quoted from Philip Allerton Smith, Neo-Stoicism in English Prose of the Seventeenth Century (unprinted Harvard University dissertation, 1939), p. 132.
15. Helen Gardner, ed., *The Metaphysical Poets* (Penguin Books, 1957), 168-172.
16. Robert Farley, *Kalendarium Humanae Vitae* (1638), sig. [G8r].
17. Robert Chamberlain, *Nocturnall Lucubrations* (1638), sig. [G6r] f.
18. *Ibid.*, sig. [H3r]-[H4r].
19. Thomas Randolph, *Poems* (Oxford, 1638), pp. 68-71. For Randolph's indebtedness to classical poets, see Kathryn Anderson McEuen, *Classical Influence upon the Tribe of Ben* (Cedar Rapids, Iowa, 1939), pp. 100-105.
20. Anthony Wood, *Athenae Oxonienses* (London, 1817), III, 225.
21. Kenneth Allott, ed., *The Poems of William Habington* (London, 1948), p. 44 f.
22. See Cowley's essay 'Of Avarice'.
23. Allott, *op. cit.*, pp. 45 f. and 51 f.
24. *Ibid.*, p. 142 f.
25. *Ibid.*, p. 92 f.
26. *Ibid.*, p. 95 f.
27. *Ibid.*, p. 85 f.
28. *Ibid.*, p. 120 f.
29. *Ibid.*, p. 125 f.
30. *Ibid.*, p. 134 f.
31. *Ibid.*, pp. 136-138.
32. *The Works of John Milton* (Columbia University Press, 1936), XII, 249 f. The quotation is taken from the English translation of the Seventh Prolusion.
33. Saltonstall, *op. cit.*, character sketch number 16.
34. See Rosemond Tuve, 'Structural Figures of *L'Allegro* and *Il Penseroso*', *Images and Themes in Five Poems by Milton* (Harvard University Press, 1957), p. 20.
35. Saltonstall, *op. cit.*, sketch number 32.
36. Joseph Hall, *Characters of Virtues and Vices*, ed. Rudolf Kirk (Rutgers Studies in English, No. 6), p. 153.
37. *Ibid.*, p. 165.
38. *Ibid.*, p. 147 f.
39. *Ibid.*, p. 148.
40. Saltonstall, *op. cit.*, sketch number 36.
41. *Ibid.*, sketch number 8.
42. *Ibid.*, sketch number 36.
43. Tuve, *op. cit.*, p. 26.
44. 'What a thing it is to grasp the nature of the whole firmament and of its stars, all the movements and changes of the atmosphere, whether it strikes terror into ignorant minds by the majestic roll of thunder or by fiery comets, [whether it becomes frozen in snow and hail] or whether again it falls softly and gently in showers or dew; then perfectly to understand

the shifting winds and all the exhalations and vapours which earth and sea give forth...; and, to crown all, the divine might and power of the soul, and any knowledge we may have gained concerning those beings which we call spirits and genii and daemons.' Quoted from E. M. W. Tillyard, 'Milton. *L'Allegro* and *Il Penseroso*', *The English Association* (Pamphlet No. 82, July 1932), p. 5. Milton's most significant addition to Virgil is his reference to 'the divine might and power of the soul'.

45. To facilitate comparison, I quote the English translation of the relevant lines in Virgil:
'Yet theirs is repose without care, and a life that knows no fraud, but is rich in treasures manifold. Yea, the ease of broad domains, caverns, and living lakes, and cool vales, the lowing of the kine, and soft slumber beneath the trees — all are theirs. They have woodland glades and the haunts of game... let my delight be the country, and the running streams amid the dells — may I love the waters and the woods, though fame be lost. O for those plains, and Spercheus, and Taygetus, where Spartan girls hold Bacchic rites! O for one to set me in the cool glens of Haemus, and shield me under the branches' mighty shade!' Quoted from the Loeb edition.

46. 'Happy old man! Here, amid familiar streams and sacred springs, you shall court the cooling shade... the hedge whose willow blossoms are sipped by Hybla's bees shall often with its gentle hum soothe you to slumber... under the towering rock, the woodman's song shall fill the air; while still the cooing woodpigeons, your pets, and the turtle-dove shall cease not their moaning from the skyey elm.'

47. '’Tis pleasant, now to lie beneath some ancient ilex-tree, now on the matted turf. Meanwhile the rills glide between their high banks; birds warble in the woods; the fountains plash with their flowing waters, a sound to invite soft slumbers.'

48. This passage from the 1642 edition corresponds to lines 25-34 of the final version. See the variorum edition by T. H. Banks, ed., *The Poetical Works of Sir John Denham* (Yale University Press, 1928), p. 64.

49. For examples of a similar use of natural description, see Horace's Ode I, 3; I, 17; II, 10; III, 1; III,29.

50. William Habington, 'Et Exultavit Humiles'.

51. The quotations from Casimire are again taken from G. Hills's translation of 1646. If Denham did actually use Casimire's epode as a pattern, he must have used the Latin text.

52. Robert Herrick, *Hesperides* (1648), pp. 269-271.

53. See McEuen, *Classical Influence upon the Tribe of Ben* (Cedar Rapids, Iowa, 1939), p. 30, and Pauline Aiken, 'The Influence of the Latin Elegists on English Lyric Poetry', *Maine Bulletin*, XXXIV (1932), pp. 48 and 69 f.

54. Herrick, *op. cit.*, pp. 35-39.

55. McEuen, *op. cit.*, p. 91 f.

56. *Ibid.*, p. 30.

57. 'His Content in the Country'. Quoted from Herrick, *The Poetical Works*, ed. F. M. Moorman (Oxford University Press, 1921), p. 198.

58. *Ibid.*, pp. 100-102.

59. *Ibid.*, pp. 132-136.

60. Thomas B. Stroup, ed., *The Selected Poems of George Daniel of Beswick 1616-1657* (University of Kentucky Press, 1959).

61. *Ibid.*, p. xix.
62. *Ibid.*, pp. 17-19.
63. *Ibid.*, p. 26 f.
64. *Ibid.*, p. 44 f.
65. *Ibid.*, pp. 169-171. The poem is dated 1647.
66. See the author's postscript, p. 168 where Daniel states that his poetic fragments 'were intended, not to the publike Eye, but his owne retired Fancies, to make Light that burthen which some grone under...'

CHAPTER IV

1. *The Works of Sir Thomas Browne,* ed. Geoffrey Keynes (London, 1931), Vol. VI, 299-302.
2. Compare John Evelyn's anonymous pamphlet, *An Apologie for the Royal Party* (1659) and John Dryden's *Astraea Redux* (1660).
3. Henry More, *Philosophical Poems,* ed. G. Bullough (Manchester University Press, 1931), p. xxxviii.
4. Plotinus, *The Enneads,* tr. Stephen MacKenna (London, 1956), p. 372. From V, i, 4.
5. Ross Garner, *Henry Vaughan: Experience and the Tradition* (University of Chicago Press, 1959), p. 70.
6. Ruth Wallerstein, *Seventeenth-Century Poetic* (University of Wisconsin Press, 1950), p. 272.
7. The quotation is taken from Ficino's commentary on *Libellus I,* chapter 1, where he compares Hermes' account of creation with that of Moses, concluding that Hermes conveyed 'Mosaic mysteries.' The translation is my own. See Ficino, *Opera* (Paris, 1641), II, 792 f. See also Ficino's introductory remarks, *ibid.,* II, 789 f.
8. S. G. F. Brandon, 'The Gnostic Problem in Early Christianity,' *History Today* (June, 1960), Vol. X, 415-423.
9. For a literary expression of this idea, see 'Disputation between Mary and the Cross,' *The Minor Poems of the Vernon MS,* Part II, ed. F. J. Furnivall (EETS, Original Series, No. 117), pp. 612-626. See also *The Legend of the Rood,* tr. F. E. Halliday (London, 1955). This Cornish miracle play describes how the cross was made from a tree which grew from the seeds of the fruit of the fatal tree in the Garden of Eden. After the Fall this tree becomes barren and dry, but in it is hidden 'A little child, new born.'
10. As Rosemond Tuve points out in *A Reading of George Herbert* (London, 1952), p. 86, the famous hymn by Venantius Fortunatus, the *Crux benedicta,* describes Christ as the vine and also as the fruit of the Tree of the Cross: 'O Tree of sweetness and glory, / Bearing such new-found fruit midst the green wreaths of thy boughs... Fast in thy arms is enfolded the Vine; from whom in its fullness, / Floweth the blood-red juice, Wine that gives life to the soul.'
11. Henry More, *Philosophical Poems,* ed. G. Bullough (Manchester University Press, 1931), p. xxii.
12. *Ibid.*
13. From the address 'To the reader' prefixed to More's first collection of poems (1642).
14. More, *op.cit.,* pp. 324-328.

329

THE HAPPY MAN

15. For an exposition of traditional garden symbolism, see W. D. Robertson, 'The Doctrine of Charity in Medieval Literary Gardens,' *Speculum*, XXVI (1951), 24-49.
16. One should compare More's poem with Horace's O'de I, 22 *(Integer vitae)*, Metre I, 4 from Boethius' *De Consolatione Philosophiae*, and with Casimire's Ode IV, 3. Casimire's ode, in its turn, is a paraphrase of the same Horatian ode and of Boethius' *metrum*, and may possibly have inspired More to attempt a similar performance.
17. Douglas Bush, *English Literature in the Earlier Seventeenth Century* (Oxford, 1945), p. 496 and Carl Niemeyer, 'New Light on Edward Benlowes,' *RES*, XII (1936), 36.
18. *The Poems of Mildmay Fane, 2d Earl of Westmoreland*, ed. Alex. B. Grosart (Privately printed, 1879), pp. 48-50.
19. *Ibid.*, p. 6 f.
20. *Ibid.*, p. 13.
21. *Ibid.*, pp. 136-140. This epistle is given in a Latin version on pp. 152-154.
22. M. C. Bradbrook, 'Marvell and the Poetry of Rural Solitude', *RES*, XVII (1941), 37-46.
23. Ralph Fisher's complimentary poem on *Theophila* appeared in his *Marston-Moore*, published in 1650. See Niemeyer, *op.cit.*, p. 41. Harold Jenkins, *Edward Benlowes* (Cambridge, Mass., 1952), p. 186 states that *Theophila* probably was finished by 1648, and on p. 212 he enumerates some of those who were privileged to read the poem in manuscript. Thus Clement Paman had read parts of the unfinished poem five or six years before it was printed (i.e. in 1646 or 1647), and Thomas Wincoll praised it in 1649. On p. 216 Jenkins expresses his belief that Walter Montague, author of one of the prefatory poems, must have read the epic before he was banished the country in 1649.
24. Harold Jenkins, *op.cit.*, pp. 112 and 162-168.
25. The borrowings are from 'On the Morning of Christ's Nativity,' *Comus*, 'Lycidas,' 'L'Allegro' and 'Il Penseroso.'
26. For an account of medieval number symbolism, see H. Flanders Dunbar, *Symbolism in Medieval Thought* (New Haven, 1929), particularly pp. 336-340, 466 f., and 501 f. See also Gunnar Qvarnström, *Dikten och den Nya Vetenskapen* (Lund, 1961) for comments on number symbolism in *Theophila* and *Paradise Lost*. Qvarnström's book is No. LX in the series published at Lund under the title *Acta Reg. Societatis Humaniorum Litterarum Lundensis*.
27. Qvarnström, *op.cit.*, 196-199. For a contemporary English exposition, see Robert Fludd, *Philosophia Moysaica* (1638).
28. For further comments on the typological interpretation of Scripture, see below under Marvell, 'Upon Appleton House'. See also Rosemond Tuve, *A Reading of George Herbert* (London, 1952), particularly p. 184, and J. E. Cross and S. I. Tucker, 'Allegorical Tradition and The Old English Exodus,' *Neophilologicus*, 44 (April, 1960), 122-127. This article quotes from a fifth-century theological treatise: 'Allegorically, moreover, the Red Sea is the baptism, Christ consecrated with red blood. The Hebrews who leave Egypt and cross by the Red Sea, are the faithful who, leaving the darkness of infidelity, cross by the baptismal font. Pharaoh and the Egyptians are killed in the sea, because the devil is killed in the baptismal font, losing the power which he had. The dead are certainly our original

sin and our committed sins, provided that such existed previously.' (My translation.)

It is worth noting that when the poet of the Old English *Exodus* breaks off his narrative of the crossing of the Red Sea to insert accounts of the Flood and of Abraham's sacrifice, he does so because these three events have the same typological significance. Also Marvell combines the crossing of the Red Sea with the Flood.

29. Qvarnström, *op.cit.*

30. By 1651 further translations from the Polish poet had appeared in publications by Henry Vaughan and Sir Edward Sherburne. Lovelace's *Lucasta* (1649), to which Marvell contributed a poem, contains three or four poems which seem to have been inspired by Casimire. Thus Lovelace's ode to 'The Grasse-hopper' seems a free imitation of Casimire's Ode IV, 23 ('Ad Cicadam'); 'The Rose' in the same manner seems inspired by Casimire's Ode IV, 18 ('Ad Rosam'), while his 'Advice to my best Brother' is completely in the manner of Casimire's Ode III, 4 ('That we ought to be of an even and upright mind, against the inconstancy of fortune.')

31. Qvarnström, *op.cit.*, p. 220 and 268.

32. The preface to Dr. Everard's translation states that his book contains 'more true knowledge of God and Nature, then in all the Books in the World besides, I except onely Sacred Writ.'

33. *The Divine Pymander Of Hermes Trismegistus... Translated... By that Learned Divine Doctor Everard* (1650), Book X, section 136.

34. *Ibid.*, X, 137.

35. Ruth Wallerstein, *Seventeenth-Century Poetic* (University of Wisconsin Press, 1950).

36. Plotinus, *The Ennead*, tr. Stephen MacKenna (London, 1956), p. 10.

37. From the introduction to J. E. Spingarn, ed., *Critical Essays of the Seventeenth Century* (London, 1957). All quotations from Reynolds's *Mythomystes* are taken from this edition.

38. Carol Maddison, *Apollo and the Nine* (London, 1960), p. 30.

39. *Ibid.*, p. 33.

40. Harold Wendell Smith, 'Cowley, Marvell, and the Second Temple,' *Scrutiny*, XIX (1953), 190.

41. L. W. Hyman, 'Marvell's *Garden*,' *ELH*, XXV (1958), 13.

41a. Particularly as expounded by Neoplatonists like Ficino, Pico, and de Foix. Philo and Origen had inferred from *Genesis* 1 : 27 that the first man was androgynous, and that the division into two sexes represented a later and lower state. When all created things returned to God, they would revert to the androgynous state. Seizing on Origen's interpretation, Pico (in his *Commento sopra una canzona de amore composta da Girolamo Benivieni)* interpreted the bi-sexual state as one in which man's intellectual and physical aspects or functions harmonised instead of conflicting. In Hermetic alchemy the Hermaphrodite represented the apex of transmutation, and hence was a symbol of perfection. See Edgar Wind, *Pagan Mysteries in the Renaissance* (London, 1958), p. 137 f.

42. *The Divine Pymander Of Hermes Trismegistus... Translated By that Learned Divine Doctor Everard* (London, 1650), p. 44.

43. From Fairfax's translation of a French commentary on the first *Libellus*. See Mercurius Trismegistus Pimander, translated by Thomas Lord Fairfax, British Museum Manuscript Number 25447. The belief that the Hermetic

books contain divine revelation is clearly stated on page [3v]:'It is verily believed had all his writings come to the view of this age, there would have been found in them a great concordance with The Holy Scriptures, seeing soe little as remains of them soe conforme to them, so as if itt had not beene writ before them, one would have verily thought he had taken the sence & substance of this present treatise out of them.'

44. Fairfax, *op.cit.,* p. [64v].
45. Everard, *op.cit.,* p. 21. From II, 23-24.
46. *Ibid.* From II, 25.
47. Fairfax, *op.cit.,* p. [42v].
48. *Ibid.,* p. [44v].
49. Everard, *op.cit.,* p. 23 f. From II, 37.
50. *Ibid.,* p. 24. From II, 38.
51. *Ibid.,* p. 60. From IV, 93.
52. *Ibid.,* p. 48. From IV, 37.
53. *Ibid.,* p. 74. From VI, 10.
54. The term is Casimire's, as translated by Hills. See Casimire's Ode IV, 21.
55. Everard, *op.cit.,* p. 57 f. From IV, 77 and 79.
56. *Ibid.,* p. 89. From VII, 47.
57. E. C. Pettet, *Of Paradise and Light* (Cambridge, 1960), p. 73. Pettet quotes from Harold Fisch, *Alchemy and English Literature, Proceedings of the Leeds Philosophical and Literary Society* (Oct. 1953), p. 134: 'Of all colours, it was the colour Green which, in the vegetable world at least, was of utmost importance to the alchemists; if the creative spirit had descended into the mineral world in the form of Mercury it had descended into the vegetable world in the form of greenness.' Fisch in his turn quotes from the preface to the reader in Arthur Dee's *Chymical Collections* (1650): 'For when he inspired in things Created, the Generation of the world ... he gave also a certain Springing and Budding, [that is greenness or strength] ... and that Greenness they called Nature.'
58. 'The mind, which is immortal, cannot establish or rest it self, naked, and of it self, in an Earthly Body; neither is the Earthly Body able to bear such immortality: And therefore, that it might suffer so great vertue, the Minde compacted as it were, and took to it self the passible Body of the Soul, as a Covering or a Cloathing. And the Soul being also in some sort Divine, useth the Spirit as her Minister and Servant; and the Spirit governeth the living thing.' Everard, *op. cit.,* p. 53 f. From IV, 59.
59. *Ibid.,* p. 138 f. From XI, 1 and 3.
60. Fairfax, *op.cit.,* p. [23r].
61. See footnote 58.
62. Everard, *op.cit.,* p. 54. From IV, 60-62.
63. In the moment of death 'the Spirit is contracted into the blood, and the Soul into the Spirit; but the Minde being made pure, and free from these cloathings; and being Divine by Nature, taking a fiery Body, rangeth abroad in every place, leaving the Soul to judgment, and to the punishment it hath deserved.' *Ibid.,* p. 52. From IV, 56. It must be explained that the soul deserves punishment if it has become corrupt through love of the body.
64. See above, p. 164 f.
65. Abraham Cowley's translation.
66. *Theophila,* XII, 96.

67. Thus Ficino writes: Ergo qui Solis est lumen? Umbra Dei: Ergo quid Deus est? Sol Solis est Deus, Solis lumen est Deus in corpore mundi. [By what means, then, exists the light of the sun? As the shadow of God. What, then, is God? God is the Sun of the sun, the light of the sun is God in earthly form.] Ficino, *Opera Omnia* (Parisiis, 1641), I, 596.
68. Third *Ennead*, Book VIII, section 8.
69. For an exposition of this literary tradition, see E. Katherine Dunn, 'The Medieval Cycle as History Play: an Approach to the Wakefield Plays,' *Studies in the Renaissance*, VII (1960), 76-89. The main point of universal history is to unfold God's plan for His chosen people. St. Augustine's *City of God* is the *locus classicus* for the Christian theology of history according to which the history of the world is divided into a cosmic 'week' consisting of seven periods: the creation, the covenant with Noah, the covenant with Abraham, the exodus, the reign of David, the Babylonian captivity, and the incarnation of Christ. In such a history questions of chronology are irrelevant, since one is concerned with the inner meaning of events, these being interpreted as types of the events connected with Christ and God's scheme of redemption.
70. H. Flanders Dunbar, *Symbolism in Medieval Thought* (Yale University Press, 1929), p. 19 f.
71. Don Cameron Allen, *Image and Meaning: Metaphoric Traditions in Renaissance Poetry* (Baltimore: The John Hopkins Press, 1960), 115-153.
72. Thus he comments on the fact that Noah's stay in the Ark for forty days is a type of Christ's retreat into the wilderness for forty days in order to contemplate his mission. If Marvell intended his allusion to the former event to provoke associations with the latter (if, in other words, he views Noah as a type of Christ), his re-enactment of Christ's passion in stanzas 77 and 78 has been carefully prepared for. See also Allen's interpretation of Maria Fairfax as a personification of divine wisdom.
73. Published by Burns and Oates, London, in 1960.
74. Rosemond Tuve, *A Reading of George Herbert* (London, 1952). This study provides interesting information about the various avenues through which certain typological significances had become sufficiently familiar for poets to be able to draw upon them for the sake of their generally accepted symbolic value.
75. Jean Daniélou, S.J., *From Shadows to Reality* (London, 1960), p. 11.
76. *Ibid.*, p. 19.
77. *Ibid.*, p. 83.
78. *Ibid.*, p. 64.
79. Compare ll. 285-288 and 349-350 with the following excerpt from the prefatory poem ('Pneumato-Sarco-Machia: or Theophila's Spiritual Warfare'):

> Then be sure
> That all thy outworks stand secure...
> Design
> With constant care a watch o'er every part;
> Ev'n at thy Cinque-ports, and thy heart
> Set sentinels. Let Faith be captain o'er
> The life-guard, standing at the door
> Of thy well-warded breast...

Quoted from G. Saintsbury, ed., *The Caroline Poets*, Vol. I (Oxford, 1905), p. 322.

79a. It is possible that Du Bartas, as translated by Sylvester, may have prompted Marvell to associate the massacring mowers with Moses and the punishment which he inflicted on the erring Israelites for their adoration of the golden calf. Du Bartas had compared the furious onslaught of the 'zealous Prophet' to that of a group of reapers:

... each where [he] strowes his way
With blood and slaughter, horror and dismay:
As half a score of Reapers nimbly-neat,
With cheerful ey choosing a plot of Wheat,
Reap it at pleasure, and of *Ceres* locks
Make hand-fulls sheaves, and of their
sheaves makes shocks;
And through the Field from end to end do run,
Working a-vie, til all be down and don.

Du Bartas His Diuine Weekes And Works (London, 1621), p. 372. The passage occurs in the Second Week, the Third Day and the Third Part ('The Lawe').

80. D. C. Allen, *op. cit.*, p. 118 refers in this context to the 'homo perfectissimus' of Renaissance painting.

81. Benlowes gives fine expression to this traditional idea in a prose passage prefaced to his epic: 'The life of a true Christian is a continual conflict... our blessed Saviour coming like a Man of War, commands in Chief, under the Father... When He offers Himself to us, He then invades us;... He binds when He embraceth us. In the cords of love He leads us captives; and he kills us into life, when He crucifies the old, and quickens in us the new man. So then here is no death, but of inbred corruptions: no slaughter but of carnal affections, which being mortified the soul becomes a living sacrifice, holy and acceptable unto God.' Saintsbury, *op. cit.*, I, 321.

82. To *plant* ordinance meant to put or place ordinance in position for discharging. The *Oxford English Dictionary* quotes the following example from 1650: 'Plantying your ordenaunce here and there on your walles and Bulwarkes...'

83. See Joan Grundy, 'Marvell's Grasshoppers', *N & Q*, CCII (1957), 142, and D. C. Allen, *op. cit.*, p. 134.

84. *Early English Text Society* (London, 1866), Original Series, No. 16.

85. Isabel Gamble MacCaffrey, *Paradise Lost as 'Myth'* (Harvard University Press, 1959), p. 167.

86. Daniélou, *op. cit.*, pp. 69-72.

87. Quoted *ibid.*, p. 91.

88. See the Latin argument prefixed to Canto XII, part of which may be translated as follows: 'This grove is a temple; the open boughs are the panelled ceiling, each trunk forms the pillar (or column) of the sacred house, the passable forest is the open door... I praise God with my voice, and the choristers fall in (harmonise) of their free will... the echo acts as clerk and says Amen.'

89. See above, p. 171.

90. Daniélou, *op. cit.*, p. 13.

91. D. C. Allen, *op. cit.*, p. 146.

92. The Authorised Version uses the word *encamping:* 'But the Egyptians pursued after them, all the horses and chariots of Pharaoh, and his horsemen, and his army, and overtook them [the Israelites] encamping by the sea...' *Exodus*, 14 : 16.
93. See footnote 81.
94. *Theophila*, IX, 81.
95. *Theophila*, IX, 91.
96. See footnote 67.
97. See footnote 67.
98. D. C. Allen, *op. cit.*, pp. 148-153.
99. See Horace's Ode I, 3; I, 17; II, 10; III, 1; III, 29.
100. E. M. W. Tillyard, *Some Mythical Elements in English Literature* (London, 1961), p. 83.
101. F. E. Hutchinson, *Henry Vaughan* (Oxford: Clarendon Press, 1947), p. 39.
102. *Ibid.*, pp. 55-71.
103. *The Works of Henry Vaughan*, ed. L. C. Martin (Oxford: Clarendon Press, 1914), I, 2.
104. *Ibid.*, I, 88 f.
105. *Ibid.*, I, 87 f.
106. *Ibid.*, I, 89-92.
107. *Ibid.*, II, 631.
108. *Ibid.*
109. *Ibid.*, II, 635.
110. *Ibid.*, I, 15 f.
111. In his epistle 'To my Ingenuous Friend, *R. W.*' lines 58-59 (*Works*, I, 3 f.) Vaughan borrowed a couplet from Habington's 'To Castara', lines 31-32. Vaughan therefore must have studied Habingtons poetry fairly thoroughly.
112. *Ibid.*, I, 10-12.
113. See footnote 111.
114. Vaughan's introductory epistle is dated from '*Newton* by *Usk* this 17. of *Decemb.* 1647'. E. L. Marilla, ed., *The Secular Poems of Henry Vaughan* (Uppsala, 1958), p. 153 offers the following information based on W. R. Parker's article, 'Henry Vaughan and his Publishers', *The Library*, 4th Series, XX (1940), 401-411: 'Parker adduces evidence that the group of poems in *Olor Iscanus* (1651) is not quite the same as that which the author was about to publish in 1647 but represents a careful selection by Powell from a larger accumulation some four years later. The love verse and war poems published years later still in *Thalia Rediviva* (1679), Parker points out, were actually a part of the work submitted to Powell's editorial judgment, but were judiciously excluded from the *Olor Iscanus.*' See also Harold R. Walley, 'The Strange Case of *Olor Iscanus*', *RES*, XVIII (1942), 27-37.
115. *Works*, I, 39-41.
116. *Ibid.*, I, 61 f.
117. For discussions of Henry Vaughan's knowledge of Hermetic treatises, see the following works: Ralph M. Wardle, 'Thomas Vaughan's Influence on Henry Vaughan', *PMLA*, LI (1936), 936-952; E. L. Marilla, 'Henry and Thomas Vaughan', *MLR*, XXXIX (1944), 180-183; F. E. Hutchinson, *Henry Vaughan* (Oxford, 1947), pp. 141-156; Ross Garner, *Henry Vaughan: Experience and the Tradition* (University of Chicago Press, 1959), Chap-

ter III; E. C. Pettet, *Of Paradise and Light, A Study of Vaughan's Silex Scintillans* (Cambridge University Press, 1960), pp. 71-85; Elizabeth Holmes, *Henry Vaughan and the Hermetic Philosophy* (Oxford, 1932) and Bain Tate Stewart, 'Hermetic Symbolism in Henry Vaughan's "The Night"' *P Q*, XXIX (1950), 417-422. Only E. C. Pettet, *op. cit.*, p. 97, realises that Vaughan 'may have owed a considerable debt to Casimirus' since 'there is a passage in his translation of *The Praise of a Religious Life* that adumbrates in a quite remarkable way many of the main ideas and sentiments that occur in *Silex Scintillans* whenever he is writing about Nature.'

118. *Works*, II, 432 f.
119. *Ibid.*, II, 438 ('Rules and Lessons').
120. G. Hills, *The Odes of Casimire* (1646), p. 129.
121. *The Poems of Mildmay, 2d Earl of Westmoreland*, ed. Grosart (1879), p. 176.
122. *Works*, II, 479.
123. *Ibid.*, II, 397-399.
124. This ode was not included by G. Hills in his selection.
   I quote from the Latin text:
   Dum per apricos revoluta flores,
   Vitreæ somnum fuga svadet undæ,
   Meque suspensamque comante perfla
      Barbiton alno.
   . . . . .
   Sic meo chordas quatiente plectro,
   Inter admisso digitos acutum
   Sibilo ludes, lyrico comes Po-
      etria vati.
   P. A. Budik, *Leben und Wirken der vorzüglichsten Lateinischen Dichter des XV-XVIII. Jahrhunderts* (Wien, 1828), I, 210-213 offers a fine German translation:
   Schweifst du dahin durch lichtumglänzte Blumen,
   Lockt zum Schlummer der flüchtigen Quelle Spiegel,
   Dann durchsäusle du mich, und meine Laut' ob
      Schwankender Erle.
   . . . . .
   So, wenn ich meiner hellgestimmten Laute
   Kunstgeübet die goldnen Saiten schlage,
   Spiele flüsternd um mich, Gefährten du dem
      Lyrischen Seher!
   One realises how poetry of this type must have appealed to a poet like Coleridge, who planned to translate all of Casimire's odes. However, only a few were completed.
125. *Works*, II, 404 f.
126. *Ibid.*, II, 440.
127. *Ibid.*, II, 419 f. ('The Retreate').
128. *Ibid.*, II, 524-526.
129. *Ibid.*, II, 652-654.
130. *Ibid.*, II, 642 f.
131. *Ibid.*, II, 466 f.
132. *Ibid.*, II, 614-617.

NOTES — CHAPTER IV

133. Walter Scott, ed., *Hermetica* (Oxford, 1924), I, 129.
134. See below, under Abraham Cowley and John Norris. For Hughes, see Vol. II, 157 f. In the early eighteenth century Casimire's ode was translated also by Lady Chudleigh (1703), Isaac Watts (1706) and Joshua Dinsdale (1741).
135. See *Theophila* IV, 21:

> I'th' ring of boundless lustre, from whose ray
> This petty world gleaneth its peep of day:
> Thou shalt be crown'd with wreaths of endless light.

The supposition that Vaughan was acquainted with *Theophila* is strengthened by two instances of direct borrowing. Thus Vaughan wrote as follows in 'The Evening-watch':

> ... Heav'n
> Is a plain watch, and without figures winds
> All ages up; who drew this circle even
>   He fils it; Dayes, and hours are *Blinds.*
>   *Works,* II, 425.

This comes very close indeed to *Theophila*, XII, 96:

> Heav'n was His watch, whose starry circles wind
> All ages up; the hand that sign'd
> Those figures, guides them; World, thy clocks are false and blind.

A second conceit was equally shared by the two poets:

> Thus doth God *Key* disorder'd man ...
> Tuning his brest to rise, or fall; ...
> Making the whole most Musicall.
>   (Vaughan, *Works,* II, 460)

> Affliction tunes the breast to rise, or fall.
> Making the whole man musical.
>   (*Theophila,* XIII, 60)

The borrowing is obvious, since it involves the very words with which these conceits are presented. But who borrowed from whom? The *Silex* poems, from which these quotations are taken, appeared in 1650, *Theophila* in 1652. We know that Vaughan had read the poetry of Mrs. Philips ('Orinda') years before it was published, and since *Theophila* was completed by 1648 and circulated freely among the poet's friends, it seems likely that Vaughan had had access to one of the manuscript copies. It is otherwise difficult to account for the borrowing. If Benlowes is the borrower, rather than Vaughan, then the stanzas involved must have been added between 1650 and 1652.
    It is highly suggestive that two poets, both of whom derived inspiration from Casimire's odes, should be connected in this manner.
136. Thomas Sprat, 'An Account of the Life and Writings of Mr. Abraham

337

THE HAPPY MAN

Cowley', *The Works of Mr. Abraham Cowley* (7th ed. London, 1700), sig. [c₁r]. First ed.: 1668.
137. *Ibid.*, sig. [c2v].
138. My quotations are taken from the seventh edition of Cowley's works. The epitaph is prefaced to Cowley's *Six Books of Plants ... Now made English by several Hands.* The original Latin version of the epitaph is given on p. 461 of A. R. Waller's edition of *Abraham Cowley. Essays, Plays and Sundry Verses* (Cambridge, 1906).
139. Samuel Johnson, *The Lives of the Most Eminent English Poets* (London, 1783), Vol. I, p. 22.
140. Thomas Sprat, *op. cit.*, sig. [c4r]
141. 'Miscellanies', *The Works of Mr. Abraham Cowley* (London, 1700), p. 21.
142. 'The Mistress', *ibid.*, p. 22 f.
143. 'Sylva', *ibid.*, pp. 41-43.
144. *Ibid.*, p. 50 f.
145. *Ibid.*, p. 53.
146. See G. Hills, *Odes of Casimire* (1646).
147. 'Pindarique Odes', *op. cit.*, pp. 41-43.
148. *Ibid.*, p. 45 f.
149. For a biography of Traherne, see Gladys I. Wade, *Thomas Traherne. A Critical Biography* (Princeton, 1944).
150. *The Poetical Works of Thomas Traherne*, ed. G. I. Wade (London, 1932), pp. 7-9.
151. *Ibid.*, pp. 9-11.
152. *Ibid.*, pp. 11-13.
153. 'Contentment is a sleepy thing', *ibid.*, p. 232 f.
154. 'Thoughts', *ibid.*, pp. 66-73.

CHAPTER V

1. Basil Willey, *The Seventeenth Century Background* (London, 1934), p. 137.
2. Walter Charleton is the author of *Epicurus's Morals* (1656), while Thomas Stanley wrote a *History of Philosophy* (1659). The introduction to the fifth volume of this history states that the desire of the author had been 'to take off from his memory [i. e. that of Epicurus] the greatest part of that unjust Odium, and Infamy which Envy and Malice on one hand, and Ignorance and Inhumanity on the other, have cast upon it.' This introduction is headed 'An Apologie for Epicurus'. Stanley himself is badly in need of an apology, since his discussion of the tenets of Epicurus is lifted out of Charleton's earlier treatise.
3. Basil Willey, *op. cit.*, p. 6.
4. Thomas Stanley, *The History of Philosophy, Part V* (1659), p. 231. Compare also Charleton, *Epicurus's Morals* (1656), Chapter V, section 4.
5. Stanley, *op. cit.*, p. 241 f. Compare Charleton, *op. cit.*, Chapter XII, section 6.
6. Sir George Mackenzie, *A Moral Essay, Preferring Solitude to Publick Employment* (1666), p. 74.
7. *Ibid.*, p. 81 f. Compare this passage with Lucretius, *De Rerum Natura*, II, lines 1-21; I quote lines 1-4 and 7-10:

NOTES — CHAPTER V

Suave, mari magno turbantibus aequora ventis,
e terra magnum alterius spectare laborem;
non quia vexari quemquamst iucunda voluptas,
sed quibus ipse malis careas quia cernere suave est.

. . . . .

sed nil dulcius est, bene quam munita tenere
edita doctrina sapientum templa serena,
despicere unde queas alios passimque videre
errare atque viam palantis quaerere vitae.

Quoted from the Loeb edition, which translates:

Pleasant it is, when over a great sea the winds trouble the waters,
to gaze from shore upon another's great tribulation: not because any
man's troubles are a delectable joy, but because to perceive what ills you
are free from yourself is pleasant... But nothing is more delightful
than to possess well fortified sanctuaries serene, built up by the teachings
of the wise, whence you may look down from the height upon others and
behold them all astray, wandering abroad and seeking the path of life.

8. Walter Montague, Esq., *The Accomplish'd Woman* (1656), p. 16 f.
9. Mackenzie, *op. cit.*, p. 100.
10. *The Miscellaneous Writings of John Evelyn*, ed. W. Upcott (London, 1825), p. 510.
11. *Ibid.*, p. 537.
12. Sir George Mackenzie, *A Moral Paradox* (1669), p. 6 f.
13. *Ibid.*, p. 8.
14. Lady Giffard, 'The Character of Sir William Temple', *The Early Essays and Romances of Sir William Temple*, ed. G. C. Moore Smith (Oxford, 1930), p. 29.
15. John Worlidge, *Systema Agriculturae* (4th ed., 1687), sig. [a₂r] and[a₁v].
16. *The Poetical Works of Dryden*, ed. George R. Noyes (Cambridge, 1950), p. 442 f.
17. *Ibid.*, p. 180 (From the preface to *Sylvæ*, 1685).
18. *Ibid.*, p. 176.
19. *Ibid.*, p. 385 (From *Examen Poeticum*, 1693, the dedication to Lord Radcliffe).
20. *Ibid.*, p. 176.
21. *Ibid.*, p. 183.
22. *The Odes and Epodes of Horace*, ed. and tr. John Marshall (New York and London, 1907).
23. Dryden, *op. cit.*, p. 199 f.
24. *Ibid.*, p. 200 f.
25. Quoted from John Hayward, ed., *Collected Works of John Wilmot, Earl of Rochester* (London: Nonesuch Press, 1926), p. 135 f.
26. Flatman, *Poems And Songs* (4th ed., 1686), p. 267.
27. Andrew Lang, *Sir George Mackenzie* (London, 1909), p. 80. From 'Caelia's Country House and Closet'.
28. Dryden, *Miscellany Poems* (1684), p. 435 f.
29. Dryden, *Examen Poeticum* (1693), p. 151 f. The text refers to the 34th Epigram, but it is clearly the 35th which is intended.
30. *Ibid.*, pp. 321-324.
31. Anthony Collins, *Discourse of Freethinking* (1713), p. 172.
32. *The Character of a Trimmer* (1684).

33. *The Rochester-Savile Letters 1671-1680*, ed. John Harold Wilson (Ohio State University Press, 1941), p. 34.
34. Collins, *op. cit.*, p. 130.
35. See W. G. Hiscock, 'Friendship: Francis Finch's Discourse and the Circle of the Matchless Orinda', *Review of English Studies*, XV (1939), 466-468.
36. Collins, *op. cit.*, p. 173, quotes the following statement by Tillotson: 'Is it not every Man's interest, that there should be such a Governour of the World, as really designs our Happiness, and hath omitted nothing that is necessary to it; as would govern us for our advantage, and will require nothing of us but what is for our good, and yet will infinitely reward us for the doing of that which is best for our selves? And we have reason to believe God to be such a Being, if he be at all.'
37. This is Rochester's translation, *Collected Works*, ed. J. Hayward (London, 1926), p. 45.
38. *Caroline Poets*, ed. Saintsbury (Oxford, 1905), I, 520-522.
39. *Ibid.*, I, 524.
40. *Ibid.*, I, 571 (from 'The World', line 59).
41. *Ibid.*, I, 572 (from 'The Soul').
42. *Ibid.*, I, 573 f.
43. *Ibid.*, I, 575-577.
44. *Ibid.*, I, 565 f. ('In Memory of Mrs. E. H.').
45. *Ibid.*, I, 558.
46. *Ibid.*, I, 556-558.
47. F. W. Bateson, *English Poetry and the English Language* (Oxford, 1934).
48. William Wycherley, 'An Epistle to Mr. *Dryden*', *Complete Works*, ed. M. Summers (Nonesuch Press, 1924), IV, 64.
49. Myra Reynolds, 'Introduction', *The Poems of Anne Countess of Winchilsea* (Chicago, 1903), p. cxxi: 'That Lady Winchilsea, in her attitude toward external nature, was so far in advance of her age as to be isolated from it, is put beyond dispute by a detailed study of her poems.'
50. *Poems By The Earl of Roscommon* (1717), pp. 100-103.
51. *Poems of Charles Cotton*, ed. John Beresford (London, 1923), pp. 45-48.
52. John Evelyn, *Fumifugium* (1661), sig. [a1v].
53. *Poems of Charles Cotton*, ed. John Buxton (The Muses' Library: London, 1958), pp. 251-257.
54. *Ibid.*, p. 240 f.
55. *Ibid.*, pp. 244-247.
56. *Ibid.*, pp. 31-35.
57. *Ibid.*, pp. 45-48.
58. *Ibid.*, p. 98 f.
59. *Ibid.*, p. 21 (stanza 43).
60. Geoffrey Walton, *Metaphysical to Augustan* (London, 1955), chapter 7.
61. John Norris, *Poems and Discourses Occasionally Written* (1684), p. 54.
62. Norris, *Poems*, ed. Grosart (1871), pp. 135-140.
63. *Ibid.*, pp. 142-145.
64. Norris, *Poems* (1684), p. 40.
65. Norris, *Poems*, ed. Grosart (1871), p. 65 f.
66. *Ibid.*, pp. 83-85.
67. From 'An Epistolary Essay from Lord Rochester to Lord Mulgrave'.
68. From the poem to a lady 'that accused him of inconstancy'.
69. Norris, *Poems*, ed. Grosart (1871), pp. 125-127.

NOTES — CHAPTER V

70. John Rawlet, *Poetick Miscellanies* (1687), pp. 96-99.
71. *Ibid.*, pp. 59-67.
72. *The Complete Works of William Wycherley*, ed. M. Summers (Nonesuch
73. *Ibid.*, IV, 205-213.
74. *Ibid.*, IV, 186 f.
75. Thomas Stanley, *Poems*, ed. Brydges (London, 1814), pp. 30-35.
    Press, 1924), IV, 13 f.
76. See Mario Praz, 'Stanley, Sherburne and Ayres as Translators', *The Modern Language Review*, XX (1925), 280-294 and 419-431.
77. *Caroline Poets*, ed. Saintsbury (Oxford, 1906), II, 332 f.
78. *Poems By The Earl of Roscommon... Together with Poems By Mr. Richard Duke* (London, 1717), pp. 507-514.
79. *Complete Works of Thomas Shadwell*, ed. M. Summers (London, 1927), V, 273-287.
80. *The Works of Mrs. Aphra Behn*, ed. A. H. Bullen (London, 1915), VI, 121. To 'die' was Restoration slang for the climax of the act of love.
81. *Ibid.*, VI, 397.
82. *Ibid.*, VI, 138-144.
83. This is maintained by George Woodcock, *The Incomparable Aphra* (London and New York, 1948), p. 171.
84. Aphra Behn, *op. cit.*, V, 135: 'He had an extreme good and graceful Mien, and all the Civility of a well-bred Great Man. He had nothing of Barbarity in his Nature, but in all Points address'd himself as if his Education had been in some *European* court.'
85. *Ibid.*, VI, 144-148.
86. *Ibid.*, VI, 224-290.
87. Nahum Tate, *Poems* (1677), pp. 14-19.
88. *Ibid.*, pp. 74-78.
89. *Ibid.*, p. 132 f.
90. *Ibid.*, p. 78 f.; p. 79 f., and p. 80 f.
91. *Ibid.*, p. 24 f.
92. Nahum Tate, *Poems* (1684), p. 105.
93. Rowland Watkyns, *Flamma Sine Fumo* (1662), p. 63.
94. John Tutchin, *Poems on Several Occasions. With a Pastoral. To which is Added, A Discourse of Life* (1685), sig. [A4r].
95. *Ibid.*, pp. 127-148.
96. *Ibid.*, p. 140 f. and p. 142 f.
97. *Ibid.*, p. 144 f.
98. *Ibid.*, p. 147 f.
99. Thomas Heyrick, *Miscellany Poems* (Cambridge, 1691), pp. 101-110.
100. *Ibid.*, pp. 24-28.
101. *Ibid.*, p. 1 f.
102. *Ibid.*, Part II, pp. 1-67.
103. [William Walsh,] *Letters and Poems* (1692), pp. 107-109.
104. John Dryden, ed., *The Annual Miscellany: For the Year 1694* (London, 1694), pp. 195-201.
105. J. S., *The Innocent Epicure: Or, The Art of Angling. A Poem* (1697), p. 52.
106. *Ibid.*, p. 14 f.
107. Elizabeth Handasyde, *Granville the Polite* (Oxford University Press, 1933), p. 18.

108. *Poetical Works,* ed. Bell (London, 1793), pp. 142-144.
109. *Ibid.,* pp. 110-114.
110. *The Poems of Anne, Countess of Winchilsea,* ed. Myra Reynolds (Chicago, 1903), pp. 68-77.
111. *Ibid.,* pp. 98-100.
112. *Ibid.,* pp. 160-162.
113. *Ibid.,* pp. 28-30.
114. *Ibid.,* pp. 268-270.
115. H. N. Fairchild, *Religious Trends in English Poetry* (Columbia University Press, 1939), I, 245 f.
116. Lady Mary Chudleigh, *Essays Upon Several Subjects In Prose and Verse* (1710), pp. 1-18.
117. *Ibid.,* p. 237.
118. *Poems On Several Occasions* (1703), p. 1.
119. *Ibid.,* p. 40 f.
120. *Ibid.,* pp. 45-67.
121. *Ibid.,* p. 104 f.
122. *Ibid.,* p. 35 f.
123. *Ibid.,* pp. 83-87.
124. *Ibid.,* p. 57 f.
125. *Ibid.,* p. 33 f.
126. *Ibid.,* part 2, pp. 1-73.
127. Thomas Franklin Mayo, *Epicurus in England (1650-1725)* (The Southwest Press, 1934), p. 191.

INDEX

Addison, Joseph, 212, 288
Allen, Don Cameron, 174, 181, 184, 189
Allott, Kenneth, 88, 89
Anacreon, 229
Ariosto, 13
Ashmore, John, 14 f., 26, 71, 72
Austin, Ralph, 122
Ayres, Philip, 280, 281

Bastwick, Dr., 82
Bateson, F. W., 261
Beaumont, Sir John, 71, 72
Behn, Aphra, 231, 235 f., 280, *283-288*, 289, 294, 308, 315
Benlowes, Edward, 83, 108, 115, 118, 129, 132, *139-152*, 153, 160, 170, 171, 173, 176, 178, 182, 185 f., 195, 200, 206, 209, 218, 220, 224, 234, 316
Blake, William, 8 f.
Bocchi, 158
Boehme, Jacob, 122, 123
Boethius, 131, 196, 201, 229, 307; metrum I, 4, 65 f.; metrum II, 4, 200; metrum II,5, 200, 222; metrum III, 12, 200
Brome, Alexander, 72
Browne, Sir Thomas, 121
Browne, William, 56 f., 65, 67
Buckingham, Duke of, 218
Burton, Robert, 162
Byrd, William, 55 f., 67

Calcagnini, 158
Canticles, 44, 118, 126, 127, 171, 186, 220, 224
Capilupus, Camillus, 13
Cary, Lucius. 50, 83
Casimire, see Sarbiewski
Castiglione, 231
Catullus, 230, 251
Cavendish, Margaret, Duchess of Newcastle, 233
Chamberlain, Robert, 86
Chapman, George, 72
Charles V, 144

Charleton, Walter, 230
Chesterfield, Earl of, 237
Chesterton, G. K., 156
Christ, 144, 147, 171, 172, 173, 175, 181, 182, 184, 185
Chudleigh, Lady Mary, 296, *300-308*, 316, 317
Cicero, 23
Clarendon, Earl of, 83
Claudian, 48, 88, 198, 206, 220; Epigram on the Old Man from Verona, 38 f., 71, 72, 86, 170, 200, 201
Cleveland, 140
Coleridge, S. T., 262, 318, 336 note 124
Collins, Anthony, 252 f.
Columella, 23
Copernicus, 51
Cotton, Charles, 72, 261, 262, *265-271*, 284, 285, 293, 320
Cowley, Abraham, 14, *15-41*, 47 f., 60, 72, 206, *212-221*, 225, 234, 238, 243, 244, 256, 257, 260, 263, 266, 271, 272, 276, 289, 290, 291-294 *passim*, 298, 301, 303, 305, 308, 315, 316, 317, 318, 320, 321
Crashaw, Richard, 140
Creech, Thomas, 47, 72, 244, 316
Crinito, 13
Cusanus, 158

Daniel, George, of Beswick, 114-117
Daniélou, Jean, S. J., 174
Dante, 141
Davies, Sir John, 166
Davies, John, of Hereford, 56
De Foix, Francois, 153, 163, 331 note 41 a
De Guevara, Don Antonio, *196-198*, 201, 206
De Viaud, Théophile, 194
Dee, Arthur, 332 note 57
Denham, Sir John, 73, 93, *107-113*, 143, 319, 321; *Cooper's Hill*, 118, 190
Dennys, John, 57

343

344

Joshua, 182
Juvenal, 247 f.

Lansdowne, Lord, see Granville,
George
Lilburne, John, 82
Lipsius, 88
Little Gidding, 83
Locke, John, 231, 306, 307, 308
Lovelace, Richard, 331 note 30
Lucretius, Chapter V *passim*, 58, 229,
232 f., 238, 248, 293, 304, 307, 316,
320; *De rerum natura*, 230, 239 f.,
249, 254

Mackenzie, Sir George, *232-236*, 249,
271, 277, 283, 301
Maddison, Carol, 13
Marshall, John, 241
Martial, 16 f., 48, 63, 72, 87, 88, 101,
113, 220; Epigram II, 90, 39 f.;
Epigram IV, 90, 15; Epigram V, 21,
213; Epigram V, 59, 39; Epigram
X, 47, 40 f., 60 f., 71, 86, 114
Marvell, Andrew, 73, 79, 115, 118, 122,
125, 129, 130, 131, 132, 139, *152-195*,
198, 200, 206, 217, 218, 220, 223,
224, 225, 234, 257, 261, 314, 316,
318, 319, 321; 'The Garden', 7,
46, 47, 100, 143, *154-172*; 'Upon
Appleton House', 151, *172-190*;
'Upon the Hill and Grove at Bill-
borow', 113, *190-194*
May, Thomas, 72, 244
Mayo, Thomas Franklin, 309
Miles, Josephine, 9
Milton, John, 7, 50, 73, *100-107*, 113,
117, 140, 152 f., 198, 231, 300, 313,
314, 321; companion poems, 45 f.,
73, *100-107*, 118; *Paradise Lost*,
151, 187
Montaigne, 265
More, Henry, 50, 115, 122, *129-132*,
143, 160, 195, 224, 225, 271
Moses, 125, 144, 147, 151, 158, 172,
175, 180, 185
Mountague, Walter, 80 f., 233 f.
Musæus, 158

Nahum, 180
Newcastle, Duchess of, 233

Newton, 275
Noah, 174, 175, 181, 182, 184
Norris, John, 206, 212, 234, *271-275*,
283, 289, 300, 301, 302, 305, 308,
309, 316
North, Dudley, 51
Nourse, Timothy, 10, 51
Numbers, 180

Ogilby, John, 72, 140, 237, 244
Origen, 175, 331, note 41 a
Orinda, see Philips
Orpheus, 158
Otway, Thomas, 248, 282, 283, 284
Ovid, 91, 229

Petrarch, 14, 47
Pettet, E. C., 167
Philips, Mrs. K., 201, 234, *252-262*, 263,
283, 300, 308, 315, 319, 320
Philo, 175, 184, 331 note 41 a
Pico della Mirandola, 158, 331 note
41 a
Pimander, see Hermes Trismegistus
Plato, 106, 123 f., 130, 158, 162, 171,
182, 183, 189, 216, 230, 234, 275
Pléiade, the, 14
Plotinus, 123, 124, 156, 183
Pomfret, John, 41, 215, 289, 293
Pope, Alexander, 21, 47, 97, 262, 275,
300; 'Ode to Solitude', 46;
Windsor Forest, 46
Porphyry, 156 f
Praz, Mario, 281
Preti, Girolamo, 281
Psalms, 224
Pythagoras, 158

Quarles, Francis, 140
Qvarnström, Gunnar, 151, 153

Racan, 14
Randolph, Thomas, 71, 72, 86, 114 f.,
243
Rapin, 47
Rawlet, John, *275-277*, 308.
Reynolds, Henry, 157 f., 159
Reynolds, Myra, 262
Rider, Henry, 71
Rochester, Earl of, 241, 248 f., 252,
273, 274, 275, 308

Roscommon, Earl of, 261, 262, 277, 280, 281, 283, 308, 309, 315, 321
Rosse, Alexander, 83
Rota, Bernardino, 13

S., J., *294-296*
St. Amant, 194, 260, 280
St. Ambrose, 175
St. Augustine, 333 note 69
St. Justin, 181
St. Paul, 185
Sallust, see Du Bartas
Saltonstall, Wye, 71, 81, *101-105*, 314
Sanderson, Robert, 82 f.
Sarbiewski, Casimire, S. J., 13 f., 73-80, 93, 95, 99, 117, 118, *126-129*, 131, 132, 140 f., 143, 146, 148 f., 152, 171, 195, 196, 201, 202, 224, 225, 307, 310, 316, 319, 326 note 3; Ode I, 1, 128 f., 140, 145, 148, 149; Ode I, 2, 216; Ode II, 5, 129, 140, *206-211*, 216, 305; Ode II,8, 216; Ode III,4, 75, 331 note 30; Ode III,6, 91, 92; Ode III,22, 81 f., Ode III,23, 198; Ode IV,3, 91, 92; Ode IV,10, 75; Ode IV,12, 75; Ode IV,15, 94, 198; Ode IV,18, 331 note 30; Ode IV,21, *126-128*, 140; Ode IV, 23, 331 note 30; Ode IV,24, 203; Ode IV,32, 129, 159, 161; Ode IV, 44, 140; Epode 1, 76, *110-113*, 140, 149, *190-193*; Epode 3, *76-78*, 126, 139, 140, 148, 159, 160, *198-200*.
Seneca, 17, 48, 58, 81, 229, 230; chorus from *Thyestes*, 21 f., 272, 289, 297
Shadwell, Thomas, 282, 288
Shaftesbury, 3rd Earl of, 34, 235
Shakespeare, 50, 140
Sherburne, Sir Edward, 72, 74, 198
Smith, John, 49, 71
Socrates, 158
Sophia Salomonos, 189
Spenser, Edmund, 231
Spingarn, J. E., 147
Sprat, Thomas, 212, 213
Stanley, Thomas, 230, 280
Steele, Richard, 212, 288
Stroup, Thomas B., 115
Switzer, Stephen, 10
Sylvester, Joshua, 66

Tate, Nahum, 261, 284, *288-290*, 294, 295, 298
Temple, Sir William, 51, 233, 236, 252
Theocritus, 47, 238
Thomson, James, 7, 10, 45, 46, 294
Thynne, Francis, 56
Tibullus, 113, 114, 117
Tillotson, Archbishop, 251, 254
Tillyard, E. M. W., 194
Traherne, Thomas, 122, *221-223*
Tutchin, John, *290-293*, 308, 316, 317
Tuve, Rosemond, 105, 174

Varro, 23
Vaughan, Henry, 23, 72, 73, 74, 79, 81 f., 108, 118, 122, 124, 129, 167, 170, *195-212*, 218, 220, 221, 223, 224, 225, 260, 261, 316, 319, 337 note 135
Virgil, Chapter I *passim*, 7, 48, 65, 72, 73, 88, 100, 101, 108, 127, 133, 145, 206, 220; *Eclogues*, 126; Eclogue 1, 106; Eclogue 5, 44; *Georgics*, 72, 316; *Georgics* II, 15, 19 f., *24-29*, 43, 49, 58, 63, 64, 66, 67, 102, 103, 105 f., 106, 113, 131, 196, 217, 237, 238, 240, *244-247*, 317

Waller, Edmund, 107
Wallerstein, Ruth, 154, 162
Walsh, William, 294
Walton, Geoffrey, 271
Walton, Izaak, 49, 51, 265
Watkyns, Rowland, 290
Watts, Isaac, 305, 317
Westmoreland, Earl of, see Fane, Mildmay
Winchilsea, Lady, 234, 261, 262, 286, 296, *298-300*, 302, 310, 317, 319, 320, 321
Wind, Edgar, 158
Wither, George, 83
Wolsley, 251
Wood, Anthony, 89
Woodford, Samuel, 220 f.
Wordsworth, William, 262, 299
Worlidge, John, 236
Wotton, Sir Henry, 56, 65
Wycherley, William, *277-280*, 309, 317

Zoroaster, 158